In Memory

It is said the true measure of a man can be determined not by how many times he falls down, but how many times he picks himself back up. Eddie Guerrero's life is a celebration of just that. It's a story about inspiration, about a man who succeeded in times when countless others would have failed. His strong family roots coupled with his faith in God gave him the power to rise above adversity and help those around him when they themselves were in need. This made Eddie a World Champion both in and out of the ring.

Eddie was unwavering in his determination to succeed in the business he loved with all his heart. He looked forward to the challenge of creating his own identity and taking the famed Guerrero name into the twenty-first century while paying homage to the family members who paved the way for him. He was the consummate performer and loved being in front of the fans. Every move he made had a purpose, everything he did had meaning. From the moment he walked through the curtain, he had you on the edge of your seat. Nothing was ever wasted or taken for granted. It's rare that someone so humble has such a profound effect on the lives of the people who were privileged enough to be around him. Eddie's influence on the professional wrestling business will be felt for generations to come as he will be immediately regarded as one of the squared circle's greatest competitors. To quote his older brother Mando, "Eddie was born to wrestle."

God bless you, Eddie, for you'll never know how deeply you touched us all. You'll be in our hearts and minds forever. Watch over us. Viva La Raza!

—Vince McMahon

Eddie Guerrero
1967–2005

CHEATING DEATH, STEALING LIFE

THE EDDIE GUERRERO STORY

BY **EDDIE GUERRERO**
with **MICHAEL KRUGMAN**

POCKET BOOKS

New York   London   Toronto   Sydney

POCKET BOOKS, a division of Simon & Schuster, Inc.
1230 Avenue of the Americas, New York, NY 10020

Library of Congress Cataloging-in-Publication Data

Guerrero, Eddie.
   Cheating death, stealing life : the Eddie Guerrero story / by Eddie Guerrero with Michael Krugman.—1st Pocket Books hardcover ed.
       p.   cm.
       1. Guerrero, Eddie. 2. Wrestlers—United States—Biography.
3. Wrestlers—Substance use—United States. I. Krugman, Michael.
II. World Wrestling Entertainment, Inc.

GV1196.G84C43 2005
796.812'092—dc22
[B]   2005049171

ISBN-13: 978-0-7434-9353-6
ISBN-10:   0-7434-9353-2

This Pocket Books hardcover edition December 2005

10   9   8   7   6   5   4   3

POCKET and colophon are registered trademarks of Simon & Schuster, Inc.

Designed by William Ruoto

Visit us on the World Wide Web
http://www.simonsays.com
http://www.wwe.com

Manufactured in the United States of America

For information regarding special discounts for bulk purchases, please contactSimon & Schuster Special Sales at 1-800-456-6798 or business@simonandschuster.com.

Para mi papa,
Salvador "Gory" Guerrero,
quien me inspiró y me enseñó todo.
Te extraño día a día.
Con todo mi amor.

PROLOGUE: NO WAY OUT

February 15, 2004

You did it, I thought as the crowd at San Francisco's Cow Palace roared their approval. *You really did it. Now you can breathe again.*

Though I'd worked my entire life for this moment, nothing could've prepared me for the reality. I was the WWE Champion! I'd reached the top of the wrestling mountain! There is no greater honor in this business.

I had beaten Brock Lesnar, a great champion almost twice my size, in an arena overflowing its capacity with fans, most of whom were Chicanos there to see me, Latino Heat, try to win the biggest match of my career.

It was truly an amazing night, made even more incredible by the fact that just two and a half years earlier I wasn't even working for WWE. I'd been let go after my lifetime of drug and alcohol addiction had finally sent me hurtling to the lowest point of my entire life.

If someone had told me then that I was going to be the standard bearer for World Wrestling Entertainment, the biggest and best wrestling company on the planet, I would never have believed it. In fact, I didn't even believe it when WWE CEO Vince McMahon first told me that he was planning on awarding me the belt.

Nobody—not even myself—had ever seen me as a main eventer, as a guy who could be trusted to represent the best a wrestling promotion had to offer. It was Vince, God bless him, who really believed in me. And his faith in me gave me the confidence to go out and give Brock Lesnar the match of my life.

For me, winning the most prestigious title in our sport was the fulfillment of a dream. I'm not talking about a dream that I had when I first started in the business—this was a dream from ever since I can remember, when I was a little boy watching my father, the legendary Gory Guerrero, wrestle, or seeing how proud my brothers Chavo, Mando, and Hector were when they wore championship belts.

Lord knows, it hadn't been easy. The wrestling business is like nothing else. It takes a very strong personality to live the life of a professional wrestler. It's not so much what goes on inside the ring—it's everything that goes on outside of it as well. The twenty minutes or more we spend inside the ring, that's the fun part. It's the rest of our lives that's the real battle—the ruthless backstage politics, the constant traveling, the endless mental and physical aches and pains.

My friend Dean Malenko says it all the time: "This business isn't for everybody."

For example, look at the brief career of Nathan Jones, the seven-foot-tall Australian wrestler who had a run in WWE back in 2003. Here's a guy that was a legitimate badass, that did almost ten years in a maximum-security prison for committing armed robberies. But a year in the wrestling business broke him.

"Fuck this," Nathan Jones said. "I can't take it anymore."

He packed his bags, walked out of the dressing room, and never came back. From what I understand, he told people that being a wrestler was tougher than being in the joint.

For those of us who don't run away, every day brings with it a new challenge. Don't get me wrong—there is an upside. For me, there's nothing quite as thrilling and joyous as being in the ring wrestling. Wrestling is like the greatest high in the world. Being able to control the crowd, making them laugh, making them cry, making them mad, making them love me, or making them want to kill me. It's like a drug to me.

But like any drug, it can take its toll on you.

My whole life, from the moment I left my mother's womb, has been about wrestling. I've been wrestling professionally for more than twenty years. I've traveled the world, working for every major promotion there is to work for, wrestling the best athletes and biggest stars in the business. I had so many blessings in my life, none more than the love of my amazing wife, Vickie, and my incredible, beautiful daughters, Shaul, Sherilyn, and Kaylie.

Then, like a fool, I threw it all away, destroying everything that was good about my life by poisoning it with drinking and drug abuse.

My addiction cost me everything—my wife and kids, every penny I'd ever made, the career that I'd worked at since I was an eight-year-old boy playing in my dad's wrestling ring. I should've died at least three times. I thought I'd hit bottom over and over again, never realizing just how far down the bottom truly was until I landed there.

But there is one good thing about reaching the bottom. When you get there, there's nothing left to do but fight your way back up or die.

Christ teaches us that in order to gain your life, first you have to lose it. I've been blessed by the Lord with the opportunity to be redeemed for my past sins. It took more strength and hard work than I would've believed myself capable of, but with God's grace and strength, I managed to lift myself up and become a better person than I'd ever imagined—I believe I have become a loving husband, a compassionate father, and a stronger wrestler.

When I came back from my wilderness, I knew the only thing I could control was what I could give from within myself. I wanted the opportunity to push myself like I've never pushed myself before. Every time I stepped into that ring, my goal was to give my best, to always give every ounce of myself to every match.

There were times when I just didn't have it. I'd been on the road for days, I was tired or sick, but I still went out there and produced. That's the true definition of giving everything you've got.

Winning the WWE championship was my reward for all that effort and energy. As I soaked in the cheers of the fans, my mom and my brother Mando applauding from the front row, all I could do was breathe a huge sigh of relief. It had been such a long journey that brought me there, from leaping around my dad's backyard ring in El Paso to the chaos I was in two and a half years before.

I know it's a cliché, but standing in the middle of the ring, holding the WWE championship belt in my hand, I can honestly say I saw my life flashing before my eyes. . . .

THE EDDIE GUERRERO STORY

MY FATHER'S STRENGTH SUPPORTED OUR FAMILY.
CLOCKWISE FROM LEFT: HECTOR, MANDO, CHAVO, CUQUI, MOM, LINDA, AND DAD.

CHAPTER 1

My father, Salvador Guerrero Quesada, was born January 11, 1921, in Ray, Arizona, a town that no longer exists. There was once a huge copper mine there, but it grew so big that all the people in the town had to move.

Like so many Mexican immigrants, my grandfather and my grandmother were migrant workers. They traveled from farm to farm, picking fruits and vegetables all over the Southwest and California. It was—and still is—a very hard life.

My dad attended school in America until he was nine years old. When his mother passed away from pneumonia, my grandfather decided to bring the family back to Mexico.

Because he spoke perfect English, my father was able to earn money working as an interpreter in Guadalajara. When he was sixteen, his father was killed in a hit-and-run automobile accident. As the oldest son, my father was left to basically raise his brother and four sisters.

Dad always enjoyed sports, and he decided to join a Guadalajara gym to learn how to box. What he didn't realize was that they didn't teach boxing at that particular gym—they taught *lucha libre*.

He fell in love with wrestling right from the start. His trainers were two local *luchadors*, Diablo Velasco and El Indio Mejía. Dad wrestled his first match on September 14, 1937, doing the job to—that is, losing to—a guy named El Rojo at the Arena Nilo in Guadalajara. He got paid 15 centavos.

Dad capitalized on his American background by working around Mexico under the name Joe Morgan. But he hated that name and started thinking about what to call himself. He knew that he wanted to use his real name, but he didn't think Salvador was catchy enough. Since he had developed a reputation for having very bloody matches, he began calling himself Gory Guerrero.

People took to my dad right away. He loved bodybuilding, so he had a great physical appearance. More importantly, he had a very aggressive wrestling style that made him one of the biggest heels in the business. Because he had had such a tough life, there was a lot of anger built up inside of him. He took out all that rage in the ring, which led the fans to give him the nickname *El Ave de las Tempestades*—Thunder Bird.

In 1943, my father got signed by EMLL—Empresa Mexicana de Lucha Libre—which was the Mexican equivalent of today's World Wrestling Entertainment. Salvador Lutteroth, the man behind EMLL, essentially controlled all of Mexico's wrestling circuit. That year, Dad ended up being honored as "Rookie of the Year," even though he'd already been wrestling professionally for some time.

He won his first championship two years later, winning the National Welterweight title—despite the fact that he wasn't a welterweight! They must've realized that was a mistake, because he dropped the title pretty quickly. A couple of months later, Dad won the National Middleweight title, which he held for close to a year. From there he went on to win a number of world titles, including the NWA World Middleweight and World Light Heavyweight championships.

In 1954, my dad was given a shot at the NWA World Heavyweight Champion, the legendary Lou Thesz. He didn't win the title, but it was a very big deal. Mexican wrestlers rarely got the opportunity to wrestle for the biggest championship in the business, so just getting the match showed how well respected he was by the NWA commission.

Dad was a star because he was such an incredible heel. Because he didn't have an easy childhood, Dad had a lot of anger to channel into the ring. He had all this aggression inside him, and the crowds were able to pick up on it. The people just hated him, to the point that he would wind up causing riots. If a fan challenged him, he would jump out of the ring, look the guy in the eye, and then knock him on his ass. Before you knew it, he'd be going at it with the whole damn crowd.

Dad might've been the toughest heel in *lucha libre,* but he was also a very elegant man and a sharp dresser. He was always very well groomed, in stylish suits and ties.

He was especially adamant about clean wrestling gear. He would even wash his shoelaces after every match. If you go back and watch footage of my dad in the ring, you can see that his laces are even whiter than the canvas!

Dad's career skyrocketed with his feud against Cavernario Galindo. Their matches were total bloodbaths, which was revolutionary for the time. People still talk about their no-DQ, no-countout fight. It was so brutal that my dad had to be taken to the hospital afterward because of massive blood loss. The Guerrero vs. Galindo battles were so successful, other promoters began imitating them by having their wrestlers bleed like stuck pigs.

In the late 1940s, my father teamed up with the one and only El Santo as *La Pareja Atomica*—the Atomic Pair. They were a perfectly matched team. My dad was a master technical wrestler while Santo was a total showman and brawler. *La Pareja Atomica* was enormously successful, the most popular tag team in Mexico for the length of their run together. In fact, they never lost a single match.

Nobody had quite the same mystique as El Santo. There's never been anyone who's had kayfabe like him. He took great care not to let anyone ever see him without his silver mask. No one knew who he was, not even the other wrestlers.

Santo was a true pioneer. When he first started, there were only a handful of masked wrestlers. Now, of course, almost every *luchador* wears a mask. The masks add to the illusion of *lucha libre.* People respond to them because they instantly create an air of mystery. It's a way of turning wrestlers into something larger than life, into superheroes. It's all about building the fantasy.

It's hard to describe the level of fame Santo had in Mexico. He was the man. I don't think there was anybody in Mexico that didn't know who he was. Calling him a legend doesn't even do justice to how big he was. In his

LA PAREJA ATOMICA
EL SANTO Y "Gory" GUERRERO

¡QUE EN PAZ DESCANSEN!

LA PAREJA ATOMICA—THE GREATEST TAG TEAM IN *LUCHA LIBRE*.

heyday, Santo was bigger than Hulk Hogan and Stone Cold Steve Austin combined.

Santo was more than just a wrestler. He was a real live superhero, appearing in comic books and more than fifty movies, with titles like *Santo Versus the Vampire Women* and *Santo Versus the Martian Invasion.* The films were very low-budget, but they were unbelievably popular. My dad appeared in a few of Santo's movies, but he didn't really like doing them. He was all about the wrestling.

Dad prided himself on his technical wrestling prowess. People use the word "pioneer" very freely, but my dad truly was an innovator. He originated at least two of the most famous wrestling moves—the Camel Clutch and a back-to-back backbreaker submission hold called the Gory Special.

The Camel Clutch—*la de a caballo*—is a submission hold where a wrestler sits on the back of his opponent, then reaches under his opponent's arms, applies a chinlock, and pulls back his head, arms, and torso. My dad started using the Camel Clutch back when he was tagging with Santo, who liked it so much that he asked if he could have it. Of course, my dad said yes and it became Santo's finishing hold for the rest of his career.

The Gory Special, he kept for himself. That's something that all the Guerrero boys use. I still like to lock on the Gory Special, though I try to save it for special occasions.

One of my dad's most successful feuds was with Enrique Llanes, who used to tag with Tarzan Lopez as *La Pareja Ideal*. One night, Enrique invited my dad over for dinner and introduced him to his family.

My dad and Enrique's sister Herlinda hit it off right away. After the dinner, my dad went to Enrique and asked for his permission to take Herlinda on a date. The rest, as they say, is history.

My mother grew up in Mexico City, but she was born in Pueblo, near the Aztec pyramids. Before my mother was born, her father worked as a telegraphist for General Emiliano Zapata, who was one of the leaders of the Mexican Revolution. He was actually a double agent, officially working for the government, but secretly passing on information to the Revolution.

Eventually, my grandfather was caught by the government and sentenced to execution by firing squad. As they were getting ready to shoot him, my grandmother and three of their children jumped in front of him.

"If you kill him, you kill all of us," she said, looking right at the firing squad. "I won't live without him."

Incredibly, the *comandante* took pity on them and let my grandfather go. They beat him within an inch of his life, but they didn't kill him. It's a good thing for me—if they hadn't let him go, there would be no Latino Heat!

From there, my grandparents had even more kids, with my mom arriving second to last. After the Revolution, the new government took very good care of my grandfather and he was able to retire.

Herlinda Llanes and Gory Guerrero were married in 1947, and started having children right away. The first was my sister Maria, who everybody calls Cuqui. A year later came Salvador Jr., better known as Chavo. Then came Armando—aka Mando—followed by Hector and Linda. Last, but definitely not least, came the baby of the family, yours truly, Eduardo Gory Guerrero Llanes.

In 1966, my dad decided to escape the complete control of Lutteroth and EMLL. He had been the NWA World Light Heavyweight champ—the most prestigious title in *lucha libre*—for more than three years. Lutteroth wanted my dad to drop the title to Ray Mendoza in a way that my dad felt was bad for business. Rather than do as he was told, Dad rebelled, leaving EMLL and taking the title belt with him.

He settled in El Paso and began working all over the United States, mainly Los Angeles, the Carolinas, and Texas. He even worked a couple of matches for Vince McMahon Sr. in the old World Wide Wrestling Federation. Of course, he continued to work in Mexico, wrestling in border cities like Juarez and Tijuana.

As he got older, Dad began cutting back on his wrestling and concentrated on training and doing joint promotion with Dory Funk Sr. They worked together all over West Texas, in El Paso and Amarillo and other towns.

When Dory passed, Dad continued to put on shows, mostly in Juarez, featuring wrestlers he trained, like my brothers Chavo and Hector, as well as such legendary stars as El Santo and Buddy Rogers Jr.

Even into his senior years, Dad's whole world was wrestling. Needless to say, it was also the world where I was born and raised.

CHEATING DEATH, STEALING LIFE

CHAPTER 2

My mom was forty when she had me. I think I came as a bit of a surprise. Everyone always said I was my dad's last effort.

ME AND MY DAD.

Having older parents means you tend to get spoiled rotten. It's funny—when I'd get sick at school and my parents had to come pick me up, the nurse would say, "Eddie, your grandparents are here."

"Grandparents? I don't have grandparents. That's my mom and dad!"

Being the youngest, I was a bit of a mama's boy. I was really protected as I grew up, almost like I was in a bubble. I especially loved being carried around. Maybe it was the feeling of security, or maybe I was just lazy, but I was happiest when I was in my parents' arms.

Even as I got bigger, I loved being carried. My mom would carry me to school. When we got about a block away, I'd say, "Put me down!" I'd run to school, do my thing. When my mom picked me up after school, I'd wait until we were a block away, and then make sure nobody could see me, and say, "Okay, you can carry me now."

I was also very attached to my bottle. I drank out of it until I was five years old. I guess you could say that I always liked to have a bottle in my hand; I just went from milk to beer.

I was a happy, rambunctious little kid. I was so wild, I actually thought I was Tarzan. I would put on my swimming trunks, then take one of my mom's short face towels and tuck it in like I was wearing a loincloth. I'd swing from a rope my dad tied to a tree in our yard, yelling like Tarzan— "Ahhhh-ah-ahhhh!" Of course, you can't be Tarzan without Cheetah, so my mom bought me this stuffed monkey. I loved that monkey—I had it with me all the time.

The Guerreros were a proud Mexican-American family, with equal attention paid to both sides of our heritage. With my dad, we spoke English, and with my mom, we spoke Spanish. When my mom first came to the States, she wasn't able to speak English, which was a real problem for her. Both she and my dad wanted to be sure that all their children were fluent in both languages.

There are huge age gaps between my brothers and sisters. Linda is seven years older than me, Hector is thirteen years older, Mando is seventeen years older, Chavo is nineteen years older, and Cuqui is twenty years older.

Chavo got married a year or so after I was born. After that it was Mando, Hector, Linda, and myself. Cuqui lived with us on and off until she got her teacher's license and moved to Los Angeles.

I was very close to Cuqui. She was very protective, just like a mom. Every Saturday, the two of us would go to the movies together. We'd get the schedule from the local multiplex, then coordinate the times so we could buy one ticket and then sneak into the other movies. Sometimes we'd see four movies in one day.

Having such older siblings was a pretty unusual situation. When I was little, Chavo was already a grown man, with a family of his own. Not only that, he was one of the top ten wrestlers in the world at that point, so he wasn't really around all that much. He was on the road, working hard.

Even though Chavo didn't spend a lot of time with me, I idolized him. I just loved to watch him wrestle. I still do. But outside of the ring, he could be a real prick.

I feel Chavo didn't treat me like a big brother should. He made me feel totally unimportant. As I got older, I began to understand that he had a lot of anger inside him. Chavo was angry at the business, because he felt like there was so much further he could've gone after his career peaked.

He was also angry at our parents, because my dad was pretty rough with him. Dad was a hard man, a strict disciplinarian, and my brothers felt the brunt of that much more than I ever did.

I know that my father was full of love for his children. He was just doing what he believed was best for his kids—being a good father meant being extremely strict. Not that we didn't have a lot of good times together. My dad loved playing with us, having fun with us. Unfortunately, I think the bad stuff outweighs the good in my brother's memories of him. The same thing happens with my memories of Chavo—the dark memories stand out over the good times we had.

Having a brother nineteen years older was almost like having two fathers. By the time I showed up, my dad had mellowed quite a bit. He was much more easygoing than he was when he was bringing up my brothers. Chavo ended up being the tough guy.

Don't get me wrong—I love Chavo. He's my brother and nothing can take that love away. When it comes to wrestling, I learned more from Chavo than anybody else other than my dad. He taught me psychology, timing, all the essentials. I'm grateful for that. I wouldn't be the wrestler I am without him.

But personally, our relationship leaves a lot to be desired. Chavo acts like he's my dad, but he hasn't earned the right to talk to me like that. He hasn't earned my respect as a man.

13

When I was growing up, my family gave me a couple of nicknames. My parents used to call me "Ewis," which I guess is like baby talk for "Eddie." Truth be told, I have no idea where it came from. My mom had short nicknames for all my brothers and sisters. Armando became Mando, Hector was called Heco. I was Ewis. It never even crossed my mind to ask why. It's just what everybody called me.

Later on, my parents started calling me "Chilaquil." That comes from a Mexican dish called *chilaquilas*. They're kind of like enchiladas, with tortilla chips smothered in spicy meat and sauce. I got the nickname from one of my uncles in Mexico, who said I was just like *chilaquilas*—a big pain in the ass.

The El Paso neighborhood where my family lived was a very close-knit community. Everybody looked out for everybody else. My best friends were my neighbors from across the street, Johnny and Dennis Nila. I also used to play with my next-door neighbor, Norma Silva. Norma was a great girl, a fabulous friend. We used to play together in this little backyard play-house we had. My dad had bought it for Linda, but when she outgrew it, I took it over. Norma and I would go in there and play house.

Like most boys and girls, we were curious about each other's bodies, so we did some exploring together—"What's this?" "What's that?" We never touched each other—we were way too young for that—but we did a lot of looking!

I think I always loved looking at girls. My curiosity about a woman's body came at a very young age. Mando had a stash of *Playboy* magazines under his bed, and needless to say, I loved looking at them. That's probably where I developed my taste for women—I like them strong and sexy, with solid legs and a good ass. Every girl I've ever loved since then fits that description.

When I was in first grade, my mom went down to Mexico to visit relatives. The first thing my dad said to her when she got home was, "Eddie doesn't seem right."

The first clue was that I couldn't hold my head up. Mom would lift my head, but it'd fall right back down. I simply didn't have the strength to sit up straight. Before long, I was barely able to walk.

Mom brought me to see our family pediatrician, Dr. Roman. He was a wonderful doctor. He took care of me throughout my entire childhood.

Dr. Roman took one look at me and knew right away what was wrong with me. He ran a series of tests, and sure enough, his initial diagnosis was correct—I had contracted spinal meningitis.

"Mrs. Guerrero," he said, "you've got to get Eddie to the hospital right away."

My mom didn't have a car, so she picked me up in her arms and carried me from his office to the hospital. Just like that. She isn't a very big woman, but that supermom adrenaline started flowing through her veins and she lifted me as if I were as light as a feather. It was only three or four blocks, but she power-walked my six-year-old ass to the emergency room.

Mom got me to the hospital just in time. They admitted me right away. I was slipping in and out of consciousness, but I'll never forget what happened next. The doctor had a huge needle—maybe six inches long—and explained that he was going to have to put it into my back to see what was wrong with me. He turned me onto my stomach so he could get at my spine, then slipped the needle in. It didn't hurt going in, but I can still feel the sensation of the needle reaching my spine. It went right in, all the way to the bone.

I must've blacked out, because the next thing I remember is opening my eyes and seeing my mom. "How are you feeling, Ewis?" she said.

The antibiotics that the doctors gave me clearly did the trick. I was still kind of weak, but I started jumping up and down on the bed. Mom was so relieved. She scolded me to lie still, but I could see that she was happy to see me moving around.

I had to stay in the hospital for two weeks. They made me do physical therapy, just to make sure my legs worked okay. The only lasting damage was that the tetracycline treatment caused a permanent discoloration of my teeth. I still had a few baby teeth, but the adult ones all came in gray.

I was self-conscious about my teeth for most of my life. When I first started wrestling, I would never give a full smile. Photographers would tell me, "Smile, Eddie," and I'd say, "I *am* smiling."

W hile I was growing up, my best friend was Chavo's son, Chavo Jr.—or, as everyone called him, Chavito. He was my true brother. We did everything together. We played together, we joked together. We fought all the time, but always made up right after. We were just super buds.

People are always surprised to find out that Chavito is my nephew, not my brother. But that's because not all families have a twenty-year age gap between kids.

Though I didn't get along especially well with Chavo, I was extremely close to the rest of his family. My sister-in-law Nancy is great, a wonderful lady. I also love Chavito's sister, Victoria—Tori. She's six years younger than me. She used to tag along with me and Chavito. She was a real tomboy back then.

In the mid-seventies Chavo decided to move his family out to Los Angeles. He was a huge star out there, wrestling all over Southern California. Chavo worked the same loop for years—Bakersfield on Thursdays, Fresno on Saturdays, San Bernardino on Sundays, Pico Rivera on Mondays, San Diego on Tuesdays, and Wednesdays and Fridays at the legendary Grand Olympic Auditorium in LA.

Chavo was unquestionably one of the greatest wrestlers of the era. A lot of today's wrestling fans are familiar with Chavo only as Chavo Jr.'s dad, Chavo Classic, but in the 1970s and 1980s he was the number one draw in Los Angeles, working for Mike LeBell's World Wrestling Association. He wrestled all the top superstars of the day—Superstar Billy Graham, Terry Funk, Greg "The Hammer" Valentine. His most famous feud was with Roddy Piper, fighting over the NWA Americas Heavyweight Championship. Between 1975 and 1980, Chavo actually held that title fifteen times!

At one time or another, Chavo challenged for the biggest championships in wrestling, including the NWA World title, the AWA World Heavyweight title and the WWWF title. And that doesn't even include all the various tag team championships he held over the years with any number of partners, including my dad and my brothers Hector and Mando.

Chavo was also very successful in Japan. He held the NWA World Junior Heavyweight Championship a number of times. That's extremely rare: not many *gaijin*—foreigners—get to hold titles over there, only the really special ones.

One of the reasons Chavo was so over was that he incorporated bits of the high-flying *lucha* style into American wrestling. My dad was much more of a mat wrestler, but being younger, Chavo was able to use a bit more flying in his matches. He was one of the first wrestlers to do a moonsault, and one of the first to do backflips off the top rope. He was definitely a pioneer.

After Chavo and his family moved out west, I would go out there every summer to spend time with Chavito. Chavo and I actually got along better during those trips than we did when he lived in El Paso. One time, he took me and Chavito camping up in the Sequoia Mountains. The plan was to put up a tent, but it was so freaking cold, we all slept huddled together in the van. Other than that, we had a blast—hiking, swimming in the river, sitting around the campfire. It's probably one of my dearest memories of Chavo.

I got along much better with Hector and Mando.

Mando was the kind of older brother that got a kick out of making his little brother—me—do crazy stuff. We were working together on the roof one time. He jumped off into the dirt—it was just one story high—then called up to me, "Hey, Eddie!"

"What?"

"Jump off. I'll catch you!"

"No way!"

"Come on, man!"

I knew he wasn't going to stop hassling me, so I did it. "One, two, three, okay, here I go." Mando totally caught me. He was an asshole as far as ribbing me, but when it came down to it, he would never let me get hurt. Never.

After that day, I'd jump off the roof with confidence. I used to run off the edge of the roof and jump into my dad's ring. Mando taught me fearlessness, which is definitely a requirement for my job in WWE.

Mando's love of jumping off buildings paid off for him down the line. He had a pretty successful run as a wrestler, working mostly out in the Southern

17

California territory. He was a seven-time NWA Americas Tag Team Champion, three of which he held with Hector. After twenty years as a professional wrestler, Mando retired to start an easier second career—in movies like *Falling Down,* with Michael Douglas—as a Hollywood stuntman!

Being the closest to me in age, Hector was the brother I got along with best. But he wasn't around for long either—he had a great career, working in just about every wrestling promotion there was, from NWA Florida with Dusty Rhodes and Bill Watts's Mid-South Wrestling, National Wrestling Association, to World Championship Wrestling and World Wrestling Federation.

Even back then, the wrestling life separated me from the people I loved most.

CHAPTER 3

It wasn't easy being the son of Gory Guerrero.

My dad lived his gimmick—he was Gory Guerrero when he was in the ring, he was Gory Guerrero when he was at home. He was a hard man, very strict and severe. My brothers did not have it easy with him.

But I was the baby. By the time I showed up, Dad had mellowed quite a bit. I got nothing but love from him.

Don't get me wrong—Dad disciplined me when he had to. When I was little, I was friends with a girl in my neighborhood, Irma Soto. One day Irma didn't want to come out and play, so I chucked a rock at her window. Then, after the window shattered, I grabbed a handful of mud and threw that in there too.

When my dad heard what I'd done, he got hot. He threw me over his lap and gave me a serious spanking.

As strong as Dad was, he was always very loving, just a tremendous father. I really felt that I could go to him and talk to him about anything.

I know he was strict as hell with my brothers, but with me, Dad was surprisingly cool. When I was about thirteen or so, he busted me with a porno tape in my room. He told me that he was in my room looking for knee pads and found this video under my bed.

CHAVITO—MY BEST FRIEND AND TAG TEAM PARTNER.

"I thought it was a wrestling tape," he said, "so I put it on to see what it was. Get rid of it before your mom finds it."

"Yes, sir!"

Wrestling was always the family business. Dad ran Monday night wrestling shows at El Paso Coliseum for close to fifteen years, and at one point or another, all the Guerrero boys worked for my dad's promotion. We did everything—we set up the ring and the seats, we passed out flyers, we sold tickets, we sold concessions during the matches, we ran all kinds of errands. As my brothers got older, they starred in the show.

There were wrestlers around all the time, from the great to the not-so-great. On one occasion, my dad invited El Santo over for lunch. It was

CHEATING DEATH, STEALING LIFE

I ALWAYS KNEW I'D BE A CHAMPION. ME WEARING DAD'S TITLES.

like a presidential visit. There was an enormous amount of intrigue just to get Santo to the house. Precautions had to be made so that no one saw him with my dad. Santo and my dad were such good friends, but they could never hang out together in public. Even if Santo wasn't wearing his mask, there was always the chance that someone might put two and two together.

Along with stars such as El Santo and Ernie Ladd, I also spent time with wrestlers that never really became famous, people like Mr. Wrestling and Ricky Romero. One of my favorites was El Dorado Hernandez, who wrestled for my dad in Juarez. He was a pretty good flyer and he had great charisma. I loved watching him work.

There were also people who were famous for things other than wrestling. My dad actually trained two guys named Billy and Benny McGuire, who

21

THE EDDIE GUERRERO STORY

were in the *Guinness Book of World Records* as the world's heaviest twins. They were huge—more than 700 pounds each. Anyone who grew up in the seventies remembers their picture, these two enormous guys riding little motorcycles.

That picture was so famous, they got a deal with Honda to drive their minibikes across the country. When they hit El Paso, my dad approached them about maybe becoming wrestlers. They loved the idea, and he ended up training them. They didn't actually take bumps—they were much too fat. Instead, other wrestlers would just run into them. They had a few high spots, like when they'd do a big splash. It wasn't exactly wrestling, but it was an attraction. They ended up doing okay, working all over the South and in Japan.

As I grew up, Dad was more involved in training than promoting. He brought the same style to his training that he did to being a father—strong and strict.

From the earliest time I can remember, Dad was always training his boys—that's all the wrestlers, not just his sons. Basically, he was creating his own talent, training the wrestlers that would work his shows. In the case of me and my brothers, he *literally* created his own talent!

Most of his training was done over the border in Ciudad Juarez. He conducted his workouts in the ring at Arena International, though he also had a ring set up in our backyard.

God, I loved that ring. Chavito and I would play in it all the time, pretending we were the tag team champions of the world. As we got a little older, Dad let Chavito and me have wrestling matches during intermission at his shows. Man, the crowd ate it up!

I'd watch my dad putting the boys through drills, and as I got older, I started joining in. To me, it was just playing, like other kids ride skateboards or play baseball. I used to do those things too, but I was also able to dropkick my friends.

Then when I was eight or nine, I started telling my brothers, "I want to wrestle! I want to wrestle!"

"Oh, you want to wrestle, do you?"

After they were done working out, I'd get in the ring with them and they'd beat the hell out of me. Hector was especially tough. He'd stiff me—actually hit me—a while and then he would grab my head and ram it into the turn-buckle hard—boom!

But after they were done messing with me, we would wrestle and they were totally cool. They would teach me all kinds of stuff—holds, moves—and totally put me over.

I didn't realize it at the time, but by kicking my ass, they were teaching me respect. They were showing me how to respect this business. They were treating me like they would treat any kid who wanted to learn how to wrestle.

In addition to his regular shows at the Coliseum in El Paso, my dad also promoted exhibition shows, at places like the local fair. When I was nine and Chavito was six, we had our first official match, wrestling against my dad at the Tigua Indian Fair. It was great! He had the ring announcer announce, "Gory Guerrero versus Eddie and Chavo Guerrero," and the fans went crazy. He totally put us over, too. The great Gory Guerrero did the job for two little boys! I hit him with a dropkick, then as he took a bump, Chavito came off the top rope onto him. I jumped on top of Chavo and the ref counted, "One! Two! Three!" The people went nuts!

I've always had an aptitude for wrestling. I can't explain it—it's like a gift. To this day, I don't always know how or why I do certain things. People ask me, "How did you do that move?"

"I don't know," I reply. "I just did it."

Vince McMahon has often come to me after matches to ask me what I was thinking when I did some move or another. He'll see the look on my face and say, "You don't know, do you?"

"Nope."

He just shakes his head and smiles. I think he understands that it's an instinct, a feeling. It's like a God-given gift for knowing what will make a match work in that particular moment, what will advance the story and light up the crowd.

Wrestling just comes naturally to me. It wasn't like there was this moment where I said, "This is what I'm going to do." It's just what I did. It was my life.

WRESTLING FOR THOMAS JEFFERSON HIGH SCHOOL.

CHAPTER 4

My mom felt I needed to participate in more extracurricular activities, so she made me join the Henderson Middle High School marching band. I wanted to play trumpet, but when I signed up, all the trumpet spots were taken.

The band director, Mr. Dove, talked me into playing the trombone. I was friends with the band's other trombonist, a kid named Mike Landa. He was actually really good. But there were supposed to be two trombone players, and they couldn't get anyone to take the other slot.

"I don't care if you can't play," Mr. Dove said. "All you've got to do is hold the damn thing out there and let Mike pick up the slack."

I was in the middle of junior high when my family moved to California. My dad had made good money over the years, from being a wrestler to running a successful promotion. Unfortunately, like so many people in this business, he had bad advisors looking out for him and he ended up getting bilked out of more than a quarter of a million dollars. He lost all his savings, his business, everything. It was bad.

My parents struggled to make ends meet. Since all her kids were now pretty much grown—it was just me and Linda at that point—my mom was able to work. She took a job subbing at the Anderson Junior High School cafeteria. Before long, she had a permanent position there.

When Mike LeBell called, asking my dad to come out west and help with his promotion, he didn't have much of a choice. He needed to support his family.

Mike LeBell ran a promotion out in Los Angeles called WWA—World Wrestling Association. He did great business running shows at the Olympic Auditorium. LeBell understood the Latino market long before the bigger promotions did. His top stars were guys like Pedro Morales, Ray Mendoza, and my brother Chavo, not to mention such icons as Freddie Blassie, Terry Funk, and "Rowdy" Roddy Piper, with whom my brother had a legendary feud.

LeBell offered my dad the opportunity to run a few of his California markets—Oceanside, San Pedro, San Bernardino, a couple of others. My dad accepted, and so my family packed up, left El Paso, and drove out west. We settled in Westminster, which is near Long Beach.

We spent two years in California. Just like in El Paso, my life was all about wrestling. I'd come home from school and help my dad load the ring into the truck. Then we'd travel to wherever the show was and I'd help put up the ring. Before the show, I'd pass out flyers, then help sell the tickets. We'd do the show, then bring down the ring and go home to Westminster. The next day, I'd get up, go to school, then come home and help my dad unload the ring.

California wasn't bad, but after a couple of years, my whole family was homesick for Texas. We loaded up my dad's truck and headed home to El Paso.

I was really happy about moving back to Texas. When we got home, my dad took a job outside the wrestling business for the first time in his life. He started selling insurance for AAA—American Automobile Association.

It was really hard for him, but he had to put food on our family's table. I don't think he especially loved doing it, but just like everything else he did, he gave it one hundred percent. He sold insurance with all the dedication he gave to wrestling. He ended up being "Insurance Salesman of the Month" for five months in a row.

Of course, Dad couldn't stay completely out of the business for long. He began working with Fritz Von Erich's World Class Championship Wrestling, promoting shows in and around El Paso. It wasn't the same as running his own thing, but he really enjoyed it.

We came back to El Paso just in time for me to start my freshman year at Thomas Jefferson High School. It was hard for me, moving back and forth, having to keep starting at new schools.

I wasn't a great student. Mostly I got Cs and Ds. I was lazy. I didn't want to do homework, I wanted to get in the ring and wrestle.

Once again, my mom pushed me to sign up for the marching band. Even though I was totally against it in the beginning, it turned out to be a great experience.

Marching band was a lot of fun, though I never did get very good on my instrument. In fact, I never even learned how to read music. Mike Landa would spell things out for me, showing me what to play, then writing down— third position, fourth position—so I wouldn't need to read the charts as we played.

Basically, I cheated. That's been my motto all my life—cheat to win! At one point or another, I cheated on everything. I was actually pretty good at cheating on tests. I would sit in my room and devise new ways to cheat without getting caught. You could just write the answers on your hand so many times!

I came up with a brilliant little scam—I'd write the answers on a little piece of paper, then roll it up tight and tuck it under my watch. When I was taking the test, I'd roll it out, get the answer I needed, then let it spring back under my watch. What can I say—cheating was a special little skill of mine.

Though with my gift for cheating, you'd think I'd have done better than Cs and Ds!

The funny thing is, you end up learning a lot by cheating. When you sit there, writing down all the answers, you wind up studying the subject without even realizing you're doing it.

THE EDDIE GUERRERO STORY

At the end of the first semester of my junior year, I came home from school and Linda grabbed me as I walked in the door.

"You're in trouble," she said, shaking her head.

"What'd I do now?"

"Your report card came."

The school would mail out our report cards, because too many students were trying to fool their parents into thinking they'd gotten better grades.

"Wait a second," I said. "I did pretty good this semester. I know I did Bs at least."

"No," Linda said, grinning. "You got straight As—you made the Honor Roll!"

"I did?"

"Yep. But you're in big trouble now. Dad had your report card framed and hung it up in his office. Now you're going to have to get good grades for the rest of the year!"

"Oh shit!"

I actually ended up doing okay in the next semester. I managed to get As and Bs and a couple of Cs. Things went back to normal from there, with an average of Bs and Cs and Ds. The only things I did well in were band and major sports.

For me, major sports meant wrestling. Looking back, I wish I'd played more baseball and football, but back then, I was all about the wrestling.

Obviously, amateur wrestling is very different from professional wrestling, so even though I knew a lot of basic mat stuff, I had to learn like anybody else.

At first, my dad refused to train me in amateur wrestling because he had run into a problem when he trained Chavo and Mando. He taught them the only mat wrestling style that he knew, which was shoot wrestling. His experience was with guys like Karl Gotch and Boris Malenko, wrestlers who specialized in stretching—legitimately hurting—their opponents.

So when my brothers wrestled amateur, they used what my dad had taught them to hurt the other boys. They'd get in there with these other kids and stretch them bad. The coaches had to talk to my dad and ask him not to teach them anymore.

When I started wrestling, I hounded my dad to teach me. Eventually he gave in, but he was careful to instill in me a respect for other wrestlers. He wanted to be sure I wasn't going to hurt anyone.

The first thing he explained was that shooters don't make money. A wrestler who hurts other wrestlers just isn't good for business.

"What I'm teaching you is only for self-defense in there," he said. "Don't abuse it, because it'll come back to haunt you."

Over the years, I've had to use the things my dad taught me a few times. It's not something I enjoy doing, but if somebody messes with me, I have no problem stretching them to teach them a lesson.

I started getting into bodybuilding in high school. My focus was on getting into top physical condition, not getting cut or bulked up. I just wanted to be in the best shape possible for wrestling.

All that training didn't prevent me from being plagued by injuries throughout my high school wrestling career. I tore ligaments in my thumb and ankle, I bruised my ribs, I messed up the cartilage in my knee, I dislocated my shoulder, I broke my collar bone, all by the age of sixteen.

One of the reasons I was injured so often was that I was always dieting. I was always trying to get my weight down, which made my body very fragile. I started out in the 105-pound weight class. From there I went to 112 and 119. Then I shot up from 119 to 138 pounds. For example, when I wrestled at 112, I had to get down from my natural body weight of 149. But my mentality was that the more weight I cut, the better wrestler I was going to be.

Of course, I could've dropped down to something like 119 or more, but there weren't any varsity spots open in those weight classes. If I'd wanted into those classes, I'd have had to wrestle for them, and in my freshman and sophomore years, I wasn't ready to beat those guys yet. In my junior and senior years, I started dominating the room. I could wrestle anyone I wanted to.

had a number of different personas in high school: I was the band geek, I was the jock, I was the son of Gory Guerrero. In a lot of ways, those experiences set me up for a life in wrestling, where you have to be comfortable playing multiple roles in life.

I was—and still am—a very shy person. I spent most of my teenage years trying to come out of my shell. It always felt like I grew up with a spotlight on me, because I was Gory Guerrero's son and Chavo Guerrero's brother.

I was especially bashful around girls. I was very far from the Latino Heat that people know and love.

My first "girlfriend" was Chavito's little cousin, Stephanie. She was Chavito's cousin on his mom's side, obviously. When we lived in California, I had a puppy-love thing going with this cute little girl named Michelle. After we moved back to El Paso, my heart was broken. I was thirteen and I thought it was the end of the world.

In my freshman year of high school, I don't think I had a single date. I was really shy, really timid and quiet. I had my first real date when I was a sophomore, with a girl from church.

The only time I would let myself out of my shell was at parties, when I was drinking beer with my homeboys. I first discovered that I had a taste for beer when I was about ten years old.

My dad wasn't a big drinker, so there was never beer in the house when I was growing up. I can count on one hand the number of times I saw him drink. A glass of wine at a restaurant, a can of beer at a family barbeque— that's about it.

When I was ten, my uncles came to visit from out of town and we had a big family party. Me and Chavito and a couple of my cousins stole a few beers from the ice chest. We went up to my room and I got drunk for the very first time. I drank two beers—the beer tasted lousy, but I liked it right away.

Like any high school student, I did my fair share of drinking and smoking pot, but only on the weekends, and not during the wrestling season. I really wanted to succeed as a wrestler, so I put a lot of pressure on myself to stay strong and healthy throughout the season. But when it was time to party, I partied with the best of them.

CHEATING DEATH, STEALING LIFE

There was a time there when I got really into smoking weed. I used to drive around with my little baggie and my pipe. One night I was getting loaded in my car. I was sitting there laughing and having this hysterical conversation with myself. I turned around and saw this lady standing there, looking at me like I was the weirdest person on earth.

When I came down, I realized, *Oh shit. I'm talking to myself? Maybe I better lay off the pot!*

Thomas Jefferson High School was almost completely Chicano. I don't remember ever seeing a white student there. There were middle-class kids like me, there were lower-middle-class kids, and then there were poor kids, from the barrio.

A lot of the barrio kids were mixed up in gangs. It wasn't as bad as the movies make it out to be, but there was definitely a fair amount of guns and drugs and violence.

I was lucky. Not only did I have my dad keeping me on the straight and narrow, I had a few cousins that were involved in the gang life, and their stories totally scared me off the idea. One of my cousins was killed in a drive-by, another one is doing life in jail for double homicide. Believe me, that stuff really opened my eyes. I knew that I wanted nothing to do with that lifestyle.

That doesn't mean I wasn't friendly with some of the gang kids. Being Gory Guerrero's son allowed me to cross the line and party with them. I was like a novelty to them.

I never had any trouble with the gangs. I got into a beef once with a member, but it was over a personal issue between the two of us, so the rest of the gang didn't get involved. We fought and that was that. The rule of thumb was that if you fight like a man, then you gain respect and everything is okay.

I got into a lot of fights during those days. It was usually at a party or at a nightclub. Honestly, I couldn't say why. It just seemed to happen. I'd be out partying and the next thing I knew, boom, here we go.

It was a way of showing I had balls, that Gory's son wasn't a pussy. I wanted to be a tough guy, I wanted to be the macho man, I wanted to be respected. It was more about respect than anything else.

I always tried to keep my fighting from my parents. There were times when I'd come home all banged up and my dad would ask me what happened. His main concern was that the trouble I was getting into wasn't gang-related. A black eye was one thing—he wanted to be sure I wasn't going to get shot or stabbed.

Dad was determined to keep me in check, to not let me get to the point where I actually joined a gang. He made sure that I knew I was better than that.

Dad was smart—he didn't stop me from going out to parties, but made me promise that I'd leave an hour before the party ended.

"C'mon, Dad! That's right when things start getting good!"

"I know, but that last hour is when the trouble starts. The beer runs out, nobody wants to stop partying, and next thing you know, a fight will break out."

That was a great lesson, because it turned out to be completely true. Trouble always went down at the tail end of the parties. I would go to a party, then the following day, I'd hear that somebody got stabbed or somebody got shot right there at the end. My dad knew.

N o matter what happened, I always knew that I could trust Dad to help me out if I was in trouble.

One Friday night—party night—me and my friend Jose Prado "borrowed" his father's car. While Jose was driving, we got into a little accident. It was no big deal—we swerved to avoid another car and hit a tree. Jose freaked out, saying his dad was going to kill him. We drove back to his house, and sure enough, his father started screaming, "What am I going to do?"

"Don't worry, Mr. Prado," I said. "Let's go talk to my dad."

We went over to my house, and even though it was two in the morning, my dad took a look at Mr. Prado's insurance policy and helped figure out how to deal with the damage. That's the kind of guy my dad was—if I was in any kind of trouble, I knew that I could go to him and not worry about him having a fit. I think he understood that I was a young man, and that there are some things that a young man is going to do, no matter what his parents tell him.

The wrestling team was a pretty tight-knit unit. We didn't hang with the other high school jocks—we were our own little clique. That's where I met my two best friends, Art Flores and Hector Rincon.

I actually met Art—I call him Tury, which is like a nickname for Arturo—when I was ten years old. We were in Pee Wee Football together, though we weren't friendly at all. Our team—the T-Birds—even won the Little Bowl, which was the Pee Wee version of the Super Bowl. There was a big banquet afterward, where they handed out trophies to all the kids.

It's funny. My first memory of Tury is from that banquet. All the kids were up on the dais. They had just handed out the trophies and we were all up there, clapping as they announced things like MVP and so forth. Tury was standing right in front of me. He stepped backward, right onto my trophy. He broke one of the eagles on top of the trophy, just snapped the wing right off! I got hot!

"Hey, man, you broke my trophy!"

"Um, I'm sorry," he said, and then he turned back around and continued clapping.

Tury and I became much friendlier when we wrestled together at Jefferson High, though we didn't truly become buds until later. At first, I was much tighter with our team's star heavyweight, Hector Rincon. He was a huge professional wrestling fan, so we naturally became friends.

The Jefferson High varsity team was good, but not great. We always did well, coming in second or third in city. But we never won it all, which would've been nice. At the end of my junior year, I decided I was done with wrestling. It was the first and only time in my life that I really didn't want to wrestle.

I think I was just fed up and a bit burnt out. I had let the stress get to me. I had put so much pressure on myself that when I didn't win, it killed me.

I told my coach that I didn't want to wrestle anymore, then went home and told my dad. He asked questions, but he didn't fight me. "Do what you want," he said. "You're my son and I'm going to support you."

At that time, Chavo and Hector were living in Tampa, working for Eddie Graham's Florida Championship Wrestling. I was talking to Hector and he suggested, "Why don't you come and spend the summer down here?"

Needless to say, when he made the offer, I jumped at the chance. My mom bought me a round-trip ticket, and it ended up being the best summer of my life.

I can honestly say that I grew up that summer. More important, I fell in love with wrestling again. And traveling around the territory with my brothers and Chavito, I fell in love with the business.

Up until that summer, I had only seen one side of the business, the side my father allowed me to see. In Florida I saw the other side—the partying, the women, the glory of it all. I got to travel for the first time, which I loved right away.

Ric Flair was one of Hector's best friends down there, so I got to spend some time with the Nature Boy. Let me tell you, that was quite the experience for a sixteen-year-old!

Ric is a tremendous man. Considering his place in the business, he's never been anything other than cool with me, just a really fun, down-to-earth guy. He was always laughing, always up for a party.

I got to meet so many legends that summer, Superstar Billy Graham, Angelo Mosca, the Road Warriors Animal & Hawk, Kevin Sullivan, Black Bart, Ron Bass. My brothers were working with Barry Windham and Mike Rotundo, feuding over the NWA tag titles.

Everybody was really cool. I wasn't treated like a kid, which was great. The boys knew that I respected them, and in turn, they respected me.

No one tried to protect me from seeing the reality of the lifestyle. Everybody kept an eye on me to make sure I didn't get hurt, but I wasn't sheltered at all.

You could say that summer was the beginning of my journey to manhood. I was at a show and got to talking to this cute little girl. She was around my age, with a big sexy ass, just the way I like. She suggested we go outside, so I ran to the back and pulled Hector aside. "Hey, man, I need the car keys."

"What for?"

"C'mon, bro. I just need the keys!"

Hector was no dummy—he knew something was up. He gave me the keys and I went and lost my virginity in the back of Hector's car. It was great—I think it was pretty clear that I didn't know what I was doing, so she did all the work. Needless to say, my first taste of a woman turned out to be a phenomenal experience. I think the dam broke that night. My Latino Heat was unleashed and I wanted to be with as many women as I could get my hands on.

Over the course of that summer, I hooked up with a couple of other wrestling groupies. I ended up spending a lot of time with an older woman. She was twenty-nine and she taught me everything! She must've thought I was cute, because she just took to me and really introduced me to the wonderful world of women. All the boys used to tease her, especially my brothers. "Hey, you're robbing the cradle!"

When I got back to El Paso, I was a new man. I was full of confidence, with a smile on my face. More importantly, I knew I was going to be a professional wrestler. Everything I did from that point on was with that goal in mind. I hit the gym harder than I ever had before. I had more focus, more direction.

I like to think my father knew what he was doing when he allowed me to go to Florida. I think he had an idea of the experiences I would have and he knew that it would be good for me.

CHAPTER 5

After I graduated high school, I had to pick a college. I decided on New Mexico Highlands University, a small college in Las Vegas, New Mexico. To be honest, they decided for me—that was the only school to offer me a wrestling scholarship.

I was never all that interested in college in the first place. I only went because my parents wanted me to get a degree, just in case my dream of becoming a pro wrestler didn't work out.

I made the varsity team in my first semester, wrestling at 142 pounds. Unfortunately, I reinjured my ankle almost immediately. They had no choice but to redshirt me. Basically, a college athlete has four years of NCAA eligibility. If you can't compete for one of those years due to injury, you can get redshirted so you don't lose one of your four years. You can practice, but you can't compete against other teams.

Since I couldn't wrestle, I decided to go home. My plan was to enroll at El Paso Community College, finish the year out there, then go back to New Mexico. But while I was in El Paso, the school decided to drop the wrestling program. I got a few calls from other colleges, but by then I had decided that I didn't want to wrestle amateur anymore. I knew that what I really wanted to do was start my professional career.

I had a long talk with my dad. I explained that I was serious about becoming a wrestler and I'd be grateful if he would help train me. He was great about it. He felt that I was sincere and agreed to work with me.

37

The first thing we did was go to California to get his old ring back. Back when he was running wrestling shows, he had owned three rings. One he sold, the other two he brought with us when we moved out west to work for Mike LeBell. When we came home, he left the rings out there—he gave one to Mando and stored the other at my uncle Paul's place.

Dad and I flew out there and rented a U-Haul truck. I loaded the ring up and we hit the road. That was one of the best experiences of my life, driving with my dad. I had the wheel and he talked, telling me all kinds of stories about his wrestling days. I was like a kid at story time, just hanging on every word. It was all wrestling—stories about his matches, other wrestlers, crazy things that happened to him on the road. Hearing those stories made me want to be a wrestler even more.

The motor burned out about halfway across New Mexico. Dad was not amused. "Did you check the oil?"

"Um, yeah, Dad," I lied. We had to rent another truck, and then he watched as I unloaded and loaded the ring all by myself.

All in all, our road trip took about twenty hours of driving. In a way, that was my dad's first lesson. Twenty hours on the road was a good introduction to all the driving I would have to do as a wrestler.

I had learned a lot over the years, just from watching my dad and my brothers. But when I decided that I was actually going to become a professional, that's when my real training began.

Dad was a great teacher, but he was my dad first and foremost. He wasn't nearly as tough with me as he was with other wrestlers. Every now and then he'd get upset with me, but instead of acting like a hardass, he'd get in there and show me what he wanted me to learn. He was just full of love.

Not to say that we always got along. There were times when I started rebelling, just to test my boundaries.

One time, I challenged him to wrestle me. I was young and I was sharp, so I was able to take him down. I thought I was real tough, taking down a sixty-year-old man. Well, the next thing I knew, Dad hooked my arm, rolled me over, and stretched me big-time. He had me on my back, screaming, "I'm sorry, Dad! I'm sorry!"

He let me go and when I got up, he slapped the shit out of me. "I'm ashamed of you," he said.

"What for?" I sobbed.

"For the way you've been acting. And for giving up like a girl."

That really hurt. Not that he had stretched me—though that really hurt too. What really stung was my ego. I was just a kid trying to be a man, and my dad had slapped my face.

By the time I decided to become a professional wrestler, my dad was too old to be getting in the ring with me. He tried, but he couldn't really teach me in the hands-on way he was used to. Dad told me to get somebody else to work out with me, someone I could really do moves with. I called my good friend Hector Rincon and asked if he wanted to wrestle with me.

Dad would stay outside the ring and tell us what to do. He'd come in and show us what to do with our bodies, even though he couldn't physically do the moves himself.

Pretty soon Tury started coming by the ring a lot; he had also left college, after a year of playing football. It didn't work out for him, and he was thinking about giving wrestling a shot.

Tury and Hector were both very good wrestlers. I truly believe they both could've made it in WWE, but instead they chose to walk a different path than I did.

Me, I never even considered another way of life. Wrestling wasn't a choice—it was my destiny.

EARLY DAYS IN MEXICO.

CHAPTER 6

I made my official professional wrestling debut on June 27, 1987, at the Auditorio Municipal in Juarez. I teamed with a *luchador* named Matemático—he had numbers all over his mask. It was us against El Vikingo and Flama Roja.

I was billed as Eddy Gory Guerrero. Everybody wanted to see the last link to the Gory Guerrero tradition. My dad actually told me to spell my name "Eddy." He knew that it would stand out more than the regular spelling I use today. Personally, I prefer the "Eddy" spelling. Sometimes I have to remind myself to spell it "Eddie."

I was nervous, but the match went okay. Matemático and I went over, which definitely helped my confidence. The crowd was very supportive, considering I was this young kid who didn't know what he was doing. They wanted to see a Guerrero live up to the family name. I had lived with that pressure my whole life, but for the first time, I had to live up to it, not just in my heart, but in front of other people.

From that point on, I took my dad's advice

DAD'S THUMBS-UP MEANT SO MUCH TO ME.

and wrestled as often as I could. "Get as much experience as you can," he told me. "There's no substitute for it. Experience is priceless."

And that's exactly what I did. I wrestled whenever and wherever I could get the work. I didn't care about anything else. When I was working in Juarez, I would wrestle twice a night if I could, sometimes even three times. I'd work in Juarez, then drive out to another show on the outside of town and do it all over again.

Needless to say, there wasn't a lot of money to be made. There were times when my expenses were more than my payoff. Other times my payoff was nothing more than a quart of beer and a sandwich. It didn't matter. I just wanted to wrestle.

I wrestled all over Mexico, in every big city and every small town. I wrestled in bull rings, I wrestled in buildings where the regular entertainment was cockfights. I worked on mats made of sand, in rings made of concrete. I worked one show and when I took just a hip toss to the mat, I thought my back was going to break. "The heck with this," I said. "I'm not taking any bumps today."

Walking out after the show, I saw the ring being taken down. It was nothing but a big cement platform, with a thin layer of sawdust under the canvas.

Nowadays, wrestlers get signed to a WWE contract after a few months' training in OVW—Ohio Valley Wrestling, WWE's developmental territory—and think that they've paid their dues. They stay in fancy hotel rooms and drive a rented town car all by themselves and still bitch about how tough they've got it. That makes me crazy. They should be grateful. They're getting paid to learn. Lord knows, I didn't have it that easy.

When I started wrestling, the partying was as much a part of the business as what went on in the ring. If you didn't drink, you weren't considered one of the boys. The attitude toward nondrinkers was very disdainful, like, "Oh, you can't piss with the big boys, huh?"

In Mexico, the boys would often have a couple drinks before they went out to the ring. Everybody had their own little *quartito*, their little bottle, and they'd take a couple of shots before the show. It took the edge off.

I had no problem adapting to the lifestyle. Partying hard was pretty routine for me, ever since I was sixteen years old. I didn't know any other way to live. Getting drunk and high every night was as normal to me as waking up and eating breakfast.

My dad saw how I was living and sat me down for a little talk. "Son," he said, "I'm going to share something with you. I've never even told your brothers about this. Back in the day, I would drink a beer after every match. Before I knew it, I was drinking three beers. And then three beers led to a six-pack.

Eventually I realized I wasn't getting anything out of it. All it did was make me feel bad. I was getting sluggish. It was getting in the way of my wrestling. So I stopped."

Dad was always a good teacher. He didn't tell me I had to quit drinking. He was just telling me about his experience, in the hope that I would absorb the lesson. Unfortunately, I didn't listen.

I t wasn't long before my knack for getting into trouble put me into a situation that could've ended my wrestling career before it even got started.

Chavo, Tury, and I went out after the matches in Juarez. We were partying in some club, minding our own business, and as we stood at the bar drinking, this geeky guy kept getting in my face. I listened to his bullshit for a few minutes, but I finally got hot and pushed him down.

Tury turned around from his conversation and he saw this guy on the floor, getting ready to come at me. He soccer-kicked the guy in the butt—hard—but the guy still managed to get up and get right back in my face. He wouldn't let up. He just kept breaking my balls. I was getting ready to punch him when Chavo got in between us. He grabbed the guy's glasses right off his face and threw them into the street. It probably would've escalated into serious violence, but someone said the police were coming, so the three of us cut out through the back door.

The next day, our faces were on the front page of the Juarez newspaper. The headline read, "Brutal Aggression from Chavo Guerrero, Eddy Guerrero, and Predator." That was Tury—he was wrestling under the name Predator back in those days. It turned out that the guy that was getting in my face was the assistant commissioner of boxing and wrestling in Juarez. The article talked about how the three tough wrestlers brutally attacked the poor, defenseless commissioner, even though it was really just a couple of pushes and a soccer kick to the ass.

The upshot was that Chavo, Tury, and I were all suspended from wrestling in Juarez. My dad made a few calls and a meeting was arranged. It was awful—I had to plead for my life back. The assistant commissioner was a real ballbuster. He didn't want to let me off. Basically, I had to kiss a lot of ass. I had to beg his forgiveness in front of the whole commission. It was humiliating, but I had to do it. I also had to sign papers, swearing that I'd never touch him or anyone else ever again. And of course, there was a fine that had to be paid. In Mexico, there was always a fine.

I got into a lot of fights in Juarez, pretty much every time I wrestled. Sometimes they'd start during the match and carry over into the locker room afterward. At the time, I truly thought there was nothing unusual about it. Fighting was normal. It was all part of going out drinking in Mexico.

In a way, I was probably looking for trouble. Invariably, it was with guys that were bigger than me. But I'd get into punch-ups with anyone that looked at me funny. It didn't matter who it was.

One night, a bunch of my friends came down to El Paso to see me wrestle—Tury, my friend Mark Graham, and a guy I used to work with, Charles. Of course, we ended up drinking tequila at some bar on the strip. Lord only knows what kicked it off, but Tury and I got into it and before long we were exchanging blows out in the middle of the street. As we stood there beating the shit out of each other, a big crowd of people gathered around, screaming "Eddy! Eddy!" Somebody would pull us apart and we'd escape and go right back at it—boom, boom, boom!

While we were fighting, somebody actually stabbed Charles with a little pocket knife. It wasn't too serious, but he was bleeding pretty badly. We knew we had to get the hell out of there before the cops showed up, so me and Mark got into one car, Tury and Charles into the other. I was covered in blood, so when Mark got me to my house he said, "I better clean you up some." But instead of washing the blood from my face, he started cleaning my boots. That's a good friend—he knew that taking care of my favorite cowboy boots was more important than taking care of my face!

Meanwhile, Tury drove Charles to a pharmacy to get some peroxide and bandages to clean up his stab wound. It turned out the wound was too nasty to take care of, so they drove around looking for an all-night doctor to get Charles sewn up.

The next day, Tury came by my house and neither of us could remember what made us start fighting in the first place. We kissed and made up, then went out and got drunk all over again.

The wrestling fans in Juarez are very passionate, to say the least. The building where we worked was the Gymnasia Municipal—the Municipal Gymnasium. It's a completely different setup than an American arena show. For one thing, there's no guardrail. There's nothing between the ring and the fans in the first row, so fans interfering in a match or a wrestler getting into a fight with a fan is not uncommon. In fact, it happens all the time!

The Mexican fans take their wrestling very seriously. They have no problem showing their hatred for a wrestler they don't like, usually by throwing stuff at him as he walks out to the ring. I got hit by so many different things, from nachos and beer to rocks, handfuls of pesos, and bags of piss. I was Maced at least three times.

One night I took a bump onto the apron and while I was out there selling, someone threw a diaper full of doo-doo at me. It didn't hit me, but it was close. It was one of those moments where you stop and think, *This is my life?*

It wasn't just rocks and dirty diapers getting thrown—there were plenty of punches thrown as well. There were nights when I had to literally fight my way through a mob just to get back to the dressing room. We had security, but there's just so much you can do when the whole audience is trying to kill you.

Even the police officers in Mexico get into it. One time I was wrestling in Tijuana, working as a heel, and when I got back to the dressing room, one of the other wrestlers pulled me aside. "Check it out," he said, showing me a pair of brass knuckles. "One of the cops gave these to me and told me to use them on you."

My dad taught me how to deal with that kind of chaos. "Whatever you do," Dad said, "don't run. If you run, if they think you're scared, they'll eat you alive."

He told me not to worry about the fans that are yelling and cussing. "The

CHEATING DEATH, STEALING LIFE

ones you have to watch out for are the quiet ones," he said, "the ones with the crazy look in their eyes. They're the ones you have to worry about."

When you're getting hit from all sides, there's just no way to take on everybody. If you try, you're a goner. Dad explained that the thing to do was to grab one person and just beat the living shit out of him. You don't stop, you take him with you to the back, punching the fuck out of him every step of the way.

By beating up one person, you change the psychology. The other fans see what's happening and think, *Man, I don't want to get my ass kicked like that guy!* And if they see their buddy getting beaten, they're more likely to try and rescue him than continue to fuck with you. I always felt bad doing it, but it was them or me.

I still have that Juarez mentality. I drive Jimmy and Jimmy—two of WWE's amazing security guys—crazy. They know that I won't hesitate if a fan screws with me. I've learned to restrain myself over the past few years, but if someone throws beer at me, my instinct tells me to go over the rail and teach him a lesson.

I suspect it has to do with my relatively small size. They look at me and think, *He's not so big. I can take him.* You don't see fans running into the ring when Big Show or Undertaker are in there.

I won my first title working with Mando and Chavo, the WWA World Trios Championship. We beat the American Mercenaries—Bill Anderson, Tim Patterson, and Louis Spicolli. Trios are very popular in *lucha libre.* They're actually more common than your standard two-man tag team.

My first singles title came in Juarez, the Latin American Wrestling Association Heavyweight Championship. I beat a talented young Cuban bulldog named Konnan, then dropped it back to him a couple of nights later. I'm not certain where Konnan got the title in the first place. It was very common in the independents to come in and get told by the booker, "Okay, you're the champ."

"I am?"

"Yeah, and tonight you're dropping the title to so-and-so."

Konnan—aka Carlos Ashenoff—went on to become one of the biggest stars in modern *lucha libre,* the Hulk Hogan of Mexico. The two of us worked together for a lot of years, going all the way to WCW. We butted heads in the beginning, but as we got to know each other, he pushed for me every step of the way. He was a big help to my career in those days.

Like any young worker, my mentality was all about getting over. I was trying to impress everybody, from the person I was wrestling to the promoters to the fans. I was so green, I thought the way to go was to do a lot of high spots—showy aerial moves that were guaranteed to pop the crowd, but didn't always have anything to do with the psychology of the story being told in the ring.

There are a lot of differences between Mexican and American wrestling. For one thing, in Mexico there's too much reliance on high flying. Mexican wrestlers would often hit a high spot, then raise their hands for applause. My dad hated that kind of thing. "Don't ever let me see you doing that," he said.

"Why not?" I asked.

"Because you're not a clown," Dad replied. "If they applaud you for a high spot, it should only be because you deserve it. Don't ask for their approval, *earn* their approval."

I quickly learned that just doing high spots is not enough. It's about how and when you use them. It's psychology that truly gets a wrestler over, as long as the work he does in the ring is delivered with skill and passion. "Make everything as realistic as possible," Dad said. "And if it's not realistic, you have to make it realistic."

To me, that's the best definition of psychology—making the unreal seem believable. You can't get tackled, bump, land on your feet, and then go up to the top and do a moonsault. That makes the tackle meaningless. You've got to sell it. You've got to make it *real.*

Lucha is a very cutthroat business.

If you want to make it in Mexico, you've got to be prepared to fight.

The first three months I was down there, I had to fist-fight my way through every match. Obviously, we were working, but there were always legit fists—called straight shots—thrown within the work.

I'd open up, just for a second, and boom, there it was. Full in the face.

Of course, you can't let a punch to the jaw go without a receipt. If you let a straight shot go, everyone is going to take advantage of you. They'll eat you up and shit you out.

In a way, it's like a test, to see if you have the *cojones* to be a wrestler. At the same time, there's a lot of animosity, like you're there to steal their spot.

There were so many incidents where I got into it with another wrestler. One night I was in the middle of a tag match. I had one guy in a bridge, and when his partner came to break it up, he kicked me as hard as he could, right in the kidney. God, it hurt! I had to roll out of the ring and gather myself before I could continue the match. The funny thing is, the guy who kicked me is now one of my greatest friends. It's just how the business works.

Another time I was wrestling in Tijuana. Back then, the rings were just horrible. They were hard as concrete and hardly ever level. The guy I was wrestling picked me up for a suplex, but on the way down, he deliberately jerked me, opening up my spine just as I hit the crooked mat. *Wham!* I lost all feeling in my legs for about two minutes.

I had to tell my opponent to roll me out of the ring, because I literally couldn't move. Little by little, the sensation came back to my legs, but for a couple of minutes there, I was pretty scared.

To this day, I have a chronic sciatic problem from that bump. If I take a bad bump or hit a turnbuckle wrong, or even if I land funny going out of the ring, it will get aggravated and bother me for about a month.

On my first trip down to Mexico City, I caught the attention of the EMLL bookers. They saw potential in me and wanted me to start working for them.

EMLL controlled most of the Mexican territories, lending their wrestlers out to independent promoters for a cut of the action. Wrestlers were based in Mexico City, and from there worked all over the country.

I decided to move down there and see what happened. In a way it was like starting from scratch. I had moved up the card in Juarez, but in Mexico City, I wasn't shit.

Along with wrestling at EMLL's regular Arena Mexico shows, they sent me out a few times a week. Among the cities on my loop was Acapulco, where I'd work just about every weekend.

It's about an eight-hour bus ride from Mexico City to Acapulco. We'd usually leave the night before, party all night on the bus, then get into town at six in the morning and check into one of the low-end hotels for some sleep.

One particular weekend, I was traveling with *Los Hermanos Dinamita*— the Dynamite Brothers, Cien Caras & Máscara Año 2000. When we arrived in Acapulco, we went to check into our usual cheap hotel, only to find that it was booked solid. The guy at the front desk told us that there wasn't a room to be found anywhere in town, even in the expensive hotels. We'd completely forgotten that it was Easter weekend!

We were completely exhausted, so we headed over to the arena to crash in the dressing room for a few hours. Wouldn't you know it, there were only two benches in the locker room. Since I was the smallest of the three of us, there was no way I was getting one of the benches. I laid a towel out on the floor, used my bag as a pillow, and fell right to sleep.

My rest didn't last long. I was dreaming happily when I felt something moving on my chest. My first thought was that someone was ribbing me. I opened my eyes and there on my chest was the cockroach from hell, the biggest damn bug I've ever seen! I swear, it was the size of a rat! I jumped up—*Ahhhh!*—and brushed it off of me! It was disgusting!

I didn't know what to do. All I knew was that I wasn't going to lie back down on that floor! But I was so tired, I had to catch some sleep. Then it occurred to me—the ring.

I went out into the arena and rolled into the ring. I closed my eyes and started to fall asleep. After about twenty minutes I felt a huge boom! I sat up to see some of the young wrestlers doing their morning workout—with me sleeping right there in the ring!

CHEATING DEATH, STEALING LIFE

Shit, I thought. *I've got to get some sleep!* I was running out of options. I decided to get the heck out of there. I put on my swim trunks and headed over to the beach.

I hit the beach and got myself a bucket of beer and some mussels. They catch them right there and, oh man, are they delicious! I sat there on the beautiful white sand, ate my mussels and drank my beer, then lay down on my towel and fell asleep, flat on my back.

I slept a good long time. Too long. When I finally woke up, I was completely sunburned. I had never rolled over, so my entire front was bright red, like a lobster.

I felt just awful. My skin hurt like hell and I had that queasy feeling you get from being sunburned. Not to mention the fact that I had been drinking and sleeping on the beach!

When I got to the arena, the boys saw me and all cracked up. Needless to say, I was the joke of the dressing room that night. A couple of guys tried to help me out, putting vinegar on me to ease the sting a bit, but it really didn't help. I was toast.

When I hit the ring for my match with *Los Hermanos Dinamita,* I knew I was in trouble. They couldn't resist chopping the hell out of me, leaving big white handprints on my bright red chest. Oh man, it hurt like nobody's business! Remembering it, I swear I can still feel the burn!

ME AND VICKIE.

CHAPTER 7

I wasn't particularly happy living in Mexico City, so I decided to head back home to El Paso. I knew that there would be work for me in Juarez, as well as in other territories like Tijuana.

One night I was hanging out with Mike Landa, my buddy from the high school band. He was gaga over this girl named Tina, and asked me if I'd do him a favor and double-date with them and her next-door neighbor, Vickie Lara. I'm not a big fan of blind dates, but Mike was my friend, so I said, "Sure, why not?"

The first thing I noticed was Vickie's cute little ass and legs—I liked her right from the start. But it was more than just the fact that I thought she was hot. She had an amazing smile, and her eyes were full of life.

We all went to a club, and Vickie and I ended up dancing all night long. At the end of the night, I walked her out and we exchanged numbers. When I kissed her good night, I couldn't help myself—I reached down and felt her butt. Nothing too serious, just a nice touch. But that was enough. I was hooked.

Vickie was from Horizon City, on the east side of El Paso. That part of town was a little less urban than where I was from. She was used to going out with country boys, real Texas guys with cowboy hats. That was the exact

CELEBRATING THE CAREER OF GORY GUERRERO.
(FROM LEFT TO RIGHT: MANDO, DAD, HECTOR, CHAVO, AND ME.)

opposite of my look. I never wore cowboy clothes. I hate that shit. I was a city guy—jeans, boots, and a muscle shirt to show off my biceps.

Somehow, Vickie and I clicked. We might not have had all that much in common, but there was some kind of spark between us from the start.

Vickie and I started dating, but I couldn't stop myself from being a bad boy. I was still young. I wasn't ready to settle down. There's a time-honored tradition in wrestling—what happens on the road stays on the road. I was partying hard and there were temptations everywhere.

I wasn't nearly as bad a boy as I could've been. I probably went out with other girls only two or three times. But that doesn't excuse what I did—it was cheating, plain and simple.

One day my brother Mando called me and asked if I could work with him at an AWA show in California. My eyes lit up. "Shit, yeah!"

CHEATING DEATH, STEALING LIFE

Unfortunately, I was already booked for the regular Thursday night show in Juarez. I decided to blow it off and go to California. But when I got back to El Paso, my dad sat me down and gave me some bad news.

"You can't go back to Juarez," he said. "The *federales* are after you."

It seemed one of the wrestling groupies that hung around Juarez had gotten pregnant. Not only that, it turned out she was underage. A complaint was filed, accusing five wrestlers of statutory rape, and I was one of those named. Since I was the only American out of the five, the *federales* decided to come after me.

The law in Mexico doesn't work the same as it does in the States. Down there, you're guilty until proven innocent. And with those kinds of charges against you, things can get dangerous. You get put into jail and end up disappeared.

My dad felt the best course of action was for me to go on the lam. El Paso wasn't safe—there was nothing to stop the *federales* from shoving me into the trunk of a car and driving me over the border. My brother Hector was working at Smoky Mountain Wrestling at the time, so we decided I'd go live with him in Tennessee.

Those five months were a huge eye-opener for me. I had never spent time in a place where there wasn't a large Chicano community before. I was very insulated as far as the way the world treated people of Hispanic background. Living in Tennessee was the first time I ever experienced racism first-hand.

I'd feel it just walking into a restaurant. People would look at me in this disgusted way, like I was somehow dirty. Let me tell you, it hurts. You start thinking, *What's the matter with me?* At the same time, it makes you angry.

Because I'm light-skinned, people weren't sure of my background. "What are you, Italian?"

"No, I'm Mexican."

"You're too white to be a Mexican."

I'd never encountered anything like it. Growing up in El Paso, I was sheltered from the way my people were treated. Had I grown up somewhere else, I probably would've experienced that sort of thing much earlier.

It was upsetting, but it didn't spark a fire in me. That came later.

O therwise, I really enjoyed hiding out in Tennessee. I worked with Hector whenever I could, continuing to gain experience with each show. While I was there, I was invited to do the job for Terry Funk at a WCW house show. I was thrilled—not only was it WCW, but it was an opportunity to wrestle one of the all-time greats in this business. A lot of guys are called legends— Terry Funk was the real thing.

But Hector didn't want me to do it. He pointed out one of Dad's cardinal rules: "Don't ever do a squash job. It's just not worth it." But I was stubborn. I saw it as an opportunity to be seen by the WCW bookers, thinking that if they liked what they saw, maybe I had a shot at getting hired.

I called my dad and told him what I was considering. He was cool, as always. He didn't try to talk me out of it. Instead, he explained to me that there were ways of doing it without burying myself. Just because it was a squash job didn't mean I had to come out of it looking like a loser.

But when I got to the arena, I was totally paranoid that I'd made the wrong decision. I told Terry what I was thinking and he was great. "Don't worry, kid," he said. "You ain't gonna do a squash job. I'll make you look good."

That really gave me confidence. Instead of being afraid, I was determined to do my best. More than just wanting to impress the bosses, I really wanted to justify Terry's support.

He was awesome. He gave me room to get in a bunch of offense. I also did a few high spots—I hit Terry with a head scissors, he caught me doing a top rope plancha. That kind of stuff just wasn't done in WCW at that time. I heard afterward that the bookers were impressed with me, but were too apprehensive about my size to give me another shot.

H iding out in Tennessee, I was surprised at how much I missed Vickie. She had found out about my bad behavior when the *federales* came after me. I was honest with her, but she got hot and broke up with me. I couldn't blame her, but it still hurt.

The whole time I was on the lam, I couldn't stop thinking about her. I'd never felt anything like that before. *Wait a minute,* I realized, *I'm in love.*

CHEATING DEATH, STEALING LIFE

Eventually, my dad took care of my situation in Juarez. Basically, he called the girl's bluff. He knew they were just looking for a payoff, so he slipped them a little grease and that was that. Once that business was all settled, the promotion I was working for in Juarez called, asking me to come back.

The first thing I did when I got home was call Vickie and try to convince her to see me again. Slowly but surely, I got back in her good graces. I've never been unfaithful again. I'd learned my lesson.

CHAPTER 8

Vickie and I had been together for close to three years—with lots of ups and downs—when she told me she was pregnant. We'd been irresponsible, not practicing birth control. We went so long without using anything, I figured I must've been shooting blanks. But then, surprise, surprise, I was going to be a dad!

I was just a kid—I wasn't ready to get married. I loved Vickie, but I didn't think that I was truly ready for the commitment. Still, the fact that I was in love with her made the decision easy. When she told me she was pregnant, I immediately asked her to be my wife.

I never could keep anything from my parents. I sat them down and just came out with it: "Mom, Dad, there's something I need to tell you. Vickie is pregnant."

Dad looked at me, and I could see him processing the information. His eyes got hard. It was his wrestling look, his Gory Guerrero look. Very calmly, he asked, "What are you going to do about it?"

"I'm going to marry her," I said.

Dad just shook his head and walked slowly out of the room. I felt so bad. I thought he was angry and disappointed with me. But Mom told me later that he was in fact very proud of me. "My son has become a man," he said to her. "He's taking responsibility for his actions."

Mom was great, as always. She took me shopping and helped me buy Vickie an engagement ring. We invited Vickie's mom and her husband over to dinner, and I officially asked their permission for Vickie's hand in marriage. When they agreed, I gave Vickie the ring I'd bought. We spent the rest of the evening making plans—setting the date, talking about what kind of wedding we were going to have.

About two weeks before the wedding, Dad's liver crashed and we had to take him to the hospital. When he was younger, he had contracted walking pneumonia and didn't even realize it. Through that, he developed hepatitis, which stays with you for your whole life. As he got older, the hepatitis took its toll on Dad's liver, and eventually he got cirrhosis.

He was so sick. His lungs had filled with liquid, so they inserted a tube to drain them. Because of his heart condition, they couldn't give him anything to relieve his pain. But he was tough, he didn't complain at all.

I didn't know he was going to die. I knew it was serious, but the thought of him leaving us never even crossed my mind. I didn't realize how bad it was until my whole family began turning up. They were there to say good-bye.

With Dad in the hospital, Vickie and I tried to change all our wedding plans. But Dad still looked at me as his baby boy. He was lying there, knowing he was going to die, and all his worries were about me. He took my hand and said, "No matter what, you marry Vickie. That baby needs a father."

I promised that I would. I even started making arrangements to have the ceremony in the hospital. It would've meant so much to him, to see me getting married.

It was so hard, seeing such a strong man brought down by illness. One afternoon I was at his bedside, feeding him lunch. He looked at me and spread his arms wide open, asking me to hug him. I held him and said, "I love you, Dad."

"I love you too, son," he said in a weak voice. Then he looked at me and said, "Pick me up."

I thought he wanted me to sit him up in his bed, but he whispered, "No, no, take me out of here. Get me out of the hospital."

CHEATING DEATH, STEALING LIFE

"Dad, you know I can't do that."

He just shook his head, "Yes, son. I know."

It wasn't until much later that I understood what he was asking of me. He knew that he didn't have much time left and he wanted me to rescue him. It was really just his way of saying good-bye.

My mom told me that later that same day he took her hand and said, "Okay, I'm ready." He had accepted it.

By the end, Dad was no longer coherent. They'd given him morphine to ease his pain, and for all intents and purposes, the man that was my dad was no longer there. His body was there, but my dad had already left us. When he finally passed, it was a very spiritual moment. The whole family was gathered around his bed, holding hands and singing hymns, glorifying and praising the Lord.

His breaths grew shorter and shorter until finally, he took one last breath and never exhaled. The whole time, he was looking straight up, just staring at the ceiling. I know in my heart that he was coming to the presence of the Lord, but at the same time, I've always wondered what it was he was seeing. I guess I always will, at least until it's my time.

Dad passed away on Tuesday. I was devastated and wanted to postpone the wedding, but everybody kept saying, "Do what your dad would've wanted. Get married."

We buried him on Friday. And I got married on Saturday.

The night before the funeral, Tury came over and said, "Come on, man, it's your bachelor party."

We smoked a joint and had a few drinks at a local bar, but I didn't even catch a buzz. I was so numb, I didn't feel a thing.

At the end of the night we went to the Lucky Café for some food. After we finished eating, Tury said, "Hey, bro, do you have money for the bill?"

Since Tury was taking me out for my so-called bachelor party, I didn't bring my wallet, figuring I wasn't going to have to pay for anything. "You're supposed to pay, man," I laughed. "It's my night."

"You don't have any money?"

"I didn't bring any. What happened to all the money you had at the bar?"

"I spent it all."

"What the hell are we going to do now? I'll tell you one thing—I'm not going to wash dishes."

Tury got all quiet. "Why don't we do a food run?"

A food run, of course, is where you eat and then run out without paying the bill. I wasn't sure it was such a great idea. "No, man, we shouldn't."

"Trust me," Tury said. "Just wait here. I'll pull the car around and when I'm out front, you run out."

"Fuck that," I said. "You wait here and I'll get the car."

We were parked right in front of the window. I walked out and got behind the wheel. As I started to reverse out of the spot, Tury started gesturing in the window, like "Keep going. Scoot back farther."

It was just so freaking obvious! I backed out from between the two cars and when I turned around, Tury came running out the door. "C'mon, man! Haul ass!"

I put my foot on the gas, but I forgot that I had the car in reverse! Fortunately, there was nobody behind us, because we just took off backward down Alameda Avenue. It was hilarious. That was probably the only time that entire week when I forgot about my dad.

And man, Tury has balls—the next day he went back to the Lucky Café and had lunch like nothing had happened.

So that was my bachelor party. It was probably the only real laugh I'd had in weeks. Sure, it wasn't exactly the big blowout I would've wanted, but believe me, I more than made up for it over the next fifteen years!

My dad's funeral was a very public event. Gory Guerrero was a beloved figure in El Paso and Ciudad Juarez. There were over two hundred cars in the funeral procession. There were a lot of wrestlers and a lot of wrestling fans at the funeral. At one point, everyone started chanting his name— "Gory! Gory! Gory!" It was startling. I didn't know how to react.

That whole week is like a blur to me now. Man, what a roller-coaster ride. I was numb for most of it. The thing I remember most is how Vickie never left my side. She cried as much as I did, but she made sure to stay strong for me.

The next day Vickie and I were married, fulfilling my dad's final wish for

me. We had wanted to get married in the Baptist church I grew up attending, but because Vickie was expecting, we were told that we couldn't get married in the sanctuary. That got me so hot. I couldn't get married at the church that I grew up in. What kind of bullshit is that?

That's the kind of thing that really ticks me off about organized religion. It doesn't say anything in the Bible about not being able to marry someone who's pregnant. It's a completely man-made concept. Rules like that turn people away from the church. I truly see that sort of thing as the manipulation of Satan, using things of God to turn people away from God.

I always tell people to read the Bible and listen to their hearts. Religion should be about your relationship with God, not what the church says you can or cannot do. God will tell you what's right or wrong. Put your faith in

THE EDDIE GUERRERO STORY

Him and He'll guide you. You don't need rules created by man to tell you how to live your life.

Don't get me wrong—churches do a lot of great things for people. But too often they're less interested in spreading the love of God than they are in things like raising money. I stopped attending one church after I watched them manipulate the word of God to raise one million dollars so that they could buy a piece of land to add on to the church. I thought, *Why don't you do that kind of fund-raiser to feed the hungry?*

My mom stopped attending the Baptist church for a while. She was really hurt by the whole experience. Vickie and I decided to get married at the Assembly of God church. It wasn't a big fancy place, but we both liked Pastor Hageman, and that was much more important.

My wedding day was a very happy occasion, with moments of great sadness. It wasn't just that I loved Vickie that made it special—it was that I was doing what my dad wanted. I knew that he was there in spirit, watching over us.

I didn't truly feel the loss of my dad until a couple of months later. That was the first time that I really wept, that I fully mourned his death. Vickie and I were planning to visit his grave, so I gave her money to buy a huge bouquet of flowers to bring to the site. I wasn't making very much money at the time, but I told her to spare no expense. She came home with this little bunch of flowers and I just went nuts. "I told you to get a big bouquet! What the heck is this?"

"I'm sorry, babe," Vickie said. "That's all the florist had left. It's Father's Day."

I had totally forgotten. Hearing that triggered all these emotions that had been building up inside me. I just started crying and crying. I wept all day. That night I had to wrestle in Juarez, and I sat in the dressing room with tears running out of my eyes. It was as if I hadn't truly released all my sadness at my dad's passing, and when I finally started, I couldn't stop.

CHAPTER 9

Vickie and I had a little apartment together, but when our lease expired, Mom asked us to move in with her. It was the right thing— she was lonely without Dad, and I wasn't making all that much money.

While I was out working, Mom began preparing Vickie for our life together by teaching her how to live with a wrestler.

Her lessons had begun back when we first started dating. Vickie would come over to our house while I was out training in the backyard. I could see her from the ring, sitting at our dining room table, waiting for me. Mom had to take her by the hand and tell her, "You need to stop waiting for him, because they're going to be out there all day."

Mom basically took Vickie under her wing. She taught her the ins and outs of being married to a wrestler, things like how to cook for me—wrestlers have very specific diets—and how to deal with a husband who was rarely around.

Most women don't get married with the idea that their spouse is going to be away four days out of the week. If I wasn't training, I was out of town working. The wrestling life is hard for everyone involved. Not just for the wrestlers, but for our loved ones.

When I was on the road wrestling, Vickie would call me and cry about how she missed me and how hard a time she was having without me. Mom taught her that she had to be brave. "If you're going to cry," Mom said, "you don't do it in front of him. Your job is to be strong while he's out earning a living."

She also taught Vickie that part of her job was to make sure that when I came home off the road, I didn't have to work. She'd wash my clothes, make my dinner, and, most importantly, be there for me emotionally.

I know it sounds old-fashioned, but it works. It's like the old saying: Behind every successful man, there's a strong woman. I couldn't do what I do without her.

It's not easy, running a household and taking care of a family. There have been times when I've had to do the grocery shopping, and let me tell you, it's hard! It's a real job.

My family also introduced Vickie to Jesus Christ. She didn't know God when she was growing up. She asked my mom, "Where do you get your strength?" and Mom told her, "You've got to believe in the Lord."

When we first started dating, she would come to church on Sunday just to be with me. As she went to church and Bible study, she started to like what she heard. She didn't know there was a God who loved her or that there was a Bible she could read. It was just a whole new world for her.

Vickie was past her due date and we were starting to get worried. I was especially anxious. Somebody told me a story about a guy whose wife was past due, so he took her four-wheeling and that helped induce labor. I didn't know whether to believe it or not, but it seemed like a good idea, so I took Vickie for a ride. I drove like a maniac, flying over all kinds of bumps.

Sure enough, the next day her water broke. The problem was, the baby hadn't dropped yet. Her labor went on for forty-six hours.

Being a starving young wrestler, the only insurance I could qualify for was Medicaid. They sent us to a hospital that was affiliated with a medical school. Basically, Vickie was like a test patient for the interns. She lay there with all these interns coming in and examining her for almost two whole days.

Finally a real doctor came in and asked, "How long since her water broke?"

He examined her and discovered that she wasn't dilating. They gave her an epidural, which relaxed her, and then induced labor. It turned out that the baby was too big. She couldn't get out of Vickie's uterus, so they had to go in with forceps and pull her out.

On October 14, 1990, my daughter was born. We decided to name her Shaul Marie. I loved her so much from the second I laid eyes on her, my little Shaul Marie. Because she was delivered with forceps, she came out with a little conehead, which went away, thank God. If not, she would be wearing a lot of hats right now!

That night, I went home from the hospital and got on my knees. I thanked God for Shaul, and asked Him to put her under His protection. I gave her to God.

I have always believed that God is our true father. I'm just Dad here on earth. God doesn't have any grandkids. We're all His children. To this day, I pray at night and I ask God to protect Shaul, Sherilyn, and Kaylie. I'm thankful to Him for the gift, but they belong to Him. I'm just His tool.

After the delivery, both Vickie and Shaul got sick with pneumonia. Being in labor for so long had weakened Vickie's immune system to the point where she couldn't protect herself from illness. Vickie ended up staying in the hospital for four days, while Shaul was there for a week.

I was worried, of course, but the doctor explained that it was relatively normal and nothing to be overly concerned about. Whatever fears I had were overwhelmed by the fact that I had the most beautiful baby daughter in all the world.

Money was incredibly tight after Shaul was born.

I was making maybe $300 for wrestling twice a week in Juarez. The fact that we were living at my mom's definitely helped. She wouldn't accept any money for rent. All she wanted was for me to contribute to the utility bills and help pay for food.

I did what I could, working odd jobs to make extra money. I took a job at the International Fitness Center, selling memberships. Mostly, I'd wrestle. Wherever I could get a job, I'd go and work.

Eventually I realized that I had to go back to EMLL, even if it meant mov-

ing down to Mexico City. It was time to start making a real living. I wanted to provide a good life for my family.

I decided to go to Mexico City by myself, because I worried that it was too dangerous for Vickie and the baby.

My cousin Javier Llanes—who worked at EMLL—kept telling me, "Bring your family down, because it's going to drive you nuts if you don't." Well, he was dead on the money. After three months, I was terribly homesick and lonely. It was so gloomy down there. I couldn't help it, I missed being home. I admit it—I hadn't grown up yet.

I couldn't take it anymore. I called Vickie and said, "Forget what I said before. I need you and Shaul here with me."

I was living downtown, at the Hotel San Diego. I switched to a bigger room, and Javier and I went out and bought a crib for Shaul.

Things got better the minute they arrived. The three of us lived in that hotel room for eight months. Sure, we didn't have much money and the space was tight, but Vickie and I had the time of our lives. We were together, and that made all the difference in the world.

The booker for EMLL in those days was Juan Herrera. He was a real know-nothing and a total prick. He started out sweeping the offices, but because he was a yes-man, he rose up the ranks to become booker. It to-

CHEATING DEATH, STEALING LIFE

SHAUL AND VICKIE IN OUR MEXICO CITY HOTEL ROOM.

tally went to his head. He used to shake his pencil at the wrestlers and say, "See this? This is power," suggesting that he could ruin our careers at any time.

Herrera was a total jerk. He used to come up to the boys and slap them on the back as hard as he could. It was so insulting. He'd stand there laughing, because he knew no one could say or do anything to him because he was the booker.

One day, when Juan came over and smacked my back, my temper got the best of me. Instead of just taking it, I turned around and pushed him.

He got nasty after that. He started fucking with me, cutting back my bookings. Finally I went to see him to ask what was up. "I am the boss," he said, shaking his pencil at me. "I am to be respected. Don't ever put your hands on me again."

ME WITH MANDO. I NEVER LIKED BEING PIGEONHOLED WITH MEXICAN CLICHÉS LIKE SOMBREROS AND BANDOLEROS.

I said I wouldn't and things started getting back to normal. He continued being a prick, slapping my back, flicking my ears, knowing I couldn't do anything about it. I had a family to feed and rent to pay—I didn't want to do anything to jeopardize my career. So I ate shit and took all kinds of abuse from a nasty little fucker who wasn't fit to lace my wrestling boots.

Christmas was coming, and both Vickie and I were getting homesick. We had been in Mexico City for almost a year, and we wanted to be home in El Paso for the holidays.

I went to see Juan. "I'd like to bring my family home for Christmas if it's okay with you," I said. "I'll come right back in January, okay?"

"No problem," he said. I was so happy. I brought Vickie and Shaul home to El Paso and we had a great holiday with our families.

After New Year's, I called down to EMLL and asked them where they'd like me to go work. I was told to call back in a week and they'd give me a starting date. I called a week later and was told the same thing. That went on for over a month. Finally I said, "What's going on here? Do you want me back or not?"

"Call back next week," I was told.

I got hot and started calling around, trying to see if I could get work anywhere else while I waited to hear back. No matter where I tried, no one would book me. The only places I could wrestle were Juarez, because that was like home, and Tijuana, where I had a good personal relationship with the promoter.

Eventually I found out what was going on. Juan Herrera had taken advantage of my asking for a Christmas holiday by blackballing me.

From that point on, the only places I could get work were Juarez and Tijuana, plus whatever independent shows I could get in the States. Needless to say, that didn't bring in nearly enough money to support my little family, so Vickie had to get a job at the local mall.

I did the best I could, wrestling wherever and whenever I got the chance. With my limited education, the only job I could get was waiting tables at a little restaurant called Louisiana Kitchens. It was pretty demeaning. I'd wrestled on local TV and people would recognize me—"Hey, aren't you Eddy Guerrero?" I would get so embarrassed, I even denied being myself a few times.

We moved into a tiny apartment, with barely any furniture to our name. Vickie and I were sleeping in her old bed, the one she grew up in. The only thing we had that wasn't a hand-me-down was something called a "first bed," which I bought for Shaul at Wal-Mart.

We were living by the skin of our teeth. There was so little money, we ate most of our meals at our moms' houses. Tury really helped us out during those days—he'd come over with bags of groceries and the occasional six-pack of beer.

I'll always hold that fucker Juan Herrera responsible for making my family live like that. He knew what he was doing when he blackballed me.

THE EDDIE GUERRERO STORY

Where was I going to go? There was no way I was going to make a living in the States. Smaller wrestlers were unheard-of at that time. It's a terrible thing to do, messing with somebody's life like that.

God bless my mom—she saw what a hard time I was having. "Son, I admire you so much," she told me.

"Why? I can't even provide a living for my family."

"You could stay at home and not do anything because you're too proud to wait tables. It takes a strong man to swallow his pride and do whatever he has to to help his family. What you're doing shows true character. That's what makes a man. Give it time and God will open the door for you."

I thought long and hard about what Mom had said. The fact that a prick like Juan Herrera wouldn't let me make a living as a wrestler didn't give me the right to sit around feeling sorry for myself. I decided to dedicate myself to wrestling by working harder than I ever had before. I began taking better care of my body by eating right and hitting the gym with a passion. My mind got sharper and my body got leaner and meaner. When the time came for me to get back in the game, I would be ready.

CHAPTER 10

Growing up, I dreamed of going to Japan. I knew that for smaller wrestlers like me, the World Wrestling Federation wasn't even a possibility. I had accepted in my mind that I wasn't going to wrestle in the United States. If I was going to have any success as a wrestler, it was going to be in Mexico or Japan.

It's sad that most American wrestling fans aren't familiar with Japanese wrestling. I loved watching tapes from Japan, seeing wrestlers like Tiger Mask and Tatsumi Fujinami. There was something so incredible and revolutionary about their wrestling, the way they combined high-flying acrobatics and classic mat work. What was most thrilling about it was the intensity they brought to the ring. There was an energy like nothing I'd ever seen before.

At that time, the greatest wrestler in Japan was Jushin Thunder Liger. He was so acrobatic, so exciting to watch in action. Liger took the cruiserweight style to the next level. The minute I saw him wrestle, I said, "Man, I want to go work with him."

But part of me wasn't sure if I could compete in that world. In my heart, there was doubt.

Negro Casas, who I'd wrestled many times in Juarez, wrestled for New Japan Pro Wrestling, the top promotion over there. When I told him about my dream of going to Japan, he was supportive and encouraging.

"You can do this," he said. "You can go to Japan and work with guys like Liger. That's your style, man. You can work with those boys. I know it."

That really opened my eyes. Negro Casas gave me the confidence I needed, at a time when I needed it most. He helped me believe that if I worked hard, I could reach that level.

Eight months after getting blackballed by Juan Herrera, I got a call from New Japan Pro Wrestling, asking me to come over and wrestle. Negro Casas had recommended me to Black Cat, who was working for NJPW on a regular basis. Cat put me over to the office and they decided to give me a shot in Jushin Liger's annual Best of the Super Juniors tournament. Not only that, they offered me $1,000 for the week, which was big money at the time! Obviously I jumped at the opportunity.

I was twenty-five years old. I hadn't seen much of the world, and all of a sudden, there I was in Japan. It was like being on Mars. It was so alien, so different. I was so happy and so nervous, but most of all, I was in awe.

A foreigner in Japan—a *gaijin*—can't help but feel like an outsider. That's only natural when you first get to any foreign country. It's a lot like the movie *Lost in Translation*. You can't speak the language, so you've got to do a lot of pointing at things. The promoters do everything they can to make it easy for you, but it's still a huge culture shock.

Black Cat was a huge help to me on my first tour of Japan. I don't think I could have made it in if it weren't for him. He's a terrific person and an awesome worker. All the *gaijin* boys loved him.

He spoke English and Spanish, so he was put in charge of the American and Mexican wrestlers. He translated for us, helped steer us through the business.

Cat and I clicked right away. He had me over to his house for dinner so many times. We'd eat, then sit around and watch wrestling tapes together. Cat was my guide in Japan, teaching me the ropes, encouraging me to fire it up when he could see that I was hesitating or was being intimidated by an opponent.

I went to Japan with a mission. I was there to live my dream. I was one hundred percent focused on wrestling.

My mind couldn't be on anything else, because I was about to start working with the best wrestlers in the business. New Japan drew from everywhere. They'd get the best workers from Japan, from Mexico, from Europe, from America. When you're given the opportunity to work with the finest wrestlers in the world, it forces you to reach deep in yourself to rise up to their level.

Despite the fact that there were wrestlers from all around the world, there was never a communication gap in the locker room or in the ring. Wrestling is a universal language. The moves are the same no matter where you're from—clothesline, headlock, dropkick, and so forth. There were times when I needed a translator to express something to one of the Japanese boys, but a true professional can communicate all he needs to with body language. A wrestler should be able to go into the ring and work with anybody. You don't have to talk to them. It's about *feel.*

In addition to being a huge star and an innovative, incredible wrestler, Jushin Liger was in charge of New Japan's junior heavyweight division. Each year Liger and New Japan would host the Top of the Super Junior tournament, with cruiserweights and junior heavyweights invited to compete from all over the world. My first year in the tournament included such incredible workers as Negro Casas, Chris Benoit (working under a mask as Pegasus Kid), Dave "Fit" Finlay, Too Cold Scorpio, Norio Honaga, El Samurai, and the great Koji Kanemoto.

It's a round-robin competition, scored by points. Of course, it's not a shoot. There's still a booker deciding who's going to be the ultimate winner. But you still need to perform as if you were in a real competition. I knew if I wanted to impress people, I was going to have to elevate my work to the highest possible level.

I was a newcomer, so I was eliminated relatively early in the tournament. I couldn't complain, though—I lost to one of the best young wrestlers in the world, Chris Benoit.

I hadn't met Chris personally until I arrived in Japan. But I had seen him wrestle in Mexico and was totally blown away by his intensity and technical prowess. I knew he was special from the moment I laid eyes on him.

THE EDDIE GUERRERO STORY

Seeing Chris wrestle stoked the competitive side of me. *I can do what he does,* I thought. *I can work with him.*

The bottom line is, nobody can touch Chris Benoit. Chris was—and is—the man. He is the gold standard. He's the Ferrari that everybody wants to drive.

I liked Chris from the moment we first shook hands. He was totally cool, one of the nicest guys I've ever met. But when the time came to get into the ring with him, I was nervous as shit, even a bit intimidated. I'd seen him work. I knew how good he was.

The match went along fine at first. The time came for us to call our finish, which had Chris hitting me with an enzuguri kick. Man, he spun through the air and nailed me so damn hard—*Boom!* I just went black.

When I came to, Chris had me in a submission hold. I swear, I had no idea where I was. Chris started calling moves to me, but I was so loopy, I couldn't understand a word he was saying.

Finally he just said, "Fuck it," and started beating the shit out of me. That's when I snapped out of it and started fighting back. I was running on pure instinct, going move by move until we made it to the finish.

Even though I was out of the competition, I was definitely pleased by how I'd performed. I had gone in the ring with some of the best and didn't embarrass myself one bit.

That changed on the last night of the tour. Most of the boys partied pretty heavily throughout the week, but I was nervous and tried to keep to myself as much as possible. But after our closing show, I decided to let my guard down and have a few beers. More than a few, as it turned out. I was the talk of the town on the plane the next day—"Did you guys see Eddie? Man, he was wasted!"

That's the way it's always been with me. I'm like Dr. Jekyll and Mr. Hyde. When I'm sober, I'm a nice, quiet guy. But get a few drinks in me and I'm telling everybody to go to hell.

From that day on, I had a reputation for being a hard-drinking party animal. It's kind of humiliating that people saw me like that, but I can't honestly say that it was far from the truth.

CHAPTER 11

I returned home from Japan more focused and more driven than I'd ever been before. The experience really elevated my confidence.

All of a sudden, doors started opening for me. In Mexico, it's a huge deal to have worked in Japan. It says to everybody, "Hey, this guy must be good."

The fact that I was working for New Japan made it even more of a big deal. I wasn't working for some small-time promotion, I was with the best. That elevated my status even higher.

The first person to reach out to me was Carlos Maynes of Universal Wrestling Association. UWA was an independent promotion that competed with EMLL. They had a relationship with New Japan, and the word had come back to Mexico that I was worth hiring.

I started working for UWA, doing a big show every Sunday at Mexico City's El Toreo de Cuatro Caminos, a bullring that was also used for *lucha* and boxing matches.

Meanwhile, the wrestling business in Mexico was undergoing some major changes. Antonio Peña, EMLL's top booker, wanted to modernize *lucha libre* by pushing the younger talent and incorporating angles that were more like American wrestling. But EMLL owner Paco Alonso was very concerned with the company's history and kept putting down Peña's ideas.

In 1993, Peña decided to break away and form his own promotion. He took some of EMLL's top stars, like Konnan, Blue Panther, and El Hijo del Santo along with amazing younger workers like Rey Mysterio Jr. and started AAA—*Asistencia Asesoría y Administración.* AAA was modern, like WWE, with wild angles and bigger production values. Needless to say, it was a huge success. There was a time when AAA was actually the hottest promotion in North America, doing better business than anybody else.

All of a sudden, EMLL found itself in the middle of a war. Paco Alonso finally understood that he was going to have to take EMLL into the future.

My cousin Javier was named booker, and one of the first things he did was try to hire me away from Carlos Maynes. Javier made me a lot of promises, telling me how Paco was going to push me hard and make me a huge superstar. But after all the bullshit I'd been put through by Juan Herrera, I was hesitant about coming back.

Javier kept calling me, telling me over and over how Paco wanted me and how they were going to turn me into a star. In the end, it came down to money. Javier offered me $500 more per week than I was getting from Maynes.

The fact that my cousin was the booker definitely influenced my decision. I didn't wholly trust EMLL, but I figured that with Javier as booker, I was going to get a good spot.

What they came up with was *Máscara Mágica.* I knew I was in trouble the minute I was told they wanted me to work babyface under a mask. It wasn't like there was a lot to the angle—basically, the mask was supposed to be magical. That's about it. To this day, I don't know what the hell they were thinking.

Being Máscara Mágica was not a lot of fun for me. Not only did I hate wearing the mask, it felt like I was stuck in the same midcard spot. Despite Javier's promises, I was in the same position that I was as Eddy Guerrero.

Meanwhile, Antonio Peña and his top star, my old friend Konnan, kept calling me. "You don't need that mask, bro," Konnan would say. "Come on over with us."

I went to Paco Alonso and told him my concerns. I let him know that AAA was making me an offer. "You made me a lot of promises," I said. "What's the deal?"

"Sorry, Eddy," he said, "but I can't give you any more money."

He was so matter-of-fact about it, like there was nothing to discuss. If he'd even tried to make me an offer, if he'd met what AAA were willing to give me, I probably would've stayed with EMLL. Instead, Paco acted like he didn't give a shit.

Fine, I thought. *If you don't give a shit, then neither do I.*

Paco's couldn't-care-less attitude really got me hot. I decided that not only would I make the jump to AAA, I would do it with an exclamation point.

A week later, Máscara Mágica showed up at an AAA event, just like Scott Hall did at WCW a few years later. The crowd was shocked as I walked into the ring. "I'm Gory Guerrero's son," I said. "I don't need to hide my identity under a mask."

I stripped the mask off my face and threw it into the crowd. "Here! Here's your mask!"

The fans went absolutely crazy. No one had ever done anything like that before. The *lucha* tradition is that the only time a wrestler strips off his mask is when he loses it in a match. I probably could've made a lot of money losing my mask in a match, but I didn't give a shit about money—this was about my pride.

It was the kind of rebellious act my father would've approved of. He would've appreciated the fact that it wasn't about business—it was personal. EMLL hurt my career by promising me the moon, then keeping me under a mask in the midcard. I did the right thing as long as I could. I worked their gimmick, sold their product, and got nothing out of it. It reached the point where I'd had enough. I had to look out for myself.

Even though I'd committed an unspeakably heelish act by stripping off my own mask, the fans responded to my rebellious act so positively that I became a total babyface. AAA took advantage of my popularity by quickly teaming me with the promotion's biggest babyface, El Hijo del Santo, as the New Atomic Pair. We were a good draw, because our fathers were so beloved in Mexico. Of course, it also put some pressure on me. Not only did

THE EDDIE GUERRERO STORY

I have to live up to the Guerrero standard, I had to live up to the legacy of *La Pareja Atomica.*

Being the sons of two wrestling legends definitely created a bond between Santo and me. There are so few people that have our shared experience, of being the son of a champion. It's especially hard when you have such tremendous shoes to fill. I look at actors like the Sheen brothers, Charlie Sheen and Emilio Estevez. You have to work twice as hard just to create an identity separate from your dad.

The shoes of El Santo can never be filled, but El Hijo del Santo is a tremendous talent. His dad was such an icon, there was no way he was ever going to live up to that. Because his son understood that there will never be another El Santo, he was able to get out from under his father's shadow and become a great star in his own right.

The people loved El Hijo del Santo. He's got so much natural charisma and talent that he has never been able to work as a heel. Having Santo on their roster was one of the things that helped put AAA over.

When we first started tagging together, I knew that I'd have to prove myself. I had to make my own mark, I had to make my own story. I knew that I could never match Hijo del Santo as far as popularity, so there was no point in going out there and trying to show him up. I remembered my dad's advice, to know my own strengths and remember my position.

That's exactly what I did. I was the workhorse and Santo was the entertainer, the one with all the charisma. Our styles meshed beautifully, and we made a great tag team. In a lot of ways, we were very similar to our dads.

Santo and I were very successful together. As the New Atomic Pair, we were one of the biggest babyface tag teams in Mexico. But I have to be honest—we were popular solely because Santo was so over. I was just riding his coattails. People cheered for me just because I was standing up for Santo.

I eventually earned the fans' respect. But no matter how much respect I got, I knew that I was always going to play second fiddle to Santo.

CHEATING DEATH, STEALING LIFE

CHAPTER 12

In addition to working for AAA, I also went over to Japan every six weeks or so, wrestling on every tour I could. I would come home for a week and a half, work in Mexico, then go right back out. There was a two-year period when I was in Japan for at least seven or eight months out of the year.

Being away so much of the time definitely put some strains on my marriage. It was very hard on Vickie, having to take care of Shaul without me around.

I was hardly ever home. If I wasn't in Japan, I'd be on the road in Mexico. As much as I wanted to spend more time with my family, I also knew that my first responsibility was to earn a living so I could put food on the table.

Wrestling in Japan was no picnic. As dog-eat-dog as the wrestling business was in Mexico, it was twice as tough in the Japanese dressing room.

One of the most ironic things about this business is that while it looks like we're competing in the ring, the truth is, that's the only time when wrestlers are working together. It's in the back, in the dressing room, where the competition goes down.

It's every man for himself back there, and that creates a very difficult working environment. Every wrestler is on his own, and there's always someone behind you, trying to get your spot. It's not malicious, it's just the way it is. So you've got to watch your back all the time, or else you're going to get stabbed.

It's like living in that movie *The Firm*. Everybody's watching you, all the time. The only way to protect yourself is to be extra careful and keep your own counsel.

Working in Mexico, my family name gave me a certain level of protection. I was Gory Guerrero's son. I was Chavo and Mando and Hector's brother. The Guerrero name afforded me a small amount of respect. Not only that, my family had been in the business so long, I had cousins and friends everywhere I went.

But in Japan, being a Guerrero didn't mean shit. All of a sudden I was on my own, and a lot of guys thought it would be funny to take advantage of me. I started having trouble getting along with some of the other wrestlers.

When I told Mando what had been going on, he lit into me, saying it was my own fault. "You're putting yourself in that position, bro," he said. "You're drinking and getting fucked up to the point where you can't protect yourself. You're in the lion's den, man. If you keep doing what you're doing, they're going to eat you alive."

I thought long and hard about what Mando had said. I knew he was right. From that day on, I made a point of being as invisible as possible. I had a few close friends—Chris Benoit, Black Cat—but for the most part, I stuck to myself.

I've learned that it's best to be quiet in the dressing room. I'm always careful about what I say and what I do. Because things have repercussions. This business is so cutthroat, somebody will take something you've said and manipulate it to make you look horrible. So I try to avoid being put in that position.

B ut try as I might to stay out of trouble, I just couldn't help myself. I partied like a madman every time I went over there. It's hard to resist when you're far away from home for an extended period of time. After a while the anxiety and the loneliness get to you. The only thing to do is party.

A lot of the boys blew off steam by having girlfriends over there, but my love affair was with drugs and alcohol, not women. The Latino Heat character I play is just that—a character. The real Eddie was never the guy that got the girls. They don't go for me. Maybe it's the big nose, I don't know, but I've never been a ladies' man.

There was one Japanese girl, really cute and chunky, that used to follow me all over the place. I used to call her my little water buffalo. Don't get me wrong—I liked the acknowledgment, but I've seen what womanizing can do to a marriage. I know the pain that sort of behavior puts a wife through, and I was determined not to put Vickie through that kind of hell.

Since women weren't an option, I got messed up, night after night after night. I'd get wasted and then I would get mean and stupid. I started a lot of fights for no reason, simply because I was drunk and angry. The boys had a nickname for me when I was drunk—they called me "The Giant." It was as if all my inner rage would come exploding out and I'd grow to eight feet tall, five hundred pounds. I was bigger than the Big Show, with three times the temper.

Because I was wasted all the time, there were a lot of incidents in my life that I know of only because I was told about them after the fact. That's one of the prices you pay for being a drunk. Every story was essentially the same—I got loaded and The Giant came out. For example, one night we were all partying in a hotel bar when I got into a thing with Road Warrior Hawk.

Growing up, I was a huge mark—fan—for Hawk. My friend Hector Rincon and I used to mess around in my father's ring, pretending we were the Road Warriors—Hector was Animal and I was Hawk. It was such a badass gimmick, and they worked it the right way for a long, long time. They drew like nobody's business. The Road Warriors will go down in history as one of the greatest tag teams ever, no question about it.

I actually met the Road Warriors when I went down to Florida the summer I was sixteen. It was at NWA's *Lords of the Ring* supercard at the Orange Bowl. They were fighting Barry Windham & Mike Rotundo for the NWA tag titles. I remember being so impressed, totally marking out when my brother introduced me to them.

But that night in Japan, I didn't care who Hawk was—I was drunk and I was looking for a fight. I started in on Hawk and he flat out told me to stand down. "Get the fuck away from me," he said, "or I'll do something about it."

He gave me a chance to walk away, but I was stupid. I didn't want anyone to think I was a pussy, so I pushed him.

But Hawk was a man of his word. When I turned away from him, he did exactly what he said he'd do—he did something about it. *Boom!* Right in the back of the head. He knocked me on my ass, then hit me a few times for good measure.

Hawk was a big man, so a few shots from him knocked me out cold. Brad Armstrong got me into a cab and had the driver take me back to the hotel. I remember waking up and thinking, *I fucked up.*

I was really angry and upset at first. When I really stopped and thought about it, I understood that it was my own fault. He told me to back off and I challenged him. I deserved what I got.

I'm not proud of that night, but the truth is, getting knocked out by Hawk got me over with the boys in a big way. Because I didn't back down. That's something all the boys respected about me. I might get my ass handed to me, but I won't back down.

Years later, Hawk and I came together as friends and had some good talks. He accepted Christ into his heart and truly tried to change his life. He told me he loved me and that he'd always felt bad about knocking me down. I told him not to be sorry, that it was my own stupidity. I'm glad we had that conversation when we did. Not long afterward, Hawk passed away, another casualty of this hard life we lead. God rest his soul.

The more wasted I'd get, the more I'd get messed with. Because we were away from home, we had to find ways to amuse ourselves.

Some wrestlers were incorrigible when it came to pulling ribs on other wrestlers.

Ribbing is a tradition in the wrestling business. Guys play practical jokes on younger wrestlers as a way of welcoming them to the business. When I was a kid, my brothers were pretty good about not ribbing me too much. They understood that I'm a sensitive guy, and for the most part, they left me alone.

Of course, other wrestlers weren't always so considerate. Most of the time ribs are harmless and even kind of funny. Hiding the new guy's luggage, or chaining it to the rafters in the locker room, that's just a way of saying, "Welcome to the club."

But sometimes ribs could turn downright nasty—literally. Two of the worst ribbers in Japan were the Nasty Boys, Brian Knobs and Jerry Sags. Those two pulled a vicious rib on me on one of my early trips to Japan.

We were traveling together from the U.S. to Japan. A bunch of the boys met up in one of the airport lounges before the flight and had a few drinks. Brian and Jerry were totally friendly to my face, but when I wasn't looking, they H-bombed me—slipped me a mickey.

While I was out, Knobs stood over me, saying things like, "I always hated your brother Hector," and slapping me across the face. Then they shaved off my eyebrows, cut my bangs, and sheared a little triangle right in the middle of my head. I looked like Frankenstein!

That goes beyond just a practical joke. That's personal. The Nasty Boys thought it was hilarious, but I was pretty pissed. To this day, I'm very bitter about it. Shaving off somebody's eyebrows, that's just vicious. I had to wrestle in front of 18,000 people in the Sumo Palace, with no eyebrows and with my hair all cut off. The boys thought it was hilariously funny, but they didn't have to go out there looking like that.

I've got nobody to blame but myself, because I chose to play the game. I understood the world I was in. If I didn't party with them, they wouldn't have had the opportunity to put something in my drink. And if it wasn't me getting ribbed, it would've happened to someone else. Getting ribbed is part of the business, so I had to accept it.

THE EDDIE GUERRERO STORY

If you don't bite the bullet and swallow your anger, the ribs just get worse.

But being on the other side of the ribbing, being the recipient of getting ribbed, is the reason I never get involved in any of that stuff. I know how much it sucks, and I would never want to hurt anyone like that just for a cheap laugh. I couldn't live with myself. I don't need to hurt people just to get some approval from the boys. That's just idiotic.

I hated the fact that I could never protect anyone from getting ribbed. If you try to stop a rib from happening, then you get all kinds of heat and more than likely become the next victim. And that's part of the culture too. You can't jump in and say, "Hey, man, leave him alone," because then you're the one betraying the game.

That was the world we lived in. The Nasty Boys were just doing what they were taught. They may have taken it to another level, but they weren't doing anything unusual.

Whatever else my flaws may be, I don't feel I'm a hurtful guy. When I'm threatened, I'll fight as hard as I can, but I get no pleasure out of hurting somebody. I know too many guys that do things like kicking a dog just for their own amusement. That's not my style.

There are wrestlers who get their thrills working stiff—actually hurting their opponents. I hate being stiff with someone, but sometimes you've got to do it. Sometimes you've got to be stiff to get respect.

To me, the wrestlers that *want* to work stiff, that *want* to hurt you, they're just stupid. People are giving you their body out there. They're trying to provide a living for their families. If you want to go stiff, go to UFC—Ultimate Fighting Championship. When somebody gives you his body and you take advantage of him, that's assault. That kind of behavior has no place in this business. Unfortunately, there are a lot of wrestlers like that.

Being a smaller wrestler, I've had to deal with assholes like that so many times. They think, *Eddie's not so big, I'll bust him up.* When that happens, I switch to survival mode. I don't want to fight out there, but if you mess with me, I'll give it back ten times over.

CHEATING DEATH, STEALING LIFE

made some great friends in Japan, people that I consider to be true brothers like Chris Benoit and Black Cat. One of my closest friends to this day is Dean Malenko. We met on my second or third tour over there.

We got booked in a match together, and I was pretty intimidated. I'd heard so much about Dean, about his shoot fighting and how good he was at stretching people. He'd learned to shoot from his dad, Boris Malenko, one of the greatest heels of all time and the master of shoot wrestling.

Dean was a quiet guy, not very talkative. He was all business—"Nice to meet you, what do you want to do out there? Okay, we'll call the rest in the ring."

I was so nervous before our match. Black Cat saw me in the dressing room, getting ready, and said, "Why are you so nervous? Malenko's easy, a total pro."

Sure enough, we went out there and Dean was great. Totally smooth. Dean's fluid, he just flows in the ring like water. He's so graceful, he makes everything look easy.

Though he wasn't the easiest guy to get to know, Dean and I hit it off. We became fast friends, a relationship that I treasure to this day.

One of my favorite things about working in Japan was that we'd get paid in cash. Brand-new hundred-dollar bills, nice and crisp. They even smelled good!

I got paid at the end of one tour, and just to be sure I wouldn't forget it, I put the envelope under my agenda. I woke up late the next morning, and as usual, I was running late for my flight. I hurried out of there and managed to make it to the Norita airport on time. I went to pick up some souvenirs and realized I didn't have enough yen to pay for them. I reached for my payoff, and that's when it hit me—I'd left it in the hotel!

My heart just dropped. I started tearing my luggage apart, throwing my clothes everywhere, hoping that I'd packed it, even though I knew that it was sitting in my hotel room.

All the boys were cracking up. Scott Norton came over to me and put his hand on my shoulder. "Hey, man, it happens to all of us," he said.

Scott suggested that maybe Black Cat could help me out. I called him and explained what I'd done. He told me to relax, that he'd take care of it.

Cat called the hotel where we'd been staying, and fortunately the maid had found my payoff and brought it to the front desk. He picked the cash up, then wired me my money.

When Cat saw my payoff—I think it was $1,000 or so—he got hot. "Is that all they're paying you? That's just not right. Let me see what I can do."

He told me that a grand might've been fine for my first tour, but after that, they should've upped my pay. God bless him, Cat spoke to the office and from that time on, I started getting regular raises every time I worked for NJPW.

I t hurts to hear what people thought of me back when I was partying all the time. But I have to remember that they didn't put me there. I did those things. It's nobody's fault but mine.

More than anything else, I'm embarrassed. People laugh and say I was the life of the party, but those laughs are at my expense.

I was out getting loaded with a bunch of the boys—Scott and Rick Steiner, the Nasty Boys, Brian Pillman, a few others.

As usual, we were all pretty lit. The Nasty Boys were so wasted, they took off all their clothes. There they were, Brian and Jerry, totally naked in the middle of the street. Rick Steiner was yelling shit at them, everybody was cracking up. Well, from what I've been told, as all this was going on, Scott Steiner got behind me with a lighter and turned me on. I'm telling you, I had no clue. Thank God for Pillman. He came over to me and very casually said, "Um, Eddie? You know you're on fire, right?"

"What?!" I couldn't feel a thing, I was that gone.

God bless Brian, he started slapping my ass to put me out! I swear, I didn't know what happened until the next morning when I woke up and saw my shorts—"What the hell happened?"

Pillman told that story all the time. God rest his soul, he was a tremendous storyteller, totally entertaining. "There was Eddie," he'd say, "standing there on fire, not selling it at all."

BLACK TIGER AND CHRIS "WILD PEGASUS" BENOIT.

CHAPTER 13

The junior heavyweight division first caught fire in the late seventies. Tatsumi Fujinami was a huge star in Japan and even won the World Wide Wrestling Federation Junior Heavyweight title at Madison Square Garden.

Tiger Mask was the next big star in Japanese wrestling. More than a star, in fact—he was a nationally beloved cultural icon.

Tiger Mask started out as an animated comic book superhero, but in the early eighties, New Japan decided to push the junior heavyweight division by turning the character into a real wrestler. Serious wrestling fans thought it was the stupidest idea ever, but with Satoru Sayama filling the role, Tiger Mask went on to become one of the greatest superstars in the history of the business. Sayama was an incredible talent, a true pioneer of the junior heavyweight style—high-flying, death-defying, revolutionary in his charisma and move set. With his unbelievably fast feet and breathtaking martial arts skills, Tiger Mask influenced just about every junior heavyweight that followed, from Jushin Thunder Liger and Great Sasuke to Ultimo Dragon and Rey Mysterio.

It wasn't just in Japan, either. Here in America, Tiger Mask was the first and only wrestler to simultaneously wear the World Wrestling Federation Junior Heavyweight and National Wrestling Alliance World Junior Heavyweight Championship belts.

Tiger Mask was such a phenomenon that when Sayama retired in 1983, the mask moved on to Mitsuharu Misawa. He wore it until 1990, followed by the amazing Koji Kanemoto, who was Tiger Mask when I came to New Japan.

Like any comic book superhero, Tiger Mask has an evil nemesis—Black Tiger. He's the Green Goblin to Tiger Mask's Spider-Man, the Lex Luthor to his Superman.

The first Black Tiger was a tremendous British worker named Marc "Rollerball" Rocco. He was a big draw in England and worked quite a bit in Japan before retiring in 1991.

I had been over to Japan a few times, doing better and better with each trip over. When management came to me and asked if I wanted to be the new Black Tiger, I said, "Yes," with not a hint of hesitation.

As far as I was concerned, my destiny was to work in Japan. If I was going to have any chance of making a career for myself as a wrestler, it was going to be there. So the opportunity to be Black Tiger was a very big deal for me. Even though my face would be hidden underneath a mask, it was a high-profile spot that could only bring me more exposure. Though I didn't know it at the time, being asked to be Black Tiger would actually have a profound effect on the rest of my wrestling career.

It wasn't the first time that I'd worked under a mask, but when I worked in Mexico as *Máscara Mágica,* my real identity was pretty much an open secret. This time, wearing the Black Tiger mask enabled me to let loose in a way that I'd never done before. The mask also allowed me to escape from the shadow of my family. I wasn't Gory Guerrero's son or Hector and Mando and Chavo's little brother—I was Black Tiger!

It wasn't a tremendous kayfabe, of course. Plenty of people knew that it was Eddy Guerrero under the Black Tiger mask, but it still gave me a sense of freedom unlike anything I'd ever known before.

Being Black Tiger liberated me as a performer. Hiding behind a mask allows you to live out the version of you that exists only in your heart. I was able to unleash my inner heel for the very first time. And you know what? I liked it a lot!

When I was Black Tiger, I was able to let my secret mean streak free. I could do things that I couldn't do as a babyface, like Pearl Harboring guys or cheating to win. With my face hidden behind the mask, my dark side was able to show itself. I turned out to be a natural heel.

The aggressiveness that emerged from being Black Tiger changed everything about my in-ring style. I think that was the moment when I really came into my own for the first time.

What was more important was that I kept growing and learning and improving. I finally understood what my dad had taught me about being a ring general. I learned how to truly lead a match.

When I look back, I see a direct line from Black Tiger to who I am now as Latino Heat. Being Black Tiger was where I first found my voice as a performer, where I uncovered the assertiveness and ferocity to unleash my inner character.

There weren't many Americans working in Mexico. Along with Latino Americans like myself, Konnan, and Rey Mysterio, there were just a few other North American wrestlers down there, people like Black Magic—Norman Smiley, King Haku, the late Mike "Tigre Canadiense" Lozanski, and Chris Jericho, who was working in EMLL as Lionheart. Chris is a great person, a loving, caring guy. We used to hang together, though he was more like a babysitter for me, looking out for me when I got loaded.

For a gringo to succeed down there, there's got to be something different about him. The old saying is true—when in Rome, do as the Romans do—but at the same time, you have to bring something new to the equation or they'll eat you alive.

There was one American among AAA's top stars—"Love Machine" Art Barr.

Art was a tremendous performer in every way—a ridiculously gifted wrestler, able to do all the acrobatic high spots the Mexican fans loved, plus incorporate the kind of character-driven charisma that gets you over in the States. He had the gift of being able to make every little thing he did mean something. Art was like the Ric Flair of lucha libre—a swaggering, conniving heel, but so entertaining that the people loved him.

Personally, I couldn't stand the guy.

I thought Art was arrogant, overconfident, and obnoxious. He was always bragging about how talented he was or how many autographs he'd signed after a show. In Art I saw a very ambitious person who would talk badly about you the second you turned your back.

But because we were among the few English-speaking wrestlers, we would hang out occasionally. One night we were having dinner together in Monterrey when Art made a suggestion that would change my life.

"You should go heel," he said between mouthfuls of steak. "Let's talk to Tony Peña and tell him we want to team up."

I was definitely interested. Being Black Tiger in Japan had me itching to try being a heel in Mexico. Plus, Art was a superstar and I knew it would be good business to pair up with him.

We brainstormed about how I would turn and what we would do once we were heels. It was my brother Mando that came up with an inspired scheme for how to turn me.

Armed with a creative angle that we knew would work, Art and I went to Antonio Peña. We laid out our idea and to our surprise, he agreed with us immediately.

Our plan was simple but brilliant. Santo and I were in a match against Art. I got powder thrown into my eyes and while I was blinded, Art took off Santo's mask and put it on himself. He gave me a couple of shots, then put the mask back onto Santo. With my vision blurred, I assumed it was Santo that hit me, so I attacked him and beat the shit out of him.

Well, Santo was so beloved, anyone that beat on him was instantly on the wrong side of the fans. They booed and threw stuff at me. The heat was un-believable. I wouldn't have been shocked if a riot had broken out right there and then.

From that moment on, I was a heel. When Art and I first started working as a team, we were called the American Machine, which just showed how Art was the star of our team. For a while, we were known as *La Pareja del Terror*. Then one night, one of the announcers said something like "Those gringos are loco," and all of a sudden we had a name that truly fit—*Los Gringos Locos*.

CHEATING DEATH, STEALING LIFE

At first, Art and I had trouble meshing. We were great as a tag team, but as people we just weren't clicking. We'd have huge arguments after every match.

I hated being in a tag team with him. I was absolutely miserable, having to work alongside a guy that I didn't like.

I've got to be honest with myself. Why did I feel that way about him? I think it was because subconciously, I was jealous of him.

In my mind, I felt I was the better worker. So why didn't people like me the way they liked him?

Art was such a magnetic guy, really outgoing and gregarious. He was the life of the party, both in the ring and out. There was something inside of me, asking, *Why can't I be like that?*

I hadn't learned yet how much personality had to do with success in this business. It didn't matter how good a wrestler I was—I couldn't touch Art as far as charisma was concerned.

Eventually, we came to find peace. I relinquished the starring role in the ring, but in the back, I became the team leader. Art was the charisma and I was in charge of the psychology.

That's always been my goal, to be the best psychological wrestler I can be. My dad taught me that psychology is everything. That's what sells the story you're trying to get over.

Art and I were both big believers in old-school ring psychology, and we did whatever was necessary to enforce it. Babyfaces—especially the top guys—hated to sell, but we made them do it. The way we did it was by shooting with the guys who refused to sell for us. We had to stretch a lot of guys, but pretty soon everybody got the message: either you sell for us or we beat the shit out of you.

At the same time, when it was time for us to sell, we sold our asses off. We'd beat the shit out of the babyfaces, but when it came time for their comeback, we gave it all back and then some. That's how we gained respect.

Our main rivals, El Hijo del Santo and his new partner, Octagon, fought us every step of the way. The whole locker room was afraid of Santo and Octagon because of their political power. Santo's spicy, the kind of guy

LOS GRINGOS LOCOS WEARING THE RED, WHITE, AND BLUE.

you've got to stretch a little bit to get him to hear you out. "Relax," I'd say, "I'm going to give it back to you."

Eventually they figured it out—the more they sold for us, the more they got over. Santo actually said, "I thought I was doomed with you guys. I didn't realize how much I was going to get over from this."

Little by little, Art and I grew closer. Part of it was simply the amount of time we spent together. If I wasn't with my family, then I was with him. If I wasn't in Japan, I was with him.

The more I got to know him, the more I started to understand who he really was. I saw the real Art Barr—the man, not the business Art.

It turned out I was dead wrong about him. Sure, he was ambitious, but he also had a great heart. It's just that in this business, you have to be so careful who you open your heart to.

Art was one of the most giving people I've ever known, buying me presents all the time. At first, I figured there had to be some ulterior motive behind his gifts. I didn't understand that he was just being a generous friend.

I saw what a tremendous dad he was to his kids, Dexter and Tiffany. When he'd go off on the road, he'd write out a bunch of little notes for Dexter. Then he'd hide them in various places so that every day, Dexter would have a surprise note from his dad. Watching Art, I learned so much about being a good father to my own kids.

There was a spirit about Art that just radiated out of him. He had the

CHEATING DEATH, STEALING LIFE

ability to make a joke of everything. He loved to rib people, he loved to tell stories. He was just a fun guy. And that's what the people saw in him.

Art made me laugh the way no one else ever could. He was a great story-teller, always exaggerating the truth for the maximum dramatic effect. If a dog took a shit in front of him, Art would say, "Brother, it was the biggest shit ever!"

That was one of the ways he broke the ice between us. He made me laugh so much, I couldn't help but love him.

Before long, we became best friends. We became brothers.

Pretty soon, Art and I were inseparable, even when we weren't working. Shaul was close with Art's boy, Dexter, and Vickie liked Art's girlfriend, Kerri, so it was easy for our families to spend time together. One time we all went to Universal Studios and had a total ball. It's funny—I think Art and I enjoyed ourselves even more than our kids!

I learned so much from Art. Before we started working together, I'd look at the more successful wrestlers and think, *I can outwrestle these guys in the ring, so why are they making more money than me?*

Art taught me that wrestling is not just about being skillful in the ring. There's so much more to it—having a charismatic personality, telling a com-pelling story with your facial reactions.

It was from working with Art that I started opening up and trying to be charismatic. I was such a shy person back then. I still am, but through Art, I learned how to unleash my inner personality in the ring.

My dad was incredibly charismatic, but for some reason, that wasn't part of his training. He didn't teach me when and how to grunt, which faces to make to sell something dramatically. I had to learn through experience.

Whenever I look back at my old matches, I'm amazed to see how little charisma I had. The look on my face was almost expressionless at times. Now, Art, on the other hand, that guy was just nonstop personality. He had charm oozing out of every pore. Art was a star, plain and simple.

It wasn't all about Art—I still brought a lot to the table. When we first teamed up, my finisher was the jackknife splash off the top turnbuckle. A wrestler named La Fiera used to do it, and I thought it was a great move. He was so graceful, flying off the top.

Art decided that he wanted to do the splash. He made it what it is today.

One night Too Cold Scorpio said to Art, "Man, you look just like a frog!" That's how it got the name "frog splash." Art was the guy that really made the splash froggy.

From that point on, our big team finish was me doing a superplex, followed by Art hitting the frog splash. It was really dramatic, and the fans just ate it up.

So while Art was the superstar, ultimately it was the chemistry, the combination of our talents, that made Los Gringos Locos work so well.

Of course, Art was only human. He wasn't always the anything-for-a-laugh guy he appeared to be on the outside. Inside, he was dealing with a lot of the same negative issues as I was.

When we were on the road, Art and I lived the way a lot of the boys did—we would stay up all night partying, go to the arena and wrestle, then start partying again.

I was basically just a beer drinker. I'd drink hard liquor occasionally—usually tequila—but beer was my first love. Though a lot of boys were taking pills, I was too scared. I'd heard too many horror stories about boys that had died from them. Not that I didn't get offered pills all the time.

"C'mon, here's a Halcion."

"No, thanks, man."

But after a while, I started overcoming my apprehensions. Art turned me on to Percocets and Percodans, which are moderate—but still pretty powerful and totally addictive—painkillers. I admit, I fell in love with the Perks. I loved the euphoric feeling I got from them, the warmth and pleasure that come from taking any opiate.

Slowly but surely, I lost all my fear and started indulging in pills. Perks came in packages of twelve, and I'd down half a dozen at a time. Soon I began taking Valium and Halcion. Eventually I reached the point where I would take whatever downs or painkillers were around.

There was one pill that I couldn't get into, an extremely strong muscle relaxer called Soma. They were very popular with the boys, but I never really liked the feeling I got off of them. Soma are really easy to get in Mexico, so I'd buy a few hundred pills at a time, then trade them out for painkillers that I did like.

As much as I enjoyed the Perks, my drug of choice remained alcohol. I never worked drunk—it was always after the show was done. We'd head back to the hotel and drink beer all night, either in the bar or in someone's room. Sometimes we'd hit a local strip club and hang out there.

I should point out that not everybody was partying like that. Chris Jericho, for example, would have a few beers, but wouldn't touch a pill under any circumstances. But for a lot of the other wrestlers, that was the lifestyle, though maybe not as extreme as mine.

Vickie never saw my partying as that big of a deal. She understood that it was part of the culture. To her, my heavy drinking was normal. It wasn't until much later that we realized I had a problem.

Los Gringos Locos kept getting bigger and bigger. We were the guys the fans loved to hate. We totally played up the fact that Art was American and I was a Mexican-American. Real Mexicans just hate Mexican-Americans, so the more American we acted, the more heat we drew.

And as we got more over, more people wanted to be associated with us. It wasn't long before Los Gringos Locos began to grow into a full-fledged heel stable, the D-Generation X of AAA.

Konnan was the first to try and grab onto our heart. That pissed Art off no end. He didn't want anyone taking away from what we'd built. He fought tooth and nail to keep Konnan out, but I knew there was nothing we could do. Konnan was AAA's leading man. What he said went. "Hey, man," I told Art, "just go with it."

Since we couldn't stop Konnan and Tony Peña from turning Los Gringos Locos into a stable, we decided we wanted some say in who joined up. We suggested Black Cat, a phenomenal talent that we were thrilled to have as part of our team. But from there, the floodgates opened. More and more wrestlers jumped on the bandwagon—Chicano Power, El Misterioso, and the late Louis Spicolli, who was working under one of the all-time bad wrestler names: Madonna's Boyfriend.

Ultimately, it didn't matter. No matter who was put under the umbrella, Los Gringos Locos was all about Art. He was the true star of the show.

On June 22, 1994, Los Gringos Locos went to Art's hometown of Portland, Oregon, to do an AAA show in association with CWUSA, an indie promotion run by Art's dad, Sandy.

Sandy Barr was a great guy. He was a pretty good wrestler back in the day, and when he became a promoter, he was still one of the boys.

Sandy was totally jazzed about the show—he had booked Tonya Harding to appear, which at the time was a very big deal. For those too young to remember, she was an Olympic figure skater who had spent six months in the headlines for conspiring to disable one of her rivals on the U.S. skating team by having her knee bashed in with a crowbar.

It was a bit of a coup to have such a big "celebrity" take part in an indie wrestling show. Sandy really went all out, spending a ton of money on promotion. He booked the show into a baseball field, thinking it was going to be a huge success. God bless him, he really thought people would travel up to the Pacific Northwest to see a tabloid celebrity and a bunch of Mexican wrestlers.

Tonya Harding was actually very nice, quiet and sweet, not at all like the crowbar-swinging ho the press made her out to be. Of course, she had no idea who we were. She was just earning a paycheck, capitalizing on whatever was left of her fifteen minutes of fame.

The big main event match was Konnan, Blue Panther, and Perro Aguayo against me, Art, and a Portland-based indie worker named Bruiser Brian Cox—who's since passed away—with Tonya as our "manager."

It was a fiasco from the word go. Under Oregon State Boxing and Wrestling Commission rules, Tonya wasn't an officially licensed manager and as such, she wasn't allowed at ringside. We all walked out together, then Tonya went and sat down in a folding chair about halfway up the aisle.

That was pretty much it. No one had given Tonya anything to do, and she didn't make a lot of effort to get involved. Art and I had to keep running up the aisle to get instructions from her and even then, she just sat there stone-faced. Her biggest contribution was handing Art a glass of water to throw in Perro Aguayo's face.

It was all pretty silly. Unfortunately for Sandy, the show turned out to be a colossal bomb. It turned out Tonya wasn't alone in not knowing who we were. No one up in Oregon had the slightest interest in *lucha libre,* and the stadium was virtually empty.

I felt so bad for Sandy. It was one of those nights where everything just went wrong. After the show, somebody stole a couple hundred dollars of my cash payoff from the locker room. Art and his dad both tried to give me some of their money, but I couldn't take it. I knew that it was a bad night for them, financially speaking.

The only good thing to come out of the whole mess was that the show got a ton of press, which made Art so happy. *USA Today* ran photos from the event and of course, Art and Konnan totally hogged the camera. I think maybe a little of my leg made it into the frame, but that's about it. As usual, I didn't mind. I knew my place.

Los Gringos Locos' biggest feud was with AAA's top babyface, El Hijo del Santo, and his tag team partner, Octagon. It went on for months, ending with a Hair vs. Masks match at AAA's *When Worlds Collide,* the first-ever *lucha* Pay-Per-View to be held and broadcast in America. We all knew that the feud had run its course. It was time for the blow-off, and in Mexico, a Hair vs. Masks match is the ultimate blow-off.

The original plan was that it would just be me against Santo, but Art was adamant that it would be better as a tag match. We made our case to Antonio Peña and he agreed.

Art was a very persuasive guy, so he was usually in charge of our team's business. But for that match, I called the shots. I knew how much my hair was worth. If I was going to have my head shaved, I wanted to get every last penny I could for it.

When the plan was just me vs. Santo, Peña and I settled on $10,000 for my hair. But when our tag partners came into the picture, Art and I were told we would get $5,000 each.

"No way," I said. "We agreed my hair was worth $10,000."

After some haggling, we came to a compromise—Art and I would each get $7,500. Which really wasn't a bad deal, considering my hair grew back.

A couple of weeks before *When Worlds Collide,* Art and I went to Japan for a few New Japan shows—Art's first. He so impressed the office that they offered him a shot to come back and work a program with their biggest star, Jushin Thunder Liger.

About halfway through the tour, I was woken up by pounding at my hotel room door.

"All right, all right! One second!"

I crawled out of bed and opened the door. Art was standing there, with no eyebrows and all the hair on the back of his head shaved off.

"Bro, what happened?"

"Those fucking Nasty Boys happened," said Art.

Right away, I got hot. I don't care how much they wanted to rib him. Cutting his hair the way they did, knowing that we had a big hair match coming up, that was beyond a rib. That was an insult. That was a threat to our business.

To be fair, they were probably a little loaded when they did it. No one thinks straight after they've got a few drinks in them. But at the same time, the Nasty Boys were the kind of guys who didn't give a shit about anyone but themselves. They didn't respect us enough not to do what they did. They didn't care about us losing money and not being able to feed our families. All that mattered was that they got their rib in.

I'll always have a resentment against those guys for doing that. Always. Art had to wear extensions for *When Worlds Collide,* because the Nasty Boys had messed up his hair so badly. He actually had to wear a fake mullet, because the whole damn point of the match was that our hair was going to be cut off.

As angry as I was about the Nasty Boys' assholish behavior, when the time finally came for revenge, I decided against it. I turned the other cheek.

It was in Japan, and of course, we were all out partying—me, Black Cat, Knobs, and a few others. I always made a point to be on my guard when I was around the Nasty Boys. I'd get a buzz on but try not to get too screwed up. And I'd always watch my drinks, just to be sure that I wasn't going to get gimmicked. It helped having a great friend like Black Cat around to watch my back.

Sometime late in the evening, Knobs passed out, right there at the table. He was totally out. We even lifted up his head and flicked his eyebrows, just to see if he was really unconscious.

Cat looked at me and said, "Now's your chance, man. C'mon, I'll go get a razor."

I thought about how much Knobs had pissed me off over the years, how him and Sags had shown me and Art so little respect. I came close, but after a few seconds decided against it. What would I gain from messing with the guy? "No, Cat," I said. "Just let it go."

While I resisted shaving Knobs's head, I did untimately enjoy some back-handed revenge on Sags and Knobs.

The office sponsored us for a couple of shows, which in Japan means they take care of everything—hotel, food, drinks, everything top of the line. They put us up in this amazing five-star hotel. It was beautiful, sitting right on the edge of a mountain overlooking the ocean. Oh my God, was it gorgeous!

That night, all the boys got together for dinner, one of the best meals I've ever had. Kobe steaks, king crabs, the whole nine yards. And of course, the drinks were flowing nonstop throughout.

As usual, the Nastys got their load on. While they were getting more and more rowdy, Cat and I started taking all the crab and shellfish waste off people's plates. We mixed it up into a little sauce.

"Hey, Brian, Jerry," I said, "have you tasted this? Mmmmm, it's delicious, bro! Here, have some!"

They started slurping it up while me and Cat tried not to piss our pants laughing. That was so satisfying—feeding those assholes a big bowl of shit. And they didn't even have a clue!

I've shared that story with a few of the boys over the years, but I've never had a chance to tell Sags and Knobs. Now's my chance—you ate crab shit, boys. I hope you enjoyed eating it as much as I enjoyed feeding it to you!

NOBODY MADE ME LAUGH LIKE ART BARR.

CHAPTER 14

When *Worlds Collide* was a special moment in my career. The event was held on November 6, 1994, at the Los Angeles Sports Arena. We had a tremendous crowd, over 11,000 strong. It was mostly Chicano *lucha* fans, but there was also a good amount of what came to be called smart marks.

At that time, the wrestling business was changing. The fans were becoming more knowledgeable about wrestling. They knew there was more going on out there than just the big two promotions, World Wrestling Federation and World Championship Wrestling. They would trade bootleg tapes from New Japan and AAA and this crazy new promotion that was getting popular in Philadelphia—Extreme Championship Wrestling. Part of the excitement surrounding *When Worlds Collide* was that the smart marks were going to see a major *lucha* event in their own country.

Our match was Best Two-Out-Of-Three Falls. According to *lucha* rules, a fall was when both members of a team were pinned. Art and I won the first fall when I took Santo down off Art's shoulders with a flying headscissors. With Santo out, I hit Octagon with a superplex, setting up Art's frog splash. "That's made in the USA," Art boasted as he covered Octagon for the three count.

Art and I started out in control of the second fall, quickly pinning Santo to leave us in another two-on-one situation with Octagon. But we got cocky—Art accidentally set Octagon up with a chance to get me with a huracanrana. The ref counted me out, but Art was so overconfident, he had his back turned and assumed it was Octagon getting pinned. Before he knew it, Art went down to a side Russian legsweep and had to submit to Octagon's finishing hold.

Both teams were even, going into the third and final fall. Art cheated to win, hitting Octagon with a Tombstone Piledriver when the ref wasn't looking. We sold that it was such a vicious piledriver, Octagon needed medical attention and a stretcher was brought out to carry him to the back.

It was times like this that Santo shone. He refused to get pinned, even after we got him with our trademark superplex/frog splash finishing combination. Santo tossed me to the outside, then hit me with a plancha from the top rope. With the referee on the outside with us, Blue Panther ran into the ring and hit Art with a piledriver. Before I could stop him, Santo rolled back into the ring and pinned Art, leaving us to face each other, man to man.

We went at it hard. The crowd was going crazy by this point, reacting to a series of dramatic near falls. It looked like I was going to pull it off when I tried a dragon suplex on Santo, but he blocked it and managed to put me down for the 1-2-3 with a huracanrana.

The fans were loving it as Art and I cut off our hair—I did Art, then he did me. We started with a scissors, then Santo and Octagon came in and gave us a buzz cut, right down to the skin.

Santo actually saved my hair to this day. He keeps it in a little baggie.

Traditionally, you get to keep your opponent's mask after winning it, but I've never heard of anyone hanging on to the hair. I guess Santo feels there was something special about that match and he wants to commemorate it by holding on to a bag full of my hair. I'm actually quite touched and honored by that, though it does seem a little freaky.

That match has gone into legend as one of the greatest matches ever, a five-star classic, but it's hard for me to see it that way. I thank the fans for loving it, but I just can't appreciate it the way they do.

CHEATING DEATH, STEALING LIFE

I don't mean any disrespect—who am I to judge the fans for what they like? But I can only see it from the perspective of a worker. When I watch that match—or any of my matches, for that matter—all I can see is what I was doing wrong. I can't help it, I'm just very critical of my own work.

That night, however, I thought it was the greatest match ever. It was definitely one of the most thrilling nights of my career up to that point. Art and I were sure that we had delivered something spectacular and innovative.

But then I got a phone call from my brothers, which totally burst my bubble. They've always been very judgmental about my work, especially my bigger matches. That's one of the reasons I'm so hard on my own work—I know that no matter how good it is, my brothers are always going to be critical.

A rumor sprang up after *When Worlds Collide.* Paul Heyman—Paul E., the co-owner and creative genius behind Extreme Championship Wrestling—saw the show, or so the story goes, and was so impressed, he decided to sign Los Gringos Locos to ECW. Paul E. envisioned a huge feud between us and Public Enemy, who at the time were the promotion's hottest tag team.

I have no idea if that's true or not. All I know is that Art heard about it and got all excited about coming to work in the States. He called me and said, "They want us, brother! They want us!"

Of course with Art, you never could tell from one minute to the next what was real and what was just bullshit.

CHAPTER 15

After *When Worlds Collide,* Art and I were given some time off from AAA. He headed home to Portland and I took off for a tour of Japan.

I was still on the road in Japan on November 23. When I arrived at the hotel that night, there was a message from Vickie, saying that I should give her a call immediately. Right away I knew something was up.

I called home and I could hear her hesitating, like she wasn't sure how to tell me whatever it was she had to tell me. Finally she just came out with it.

"Art's dead," she said.

My first thought was that she meant Art Flores—Tury, my best friend.

"Tury's dead? Oh God, what happened?"

"No, not Tury," Vickie said. "Art."

"Art's not dead," I said. "He can't be dead. It's a lie."

I refused to hear what Vickie was telling me. I called her back three times, asking her to tell me what hospital Art was in. Each time, she tried to make me understand the truth—Art was dead.

I couldn't believe it. Actually, I could believe it—I just couldn't *accept* it.

"It's true, baby," Vickie said. "Art's gone."

She then told me everything. Art had been home with his son, Dexter, getting ready to have Thanksgiving the next day. That morning, Dexter tried to wake Art up, but he couldn't get him up. He saw his dad was cold, so he covered him with extra blankets.

Meanwhile, Art's mom, Jodi, had been trying to call, and after not getting an answer all morning, she decided to drive over to the house. She went to the door and started knocking. Dexter tried to let her in, but he couldn't reach the lock. He just kept saying, "Grandma, Daddy won't wake up."

Jodi—who's a wonderful woman—went around back and looked in the window. She saw Art lying there, all pale and still, and knew right away that he was gone.

To this day, nobody knows what happened. The cause of death is officially undetermined. People always say it was an OD of some kind, but that's never been proven. When the medical examiners did their autopsy, they didn't find an excess of anything in his body that might have killed him.

Some say it could've been a stroke, others think maybe it was a heart attack. But the fact is, the reason for Art's death remains a mystery.

I was shocked and heartbroken. All I wanted to do was get back to the States so that I could attend Art's funeral. Unfortunately, I was booked in a championship match against Jushin Liger, and New Japan management refused to let me leave. I could've said "Screw it" and gone home, but I would probably have lost my job. I had no choice, really. I had to stay and wrestle. That's probably what Art would've wanted anyway.

Because I was stuck in Japan, Vickie flew up to Portland and represented me at the funeral. When the time came for me to come home, I flew straight into Portland so I could visit with Art's folks.

Art's death was one the hardest experiences of my life. I don't think I've ever fully gotten over it, though I've learned to live with it.

It took a long time for me to come to peace with Art's passing. I cried every night for two or three months straight. I used to call my mom and cry to her about how much I missed him.

Then one night I had an incredibly vivid dream that I believe was sent to me by God. I was in the dressing room. I turned around and there was Art. He was so bright and happy, he was glowing. I asked him, "Are you okay?"

"I'm okay, Eddie," he replied, smiling.

I kept asking him, "Are you okay?"

"I'm okay," he said. "I'm okay."

"Did you make it to heaven?"

"Barely," Art said, "but I made it."

"Did you meet my dad?"

He smiled even wider. "Yeah, I met your dad."

All of a sudden I was in the ring, wrestling. It was weird, like two different camera angles. I was in the distance, watching myself, and there was Art, in my corner. But then I'd be in the ring. When I looked back over my shoulder to see Art, he wasn't there.

It sounds crazy, but it was completely real to me. When I woke up, I felt at peace for the first time since Art died. That was the moment when I finally came to grips with his death.

Art elevated me to the next level. The time we spent working together made me realize just how important charisma and showmanship were to getting ahead in this business.

But all of that is secondary to how much I loved Art as a friend. He was such a jokester. He made me laugh more than anyone I've ever known. Art's friendship was a true source of joy in my life, and I miss him to this day.

After Art's death, Vickie and I tried to stay in contact with his family. We would talk on the phone and exchange letters, but after a couple of years, they stopped returning my calls. It hurt, but I understood that hearing from me was a painful reminder of what they'd lost. If not talking to me was what they needed to do in order to move on, I was totally cool with it.

For a long time, I thought about Art every single day. I don't anymore, though he'll always be in my heart. Sometimes moving on is the only way to put death behind you. Otherwise it'll haunt you forever, and that's not a healthy way to live.

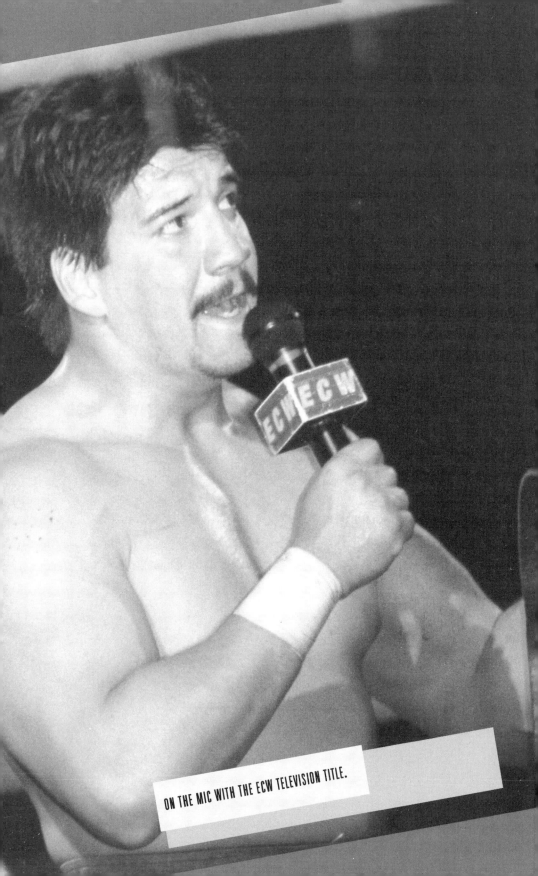

ON THE MIC WITH THE ECW TELEVISION TITLE.

CHAPTER 16

Art was the first of many wrestlers I've known that left us before their time.

The list goes on and on—Louis Spicolli, Brian Pillman, Moondog Spot, Curt Hennig, Crash Holly, Road Warrior Hawk. All gone, all way too young.

It happens so often. It breaks my heart, because in our business, death is no longer a surprise. I don't have an answer as to why so many of us don't make it. All I can do is shake my head and thank God that I'm still here.

There's no getting around the fact that wrestling takes its toll on people. Not just physically, but emotionally as well. This business is so stressful—it requires you to beat up your body night after night. It causes you to be away from your family most of the time, living your life in hotel rooms and rental cars.

And because we're all independent contractors, the politics involved in protecting your position is incredibly isolating. It all adds up to a massive emotional weight on your shoulders.

Part of the appeal of wrestling is that it allows grown men to act like fifteen-year-olds, to be a little bit crazy. In fact, it encourages it. So when you're done with the business—or when the business is done with you—you're really not prepared for the next stage of your life. The wrestling business doesn't equip you for the real world. It doesn't teach you how to be a real person.

It's a hard life, and for some people, the only way to deal with it is by getting high. I know that's what I did.

Art's passing was a major turning point in my life, one of the most profound experiences I've ever had. I prayed a lot after he died. I questioned God, asking Him why He took my brother from me. I simply couldn't understand it. My heart ached, but my love of wrestling, my desire to make it in the business, never faded.

If there was any small positive effect from Art's passing, it was that his death scared the living shit out of me. I continued to drink, but cut out all drug use.

At the end of December, I went back down to Mexico. I was still pretty devastated, but I had to work. I did one match and then everything went to hell.

The peso had been slowly crashing over the past year, and by December the government was forced to devalue the peso by fifty percent. That ultimately led to the collapse of the Mexican stock market and a terrible recession that was stopped only when the U.S. government bailed them out.

As a result of the peso crisis, Antonio told me that he simply couldn't afford to pay me anymore. To be honest, I didn't really care. With Art gone, my heart just wasn't in it anymore. I did a little work in Juarez, because I was getting paid in American dollars, but as far was AAA was concerned, I was done.

Konnan and Peña milked the Los Gringos Locos gimmick for a while longer, but without me or Art, it was just sad. They had a bunch of Mexican boys pretending to be American, waving the American flag, but nobody bought it. Finally the gimmick just petered out, and good riddance to it.

When Antonio let me go, I was content to go home and figure out my next move. I assumed that the only way I was going to continue my career was by working in Japan. There was still no chance of finding work in the States, despite the underground buzz growing about my work.

Art's dream was always about going to work in America. He used to go on and on about how we were catching on with the smart fans. "Brother, we can definitely get over in the States," he'd say. "I'm telling you, the time is right."

There were so many obvious reasons why I didn't think it could happen—my size, my wrestling style, my ethnicity. I'd seen what had happened to my brothers' careers, and I couldn't imagine that it'd be any different for me.

Still, I kept hearing great things about ECW. Chris and Dean had been working there and they would tell me stories of how wild it was, from the fans to the locker room.

"It's like a cult," Dean said, shaking his head. "You've got to see it to believe it."

When I told Dean that Paul Heyman had supposedly shown interest in Los Gringos Locos before Art passed, he said that he would reach out to Heyman and see if it was true.

It turned out that Paul E. was indeed a fan of my work. He called and told me how he wasn't only interested in putting on bloody garbage matches—he wanted ECW to also be home to the best serious wrestling in the world. When he asked me if I'd like to come up to Philadelphia and work a few matches for ECW, I agreed immediately. All of a sudden, wrestling in America didn't seem so unrealistic after all.

ECW came at exactly the right time in my life. I was feeling a little cocky after *When Worlds Collide*, thinking, *Hey, maybe I am pretty great*, but life quickly knocked me back down. I lost Art, I couldn't get work. I had been humbled.

When I got to ECW, I had no idea how much fun I was going to end up having there. I'll be honest—I really wasn't expecting much, and it turned out to be a great experience.

That locker room was so crazy. Everybody there was so passionate about wrestling. There were some incredible people working at ECW—Dean

Malenko, Chris Benoit, Mick Foley, Terry Funk, Tazz, Tommy Dreamer, the Pit Bulls, the Public Enemy. They might not have been the biggest stars in the world, but they were definitely amazing talents.

There was more mutual respect in the ECW locker room than anywhere else I've ever worked. I wasn't treated better or worse than anyone else, but the quality of my work was genuinely appreciated. Sure, I didn't make a lot of money at ECW, but nobody else did either. The fact is, Paul E. gave me work when I didn't have any. Whatever I made there was a blessing.

My first ECW match was on April 8, 1995, at the South Philly bingo hall that was known to smart wrestling fans as the ECW Arena. When I arrived at the building, Paul E. introduced me to the locker room and put me over like a million dollars. "This guy here is one of the best workers in the business," he said.

I was blown away. I never expected anybody to talk about me like that, much less in front of the boys. Hearing Paul E. say such nice things about me really made me want to deliver for him.

That night I was booked in an ECW TV Championship match against Too Cold Scorpio, a terrific wrestler that I knew from Japan. He was a tremendous athlete, trained in the New Japan dojo. To this day, I've never seen another person of his size that can do the kind of aerial work he does in the ring.

When I walked out into the ECW Arena for the first time, the response from the fans knocked my socks off. I had thought I was going to be working as a heel, but when I went out there, the place just exploded with a total babyface pop. My first thought was, *Wow, they think I'm a babyface. Well, I'll turn them, no problem.*

I sucker-punched Scorpio and to my surprise, the fans popped even more. I couldn't believe it! I tried every trick I knew, and the more heel shit I pulled, the more they popped. I couldn't do anything to make them hate me that night. I could've stood in the middle of the ring and farted and the fans would've cheered me.

It's like I've always said—the fans decide whether you're a baby or a heel. That night, the ECW fans were excited to see me and they wanted me as a babyface. I didn't have a choice. I became a babyface.

Scorpio and I gave the fans what they paid to see—a hell of a wrestling match. The cheers and chants really spurred me to give them my best work. Everybody was yelling, "Eddy! Eddy!" and "We love Art!" It was a tremendous night.

I became the new ECW TV champ that night, a pretty cool way to start things off. It showed me how strongly Paul E. and ECW co-owner Todd Gordon felt about my work, how they saw me as having the potential to help put their business over.

To come into a promotion and win a title on the first night is a very big deal—it's practically a guarantee that you're going to be working there for at least a little while. Titles are given to a wrestler for two reasons, to help elevate him, or so he can help elevate other people. I've been on both sides. In a way, carrying a title to put others over is more of a badge of honor. It shows that you're seen as popular and professional enough to help somebody else to the next level.

I was fortunate enough to spend most of my career in ECW working with good friends—people like Too Cold Scorpio and Dean Malenko. That allowed me to keep to myself and avoid any dressing room politics. All I had to do was hang on to Dean's coattails and I was set.

I wore the ECW TV title for a couple of months. Night after night, I was blown away by how much the ECW fans respected wrestling. I'd never seen anything like it. They were as passionate about the business as the wrestlers. Not only that, they were sharp—they understood the ins and outs of wrestling better than any fans I'd ever encountered. As a result, I felt an appreciation for my work that I'd never felt before.

Dean and I feuded over the TV title, with every match going to a freaking draw. It was crazy—every night we'd go out there and do half-hour matches. Working with Dean has always been magical for me. He's like the Baryshnikov of wrestling—so smooth, so fluid. Every move he does flows perfectly into the next.

My style at the time was very much a mix of the Mexican and Japanese— high flying, some suplexes, and a bit of old-fashioned mat wrestling. Dean, on the other hand, was trained as a shoot wrestler—lots of mat work and submission holds. But he's so talented, he can pretty much go with anyone he's matched against. His knowledge of shoot wrestling makes him very dangerous. He applies holds that could easily break his opponent's leg or pop his ankle.

Though our styles are very different, they meshed together perfectly. If there's one thing I've learned in my career, it's that you can't explain chemistry. It just happens. No matter what the circumstances are, Dean and I can go out there and tear the house down. Our worst matches are still good matches in the fans' eyes.

Dean and I went back and forth for weeks, trading the TV title between us. We reached the point where we developed a true psychic connection. It's an amazing feeling, being able to know just what the person you're working with is thinking, to know exactly where he's going next. It works both ways—they're as connected to you as you are to them. And once you know that you've got the wrestling chemistry down, you can add to it, intensify it with more drama, more emotion. When that chemistry is right, two wrestlers can go out there and tear the house down, night after night, and never do the same match twice.

It also creates a situation where you don't necessarily need to talk about what to do in the ring together. One night ECW was doing a show down in Florida. That afternoon Dean and I went out for a few beers and lost track of time. Eventually we realized that we were supposed to be at work and quickly rushed over to the building. When we got there, Paul was definitely a little hot.

"Sorry, sorry," we said, and ran straight out to the ring without the slightest discussion of what we were going to do. As usual, we had a hell of a match.

had only been with ECW for a couple of months when I got a call from WCW booker Kevin Sullivan. I'd known him since I was a kid, hanging out in Florida with Hector and Chavo.

Word had spread that Dean and I were tearing the house down every night. Kevin was looking to spark things up in WCW by signing a few wrestlers that could bring something different to the table.

Gossip travels pretty quickly through the locker rooms, so Dean, Chris, and I all had some idea that WCW was interested in bringing us down south. When the rumors went from just gossip to something more reliable, the three of us sat down and had a talk. We all pretty much came to the same conclusion—that it wouldn't be in our best interests to go there. So many people had told us the same things, that WCW treated smaller wrestlers like crap and that the locker room was a political nightmare.

So when Kevin finally called me, I told him thanks, but no thanks. "I'll be honest," I said. "I don't really have any confidence in you guys."

Kevin was cool, telling me that I should think on it. After I hung up, I called Dean and Chris, both of whom told me that they'd also spoken to WCW and that they'd accepted their offer. *Damn,* I thought, *maybe I made the wrong move.*

Dean and Chris are both very smart businessmen. If they had changed their minds and decided that there was a shot of making something happen in WCW, then who was I to disagree?

My brothers, as always, had conflicting opinions. Mando was very positive, telling me to go for it. Hector and Chavo, on the other hand, were both against it. "They're not going to treat you right," Hector told me, reflecting on his own bad experiences with WCW.

I thought back to my mom's advice when I was debating whether to jump from EMLL to AAA. "You'll never know if it's right or wrong unless you go and find out for yourself," she said. "Sometimes in life you've got to just hold your nose and dive into the water. I know you, Eddie. You're a fighter. You're not going to drown."

Mom's guidance helped give me the strength to make what turned out to be a great move, so I tried to apply the same advice toward going to WCW. What did I have to lose? The worst thing that could happen was that I'd flop in WCW and go back to working in Japan.

After carefully weighing all the pros and cons, I decided to go for it. I called Kevin back and very apologetically asked, "Are you still interested?"

THE EDDIE GUERRERO STORY

SHERILYN, AGE FOUR MONTHS.

Money was definitely an issue as far as my deciding to sign up with WCW. We had just bought a three-bedroom house in El Paso, my family's first real home. More importantly, my second daughter had just been born, so the fact that WCW had offered me more money than I'd ever earned before was definitely a blessing.

Vickie was in her ninth month when I went off to do a tour with New Japan. On July 8, we had a six-hour road trip between shows, and right before we left, I found out that Vickie had gone into labor. I was so excited! Every time we pulled over, I'd run to a phone and call home for an update.

CHEATING DEATH, STEALING LIFE

Finally we stopped for dinner and I reached my mother-in-law, who told me that I had a new baby daughter—Sherilyn Amber Guerrero.

I was so happy. All the boys were just as excited for me. I think they all could relate to how I must've been feeling, how I wasn't around for the birth of my child. It happens all the time, wrestlers being out on the road, earning a living while their wives give birth to their babies.

Needless to say, we celebrated that night with a bunch of beers after the show. Not that I needed an excuse to drink, but having a baby gave me a hell of a good reason to party.

When I first heard that WCW was interested, I talked to Paul Heyman and told him that I was going to stick around with ECW. He was, of course, very grateful and positive about my future in the company. So after I changed my mind and decided to sign with WCW, I immediately called Paul to tell him that I was leaving. I explained that it had nothing to do with him or ECW, that it was simply a business move that I had to make.

Paul was very quiet on the phone—unusually so—and then just said, "Okay. I understand."

The first thing Paul did was book me in a title match with Too Cold Scorpio so that I could drop the TV title. I know some guys think it makes them look bad to lose a championship belt, but "doing the honors"—that is, passing a title along when you leave the company—is the right thing for a wrestler to do. That was one of my dad's most important lessons—the business of professional wrestling is about more than just an individual worker.

Paul E. suggested that Dean and I should say good-bye to the ECW fans by putting on a series of farewell matches, wrapping it up at the ECW Arena with a guaranteed showstopper, a Two-Out-of-Three Falls match.

We blew the roof off every night of the farewell series, but when we got to the ECW Arena for the closing match, I was so nervous. I knew that the ECW fans really let a wrestler have it when he left to go work at one of the two big companies. They even had a special chant—"You sold out!" I didn't want my ECW run to end on a sour note. It was a very special couple of months, and I was anxious to close it out in as positive a fashion as I could.

I needn't have worried. The crowd was just electric, responding to everything, even the little bumps in the road.

We went back and forth for ten hot minutes and after a number of near falls, I managed to roll Dean up for the first three count. But minutes later he caught me in a Texas Cloverleaf and forced me to submit, tying things up.

The finish was where the best action was. We had the fans on their feet with false finish after false finish. Finally, Dean hip-tossed me into a Pat O'Connor roll-up. But I popped Dean's ribs, pulling his arms so all four of our shoulders were down to create a double pinning combination.

Usually fans feel cheated after a match like that goes to a draw, but in this case, it was just a total love fest. I've never felt anything like that ovation. Instead of "You sold out," they chanted, "Please don't go!" It was a very special moment, one of the greatest of my career.

The intensity of the emotion in that room was just incredible. As I stood there, taking in all the love, the entire locker room came out to honor Dean and me. The fans' appreciation was special, but getting the respect of our peers was even better.

Even after all that, I walked to the back thinking, *Damn. It wasn't the best I could've given them.* It happens after just about every big match—no matter how good it was, I can't help but wonder if I could've given it just a little bit more.

I'm not saying it wasn't a good match. I know how much the fans loved it, and I've got to trust their opinion. But for myself, it was not what I wanted our last ECW match to be. I wanted to leave them with a lot more.

Though ECW ultimately had to close its doors, when you look back at what they accomplished, it's pretty impressive. Paul E. competed against two huge companies with pretty much nothing except a bunch of talented wrestlers and an incredibly loyal fan following, and ended up having a huge influence on the business.

LEARNING ALL I COULD ABOUT *LUCHA LIBRE*.

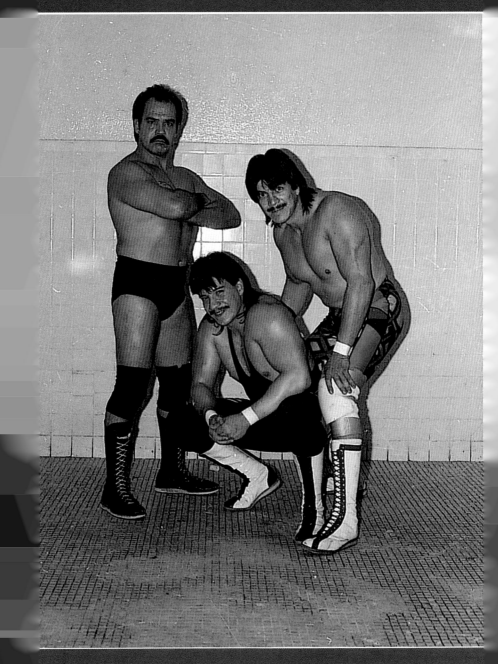

THAT'S ME WITH MY BROTHERS HECTOR (LEFT) AND MANDO (RIGHT) WHEN WE ALL WERE WORKING IN MEXICO.

COURTESY OF THE GUERRERO FAMILY.

"Los Gringos Locos"—
me and Art Barr.

SELLING LATINO HEAT WITH
"CHYNETTE," MISS KITTY.

LANDING A FROG SPLASH ON KURT ANGLE AT *WRESTLEMANIA XX.*

My girls:
Sherilyn and Shaul.

I'm so lucky to have
found my love again
with Vickie.

You'd think by
now Rey would
learn....

So many great wrestlers got their first opportunity to shine in ECW, wrestlers that probably wouldn't have had that same opportunity anywhere else. No question about it—you've got to include me in that list of names. Without my run in ECW, who knows what path my career might've taken?

CHAPTER 17

At the end of August, Dean and I went down to Atlanta to pay our first official visit to World Championship Wrestling. We stopped at a taping of *WCW Saturday Night,* which they used to do at a studio called Center Stage, near the Turner Broadcasting headquarters.

Dean and I had spent our entire adult lives as wrestlers, but stepping into the WCW dressing room made us both feel very timid. We'd heard so many stories about what went on down there, how smaller wrestlers like us were treated like shit and how we were going to get eaten alive by the politics. Sure enough, everyone there looked at us like we were there to steal their spots. It was just horrible. I had never felt anything like that before in my life.

Even with the negative vibes, I was still pretty excited to be there. I was in WCW, an opportunity I'd always wanted, but never in a million years expected.

There were two dressing rooms at Center Stage—one for the top boys, then another for the rest of the roster. Dean and I were in the second locker area, saying hello to the wrestlers we knew and introducing ourselves to the rest, when all of a sudden we heard yelling from the other room.

"Fuck you!"

"No, fuck you!"

"No! Fuck YOU!"

Then the pounding started—*Boom! Crash! Boom!*

Everybody ran to see what was going on. Standing in the middle of the dressing room were Paul Orndorff and Vader, right in each other's faces, red-faced and screaming at each other. It wasn't long before Vader had enough yelling and punched Orndorff right in the gut.

That wasn't enough to stop Orndorff. Here's this older guy with a bum left arm—which he'd injured in the middle of his legendary feud with Hulk Hogan, then never took time off to get it taken care of—and he just started beating the living shit out of big Vader—*boom, boom, boom!*

Down went Vader, but Mr. Wonderful wasn't finished. He started soccer-kicking Vader's face—*boom, boom, boom!* Thank God he was wearing flip-flops, because if he'd had shoes on he'd have done some serious damage.

Kevin Sullivan and Meng finally got in between them, trying to separate these two bulls.

Meanwhile, me and Dean are standing there with our mouths open, both of us feeling like we'd stepped into a movie, thinking, *What have we gotten ourselves into?*

Dean and I walked out of there, smiling and shaking our heads at what we'd just witnessed. We looked at each other and simultaneously said the same exact thing: "Welcome to WCW."

We later found out the backstory. Vader had finished taping his promos and had started to get changed when Orndorff—who was working as a road agent—came in and told him he had to shoot another interview. Vader refused, the two started arguing, and all hell broke loose.

Vader was let go by WCW after the incident. I had known him slightly from working with him in Japan. We got along well enough to say hello in the dressing room, but that was about it. Needless to say, I didn't get a chance to get to know him any better in WCW.

As for Mr. Wonderful, he was exactly what he appeared to be—a total badass. He was always very nice to me, though for some reason, he wouldn't call me Eddie. I don't know why, but he called me Edgrove.

"Hey, Edgrove . . ."

"Paul, my name's Eddie."

"Okay, Edgrove."

Whatever you say, I thought. The first lesson I learned in WCW was that you do not mess with Paul Orndorff. If he wants to call you Edgrove, you're Edgrove.

I'd been a WCW employee for just a few short weeks when Eric Bischoff, the senior vice president of WCW, flew me to Atlanta for a face-to-face meeting. I met with him at the WCW offices in the CNN Tower.

He was very nice, putting me over, telling me how he needed workers like me and Dean and Chris on the roster. He explained he was determined to truly compete with Vince McMahon and the all-powerful World Wrestling Federation. He was getting ready to launch his own Monday night wrestling show, a live broadcast, called *WCW Monday Nitro.* I wondered aloud where I fit into his plans.

"Well, Eddie," he said. "I have the guns, but I don't have the bullets. You guys are going to be my bullets. You guys are going to be the car crashes in the middle of my movie."

I understood his meaning right away. He had his main event players, guys like Hulk Hogan, and he needed some action to fill in the rest of his time slot. I had no problem with the concept. I never expected to make it to WCW in the first place, so just being part of the show was all right by me.

I got a very positive feeling from Eric. I believe his heart was true as far as wanting to innovate the professional wrestling business. Hiring guys like us was Eric's way of trying to add some excitement to the show, a way of bringing something new and different to Monday nights.

On September 18, Dean and I made our official WCW debut, in Johnson City, Tennessee. It was at the second-ever episode of *Nitro,* though we weren't on the actual broadcast. We wrestled a dark match after the show, what's known in the business as a DFL—dead fucking last.

A dark match isn't really done for the fans—it's more about showing management and the road agents what you can do in their ring. Dean and I were both pretty jazzed about being there and tried to give them our best, though our match didn't come close to the high standards we'd set for ourselves in ECW.

A week or so later I made my first WCW TV appearance, going to a draw against "Das Wunderkind" Alex Wright on *WCW Saturday Night*. Alex was a good guy. He always reminded me of that comic book character Plastic Man—tall, skinny, and incredibly limber. He was a classic pretty boy, always checking himself in the mirror. But like all those *GQ* guys, he was really paranoid about his looks. He had started losing his hair and it really freaked him out.

One thing you can say about me—I've never been called a pretty boy. I've always had to rely on my talent to get me over. Lord knows, no one would ever cheer for me based on my looks!

My first *Nitro* was in Denver, working with Dean. It was my first big match at WCW, and I was a bundle of nerves. Denver was one of the hardest cities to wrestle in. Not because of the fans or the condition of the arena, but because of the high altitude, which makes it incredibly difficult to catch your breath.

It was a good match, short and sweet. We weren't given enough time to blow ourselves up, and even if we had, Dean and I didn't want to pull out all the stops on our first TV match together. We figured we'd save that for later.

Right from the start it was clear that the WCW creative team had no idea what to do with me. The first time I came out on *Nitro* they played some damn Mexican trumpet music, which got me so hot. After the match, the first thing I did was go to the back and say, "You've got to change my entrance music."

I had no problem acknowledging my Mexican background. I'm proud to be a Mexican-American wrestler. But that didn't mean I had to be pigeonholed. I'm not some mariachi in a sombrero. I'm a Chicano, which is a completely different culture.

One way a new wrestler is defined on TV is through his finishing move. I figured I'd keep using the superplex I'd used in Los Gringos Locos. But Terry Taylor suggested, "What about the frog splash?"

When I joined ECW, Paul Heyman also thought that I should use the frog splash. "You should do it in Art's memory," he said. I hadn't planned on ever doing it again, but I realized that Paul and Terry were right. There could be no better tribute to Art than my using his finishing move.

It's been my finish ever since.

Being the new guy, I wasn't given a storyline to work with. My job was to wrestle, and so most of those early days in WCW were spent working five-minute matches with Chris and Dean.

It really helped me make the transition to WCW. The three of us had created a bond in Japan, as friends and as workers. I think we all felt good about working together, like, "Let's go show these guys what we can do."

When I wasn't wrestling Dean or Chris, I was working matches with lower-card guys like Jerry "J.L." Lynn, Scott Armstrong, Big Bubba, Joey Maggs, and Sgt. Craig Pittman. I also had a nice little feud with the late, great Brian Pillman.

I had first met Brian in Japan. He told me how he and Steve Austin used to watch tapes of Los Gringos Locos when they were tagging together as the Hollywood Blondes. "Yeah, right," I said. "Don't blow air up my ass."

"No, really," he said. "I love your stuff."

Looking back now, I wish I could've appreciated the compliment, one wrestler showing respect to another. But at the time all I could think was, *What does this guy want from me?* It was a classic case of paranoia. I couldn't see what a nice guy Brian was, because I was too busy watching my back.

Pillman was different from most of the boys. He had no problem telling you shit to your face. You might not like what he said, but he'd tell you straight up. When Brian first started in WCW, he called me and said, "Hey, man, I'm going to use your swinging DDT on TV. Sorry, but it's just too good a move for me not to use."

"Go for it, bro," I told him. At least he respected me enough to call and tell me. Most guys would've just stolen my stuff and not given it a second thought.

Brian passed away in 1997. His death was especially hard for me, because it hit close to home. Brian was going through a lot of personal issues that I could relate to. There was real emotional pain in his life, things that I could definitely identify with. Sadly, he wasn't able to beat his demons back before it was too late.

In December I finally got a chance to wrestle one of the top guys. Not one of—*the* top guy. The Nature Boy himself, Ric Flair.

Ric is the man. I've learned so much from him and his career. When I think of how to conduct myself in a professional way, it's Ric that pops into my mind. As far as I'm concerned, Ric Flair *is* the wrestling business.

I've been a mark for Ric for as long as I can remember. My dad had so much respect for him. When he came and wrestled for my dad, he put him over as much as I ever heard him put a wrestler over. "Watch him," Dad said. "Look at what a ring general he is. See how he guides everything."

At the time I couldn't see what my dad was talking about. I was so young. But my dad's words stuck in my mind.

Getting the opportunity to work with him was huge. I was in awe. *Wow,* I thought, *I'm going to wrestle Ric Flair!*

I badly wanted to impress him, to win his respect. We ended up having a decent little TV match. What I remember most was how good it felt to be in the ring with him. Ric made me look good, which is one of the things that makes him great. He understands that he's Ric Flair—making a younger wrestler look good won't do anything to damage his legacy.

Unfortunately, that attitude was rare among most of the top stars in WCW. They were so concerned about their spot, I don't think the idea of putting one of the younger boys over ever even crossed their minds.

Starrcade was WCW's biggest Pay-Per-View of the year. It used to be known as "the Grandaddy of 'Em All" because it actually predated *WrestleMania* by a couple of years.

My first *Starrcade* was centered around a big battle between Team WCW and Team New Japan, with whom WCW had a longstanding business relationship. It was a good arrangement—New Japan benefited from having a connection to American wrestling, while the Japanese talent added some international excitement to the WCW roster.

I was matched up against Shinjiro Otani, who I'd worked with many times over in Japan. Because we'd wrestled before, I was pretty laid-back that night. Otani, on the other hand, was incredibly nervous. Being in America, on a huge Pay-Per-View, had him shaking in his wrestling boots.

I don't know what he had to be worried about—we had always had great matches together, plus, he was going over that night. In fact, every one of my Pay-Per-View opponents went over.

Win or lose, it didn't matter all that much to me. My only concern was giving a good match. Besides, being in WCW was like this amazing surprise, a dream I never expected to come true that turned out to be even better than I'd imagined. As long as I was working, I was cool.

THE EDDIE GUERRERO STORY

WRESTLING CHRIS BENOIT IN LAS VEGAS.

CHAPTER 18

O n May 27, 1996, the wrestling business as we knew it changed overnight. Scott Hall jumped straight out of the World Wrestling Federation. Nothing like that had ever happened before. Traditionally, a new superstar would only appear after weeks, if not months, of promotion. But Hall's appearance came out of nowhere, and the fans loved it!

He jumped the rail and started badmouthing WCW, making the fans think he was representing Vince's company. He said if Bischoff wanted war, well then he had one. He also promised that he had a "big surprise" for the following week.

Hall came through the next week, introducing Kevin Nash to the WCW crowd. Over the next few months, the two Outsiders ran roughshod over WCW, interfering in matches and doing whatever the hell they pleased.

When Hulk Hogan saw that the Outsiders were getting hot, he saw an opportunity to spark new life into his character. He turned heel at the *Bash at the Beach* Pay-Per-View, teaming up with Hall and Nash to create the New World Order—the nWo.

That was the angle that put WCW over the top. Fueled by the red-hot nWo, WCW began dominating the ratings in the so-called Monday Night Wars. The TV audience expanded, house show business went up by one hundred percent. For the first time ever, WCW began looking like a real threat.

But behind the scenes, the company became an out-and-out nightmare. What people didn't realize was that the things that were happening on TV—like the nWo taking virtual control over the product—were happening for real in the back.

Hall and Nash came into WCW with a lot of pull. It was a very big deal for WCW to get these guys—they were huge stars. But at the same time, when they arrived, it was like somebody threw a couple of vipers into the dressing room. It went from being a reasonably content room to a full-blown snake pit.

The nWo might not have been spray-painting their initials on the rest of the roster, but they were definitely sticking knives in our backs. They acted like they were the only reason for WCW's success. And since they were the company's saviors, they could treat it as if it were theirs and theirs alone.

Nash was the leader of the team, no question about it. I never had a problem with Scott Hall. As far as I was concerned, he was always an okay guy. Sure, he told you what you wanted to hear, but I could never hold too much against him because at least the guy could wrestle.

That's not something anyone's ever said about Kevin Nash. Considering how little talent he had in the ring, Nash is one of the most arrogant people I've ever had the displeasure to know. He'd walk right past you and not acknowledge your presence unless he thought there was something he could get out of you.

I don't say this lightly, but I genuinely feel Nash is evil. He's never done anything for this business. The only person he cares about is himself.

What gets me is that Kevin Nash became a rich man from this business, and then shit on the people that really cared about wrestling. From the day they arrived in WCW, he and his clique saw me and my friends as second tier. They used to call us the Vanilla Midgets, which was hugely insulting.

As the nWo phenomenon got bigger and bigger, Eric Bischoff began hanging around with the main-event clique, most of whom didn't like me or my style of wrestling. Eric had been up front with me right from the start. He made it perfectly clear how he viewed my contribution to the company—my

CHEATING DEATH, STEALING LIFE

job was to be the car crash, to be high-flying filler. But it wasn't until the nWo showed up that I truly began to feel like nothing more than cannon fodder.

Bischoff stopped acting real to me. Every time we spoke I felt like I was being manipulated and bullshitted, so eventually I decided not to talk to him anymore. I knew he was full of shit, so why waste my time with him?

I understood that it wasn't personal, that it was about business. Eric was under a lot of pressure from bosses and he had to make whatever business decisions he saw fit in order to deliver ratings. But it still bothered me. Guys like me and Chris and Rey Mysterio had done the grunt work that helped make the show a hit, and then we were pushed aside. In my mind, it felt like a big fuck-you. From that moment on, I started to rebel. Fuck me? No, fuck *you*.

Ultimately, Bischoff became a victim of his own dreams. He wanted to beat Vince so badly that he was willing to give Nash and Hogan everything, including creative control. What ended up happening was that no one was able to manage the overall product.

The nWo clique had a say in everything that was going on, to the point where it became damn near impossible to put the show on without pissing somebody off. Things were constantly changing, all the way up to the final minutes before *Nitro* went live. There was always someone saying, "I don't want to do this," or "I'm not going to do a job." And nobody—meaning Bischoff—was willing to tell them to shut up and do what was best for the whole show.

Everybody was looking out for Number One. Nobody gave a damn about what was right or wrong for the product. It was the most selfish behavior I've ever seen, and it wasn't long before things at WCW started spinning out of control.

In June, I got a much-needed break from the turmoil in WCW when I headed off to New Japan to compete in their annual tournament, now called Best of the Super Junior.

I'd wrestled in the tournament a number of times by then, as Eddie Guerrero and as Black Tiger. To me, just doing well in the tournament was honor enough. Winning never even crossed my mind.

So you can imagine how surprised I was to be told that I was going to be that year's champion. I never expected to be put over in Japan. My job in Japan was to get *other* people over. I've always been comfortable with the idea that by getting other people over, I was getting myself over.

Winning the Super Juniors was a tremendous pat on the back. From what I've heard since, it was New Japan bookers Jushin Liger and Riki Choshu's idea for me to win the tournament. It was their way of saying, "We're really proud of the work you've done for us, here's something in return." I'll always be grateful to them both for that.

Chris Benoit and I met in the semifinal, and man, did we have a knock-down, blowout match! We were both working at the top of our game. I think we each had similar frustrations with WCW and were able to release it all in the ring.

I was determined to top that match when I met Jushin Liger in the finals. Unfortunately, it didn't happen. We had a pretty good match, but it wasn't the five-star classic I was shooting for.

That's just the way it goes sometimes. Liger and I had good chemistry, but that's not always enough. Sometimes it's just circumstances—on a different day, in a different town, Liger and I could well have put on the best wrestling match of all time.

Winning the Super Juniors tournament was a great acknowledgment of my work and my value to the business. Of course, at the time, I was too dumb and too naïve to see it. Now I can appreciate what it represented, but when it happened, I didn't realize that it was something special. It was just another day at the office.

Though I'd risen to a new career high in Japan, things weren't going as well for me back home. With the nWo taking over all aspects of WCW, it was pretty clear to me that I was never going to get past a certain level.

Everything and everybody that wasn't involved in the main nWo storyline was basically just filler. The rest of us were simply seen as a way to kill time between the nWo segments.

I accepted my role and tried to do the best I could with whatever was given me. I was booked into a match with Ric Flair at *Road Wild,* the Pay-Per-View we did every year at the annual biker rally in Sturges, North Dakota.

Road Wild was every wrestler's least favorite event. It was always hotter than hell and twice as dusty. Plus, everybody there is as drunk as can be. It was also a free event, which meant that none of the boys received any money from the house.

My match with Ric was not one of my better efforts, to say the least. It was one of those days where I really wanted to give my best, but nothing came together. I was trying so hard, but everything I did just fell flat. It was like a domino effect—nothing went right.

The following week was the annual WCW supercard, *Clash of the Champions.* That night—almost one year to the day after I'd first arrived in WCW—I finally went over at a major event, scoring a victory over Diamond Dallas Page.

The two of us had been feuding for months, fighting over the *Battle Bowl* ring he'd won at *Slamboree.* I remember very little about the match—when it comes to Diamond Dallas Page, I just naturally put up a mental block. The two of us never hit it off. It was every man for himself in the WCW locker room, and no one was more for himself than Page.

We went back and forth through the fall, though our feud was really only an add-on to Page's main storyline program with the nWo. Finally the time came for our big blow-off match. There was a tournament for the U.S. Championship at *Starrcade.* I made it through the brackets, beating Konnan and Benoit, leading up a title match with—who else?—DDP.

That match totally changed my career, though not necessarily for the better. Page was different from the kind of wrestlers I was used to working with. He couldn't just call a match in the ring, he needed to plot out and memorize every last move. A week before *Starrcade,* he called me at my mom's house on Christmas Eve, and we spent an hour on the phone going over the whole freakin' match.

Finally he tells me, "Scott Hall and Kevin Nash are going to come down. Hall is going to knock you out of the ring, then him and Kevin Nash are going to come in and give me their finishes. While I'm out, you come up, frog splash me, and win the title."

I didn't know what to say. I knew it wasn't going to be good for me. I was a babyface, and winning the U.S. Championship like that was going to make me look like shit.

Sure enough, people started booing me after that match. It killed me, putting a stop to any career momentum I had made over the past year. On the other hand, Page got over like a million dollars.

That was the moment when I finally understood how little anybody cared about me in WCW. What happened to me wasn't the issue. For all intents and purposes, I was just a prop in the big storyline.

To make matters worse, nWo member Syxx—better known to WWE fans as X-Pac—ran out after the bell and stole my U.S. Championship belt, setting up my next program.

Pac and I have always had a good relationship. We did a Super Juniors tour together, just before he started working for Vince. All the boys ribbed him because he was the youngest wrestler on the tour. I never was one for ribbing, and we ended up hanging out and becoming friends. There's a definite bond between us. We share a lot of the demons.

We wrapped up our feud pretty quickly, with a Ladder match at the next Pay-Per-View, *nWo Souled Out*. Simply put, the match sucked.

The thing about Ladder matches, or any hard-core gimmick match, is that you can only get better by doing them, by gaining the experience to know what to do with them. Ladder matches are particularly brutal. They're more dangerous than just about any other match because there's no way to work it. You've just got to take it. There's no way to make getting hit with a steel ladder any easier, or that fall from the top any shorter. When you take the bump off the ladder, all you think is, *Wow, it sure is high*.

Neither Pac nor myself had ever done a Ladder match before. Neither of us had any idea what we were doing in there. We never got the chance to go over what we wanted to do, and once we hit the ring, I think we both knew we were in trouble.

Pac and I both felt horrible after that match. We did our best, but it was just one of those nights.

CHEATING DEATH, STEALING LIFE

For the first time in my life, I actually hated going to work. The backstage politics took all the fun out of what I loved to do. It started taking my soul.

I began drinking more, partying harder. All the bullshit I was forced to deal with became a trigger point for me. Of course, I know now that that's just an excuse—ultimately, it comes back to me. They were my decisions. I can't blame the situation for making me do what I did. I was already on that road.

Partying was very much part of the WCW lifestyle. There was a culture there that totally excused constantly getting loaded. In a way, that was just another nail in WCW's coffin. Things reached the point where some of the boys were partying before the show, then going out to the ring all lit up. That was never me—I was always professional when it came to the show. When the show ended, that's another story.

As I got more and more down about my situation, I started keeping to myself as much as I could. I'd only speak my mind in very indirect ways. I didn't want to call any attention to myself. Paranoia was in full effect at WCW—everyone was so scared of saying the wrong thing, of burying themselves and losing their jobs.

Finally I spoke to Kevin Sullivan. "Just turn me heel, already," I said. "Please!"

I was told that it wasn't time yet, that they'd turn me when they felt it was right. In the meanwhile, I'd be dropping the U.S. title to Dean Malenko in a no-DQ match at *Uncensored*.

That turned out to be a fortunate piece of booking. The initial idea for the finishing sequence was to have Dean on the outside. I was going to dive out off the turnbuckle, but he was going to duck and send me into the barrier. The problem was that Dean was in a car accident when he was in high school and can't bend his neck down to lower his head.

When I dove, Dean did his best to get his head down, but he couldn't quite get it low enough. At the same time, I didn't have my arms high enough, so that the top of my left arm hit the top of his head. As I hit the barrier, my left pectoral muscle popped. Watching the match on tape afterwards, I could actually see the muscle tear. There's a little flicker under my skin—*pop!*—and then you can see the deformity.

It hurt like hell, but we kept going. As the match progressed, we traded finishing holds—he hit me with a frog splash and I locked him in the Texas Cloverleaf. As I applied the hold, my grip kept slipping. I couldn't hold on. That's when I knew something was wrong. We managed to finish the match—Syxx interfered, allowing Dean to clock me with his video camera for the win.

The bell rang, and I immediately went to the back and found a trainer. "It's nothing," he said.

"Nothing?" I shouted. "Look at it, you moron! You can't see that one side of my chest is all messed up?"

My pectoral muscle was completely knotted up. The pec is like a rubber band—when it's torn, it snaps back into the body. You can actually see the lump.

The muscle was never reattached. Normally that would have been the procedure, but being a wrestler isn't normal. My doctor told me that if I continued to wrestle, more than likely the muscle would tear again. Fortunately for me, I would get 99 percent of my strength back, even without the surgical reattachment, so there was no reason to worry.

The bad news was that I was going to be out of action for a while.

CHAPTER 19

No one wants to get injured, but in a weird way, it's the only chance a wrestler gets to take an extended vacation. You have to accept the fact that you're screwed for six months or however long you're out for, then learn to appreciate the free time. It's crazy, but getting hurt allows for the only breaks you get in your career.

Vickie and I had recently moved away from El Paso. I needed to be near the company's hub, so it was a choice between Atlanta or Tampa, which was where Dean and a few of the other boys lived. I've always craved warm weather, so I packed up the family and relocated to sunny Florida. It was totally the right decision—I love Tampa.

I was so happy to be around my wife and kids for an extended period of time. The girls had never really had me around like that. They had grown up with me on the road. As far as they were concerned, Daddy was always away.

Sherilyn was still just a toddler. Because of my lifestyle, I had missed most of her growing up to that point. It was a blessing to be able to enjoy her for a few months. I loved watching her, seeing her learn how to walk or singing along to Barney on the TV.

As much as I cherished being with Vickie, Shaul, and Sherilyn, it wasn't long before I started going stir-crazy! The days went so slowly. I couldn't work out, I couldn't train, I had no clue what to do with my time.

My in-laws came to visit one weekend and we took them out deep-sea fishing. On the way back in we saw people fishing on the pier. *That looks like it could be fun,* I thought. I went and bought some rods and started pier fishing. It turned out to be just what the doctor ordered. It was perfect, because it was something I could do by myself or with the whole family.

I was out for three months, the longest I'd ever gone without wrestling in my entire professional career.

On June 9, I made my long-awaited—by me, at least—return at the Fleet Center in Boston. Malenko was in the middle of a match with Jeff Jarrett when I came out of the crowd with a sling on. I whipped off the sling and gave Dean a frog splash, allowing Jarrett to score a submission with a figure-four leglock.

Yes, I was finally a full-blown heel.

I guess I should thank Diamond Dallas Page, because turning heel was the best thing that could've happened for me. After almost two years in WCW, I started enjoying myself again.

Being a heel really turned things around for me. It was so satisfying, hearing twenty thousand people yelling "Eddy sucks!" at the top of their lungs. There was a time in WCW when I could literally feel the arena vibrating, they were screaming "Eddy sucks!" so loudly. It made me feel so good, so proud of my work. To a heel, that sound is applause.

While I wasn't expecting to go to the top of the card, I began to feel that I deserved more of a push. I was drawing amazing heat as a heel and thought there was so much more we could do with that. It was Terry Taylor who suggested, "Why not get into something with Chavito?"

Chavito had been wrestling in WCW for about a year. Though we had grown apart when Chavo moved his family to California, the business brought us back together. When Chavito was in his teens, he decided that he wanted to be a wrestler. I'll always be grateful and honored that he came to me.

I took him into my house and helped him get work in Juarez. By the grace of God, he got an opportunity to perform for Eric Bischoff, who loved him right away. Eric saw a good-looking kid with a lot of talent. He offered Chavito a developmental contract, with one condition—that he move to Atlanta.

He worked steadily in WCW, mostly doing undercard matches with *luchadors* and other cruiserweights. Incredibly, until Terry brought it up, no one had ever suggested a program between the two of us.

I thought it was a great idea. I love Chavito and thought it would be a blast to work with him.

The basic storyline was that I was trying to light a fire under Chavito's ass, to teach him how to be a true Guerrero. But since I was a heel, I did it through tough love, letting him get his butt kicked by guys like Scott Hall and Scott Norton while I shook my head in disappointment.

It was difficult in the beginning. Chavito didn't get what we were doing. He thought he was being buried. What he didn't realize was that at the end of the program he was going to come out smelling like a rose. The story wouldn't make any sense without him getting his in the end.

"Trust me, man," I told him repeatedly. "It's going to pay off for you."

But in his mind, all Chavito knew was that he was getting shit on. He was genuinely embarrassed by the things I did to him in the ring. He couldn't separate the storyline from the reality. He had only been wrestling for a couple of years and this was his first real program. He was still too naïve to see that all the "Eddy sucks!" chants had a lot to do with him. The fans were booing and jeering me because they hated what I was doing to him.

Chavito is a lot like me—we're very proud people and we live what we do in the ring. It tore him up inside to have to take all the abuse and humiliation I was throwing at him. He'd hear it from his neighbors and people on the street: "Why do you let Eddy treat you like that? Stand up for yourself! Kick your uncle's ass!"

In terms of the storyline, Chavito was the sacrificial lamb, and that's a hard role to play, let alone live. I think some of his concern came from real life. He had to play second banana to me, and it wasn't a lot of fun. I should know—I've been there.

143

When I first started wrestling, I was always served up as the sacrificial lamb for my brothers. I'd get beaten up, then my brothers would show up and get me my revenge. But as time wore on, I became the center of attention, with my brothers supporting me.

That's what happened this time—WCW brought in my brother Hector to help protect Chavito from my tough love. It was wonderful having him around. Even after all my years in the business, there were still new things to learn from him.

At the same time, seeing how Hector was treated by management just about broke my heart. He had been involved with WCW for years, going back to when it was still NWA and Jim Crockett was running the show. That basic foundation was still in charge of things, and they simply didn't perceive Hector as being important.

God bless Hector, he deserved a lot better and he knew it. After about a month, he sat Chavito and me down and told us he was leaving. I understood his frustration and completely supported his decision. I also admired his courage, to stand up for himself and not eat any more shit.

Meanwhile, my feud with Chavito just kind of petered out. I guess it wasn't working out how they'd hoped, because before it could really get going, I found myself in a loose heel partnership with Jeff Jarrett. We tagged together and interfered in each other's matches, usually against members of Ric Flair's Four Horsemen.

On August 8, I had my very first singles match with Rey Mysterio.

I first met Rey Mysterio when we were both wrestling down in Tijuana. He was just a little kid, but my God, was he talented! He was doing things that were beyond the imagination.

Rey is blessed with what we call "angel." It means he's got "it," that little something extra that makes you special. He's unique. I've seen other wrestlers do amazing high flying, but they don't have what Rey has. Every time you look at him, you smile. Not just in the ring, but in real life. Rey's got something about him, a big smile and a good word, that makes you want to take him into your heart. I don't think there's a person in this business that doesn't love Rey.

We got along right from the start. I consider Rey to be my little brother. I love him that much.

The two of us had worked together in AAA, with me and Art going against him and his babyface tag partner. Incredible as it sounds, we had never wrestled each other in a one-on-one singles match.

It turned out that our personal connection extended into the ring. Rey and I were among the only guys in WCW who were able to mix the Mexican and American styles, and as a result, we meshed together beautifully in the ring. We had *chemistry.*

I really enjoyed working as a cruiserweight. I started shredding up, working out hard, cutting a lot of weight. I looked good, lean and strong. It felt like the cruiserweight division was the best place for me. I could relax and focus on my wrestling, without worrying about what was going on in the main event.

I don't usually get excited about titles, but I definitely wanted the WCW Cruiserweight Championship. With that in mind, I pushed for a feud with the then Cruiserweight Champ, Chris Jericho.

We met up at the *Fall Brawl* Pay-Per-View. Because he'd worked down in Mexico as Lionheart, Chris was coming from the same place I was. He knew how to mix Mexican high spots with American psychology. We were a good match. At *Fall Brawl,* Chris and I made a point of slowing our match down so that it was more than just a spot fest. We *wrestled.*

In the finish, I reversed a superplex, then nailed a perfect frog splash for a clean win. It felt good—the Cruiserweight belt was the first championship I had won without getting the pin through a big freaking angle. Look at the way I got the U.S. title from DDP! This time, I became the Cruiserweight Champion by going over in the middle of the ring. From *wrestling.*

I really felt that WCW missed the boat with the Cruiserweight Division. There was the potential to do something truly innovative, to combine the Mexican and American styles to create a kind of wrestling different from what most mainstream fans were used to.

THE EDDIE GUERRERO STORY

Blending aerial high spots with traditional wrestling storytelling could've really changed the business. Unfortunately, too many people—Bischoff and his pals—felt that our smaller size would prevent us from ever going beyond the middle of the card. Either that, or they were afraid of us.

As the new Cruiserweight Champ, I immediately entered a program with the obvious Number One Contender, Rey Mysterio.

I began interfering in all his matches, even to the point of working under a mask as El Caliente. The mask didn't seem to fool anyone, however. In the middle of the match, the crowd figured out that El Caliente had a similar style to mine, and started the "Eddy sucks" chants.

The following week I ran into Rey's match with Dean Malenko. I ripped his mask off and asked, "Did you lose this?"

His face was visible for a couple of seconds, which was serious business in Mexican wrestling terms. That kind of thing just wasn't done—unless there was money to be made.

When we were told how the angle would play out that night, we tried to explain that taking off Rey's mask should be something special. The agents listened, told us they appreciated our input, and then said that we should do what we were told. We were like puppets.

Bischoff got it into his head that the time had come to unmask Rey and booked us in a Title vs. Mask match at *Halloween Havoc,* at the MGM Grand in Las Vegas.

It's a huge deal when a Mexican wrestler loses his mask. It's like losing your identity. Because it represents a major career milestone, wrestlers usually make a lot of money for losing their mask. Rey argued that if he was going to sacrifice his mask, he wanted to get his payoff. "Give me a chance to lose it in TJ," he asked Bischoff.

But Eric didn't care. He didn't give a shit about the heritage of the mask. He just wanted to do what he wanted to do. It was almost as if he was doing it just to show his power, like, "You're going to lose your mask because I say you're going to lose your mask."

The afternoon of the show, Rey came to me and said he was going to try one more time to change Eric's mind. "Will you support me on this?" he asked.

I knew how upsetting this was to Rey. I understood the value of the mask and didn't want to see him screwed out of his payoff. "Of course, bro," I said. "You know I'll always stand behind you."

I don't know what was said behind closed doors, but just before show-time, Terry Taylor pulled me aside. "Hey man," he said, "I know we've been building to something different, but do you mind doing the job for Rey?"

I didn't have a problem with it. I knew letting him take my cruiserweight title was the right thing to do. I did, however, get insulted when I was told we were going to be the first match. Rey and I were too good to be jerking the curtain. *Okay,* I thought, *that's how you feel about us? We'll give you something to follow.*

When the time finally came to go out and wrestle, I was completely moti-vated. I wanted to tear the house down. For Rey and for myself. I wanted to prove that we were more than just filler.

We went out there, and our match was amazing from the word go. Rey and I couldn't do anything wrong—the timing, the psychology, everything was right on the money. The crowd was tremendous, responding exactly the way we wanted them to. The "Eddy sucks" chants began the second I walked down the ramp and never let up.

We made a point of trying out innovative new moves, things we'd never even thought of before that match. Sometimes that can screw you up, but that night was special. Everything flowed. Everything fell right into place.

At one point, Rey did this awesome move, flipping off the top rope and hitting a crazy backflip DDT on me. To this day, we haven't been able to du-plicate it. We've tried, but it never comes off the way it did at *Halloween Havoc.* It was just one of those nights.

It turned out to be one of the best, most memorable matches of my career. I'm usually pretty critical of my own work—especially in the matches that peo-ple consider to be classics—but whenever I watch that one, I just think, *Shit, that was good.*

Rey and I knew we had ripped it up out there, but when we went to the back there was hardly any reaction from the rest of the boys. A few of our friends came over and patted us on the back to say, "Good match," but that was it. For the most part, everyone was pretty quiet and didn't say shit to us.

That just confirmed it in my mind—nothing says success quite like having the top boys refuse to acknowledge you.

Unfortunately, there's a lot more to the business than just having a good match. Even though we proved at *Halloween Havoc* that we could tear it up with the best of them, it did nothing to elevate us in the eyes of the company.

Two weeks later, I took the Cruiserweight Championship back from Rey on *Nitro,* setting up a rematch at the next Pay-Per-View, *World War III '97.*

That happens almost every time you have a very special match. The first thing they try to do is duplicate it, which of course never happens. That's exactly the way it went down at *World War III.* No matter how hard we tried, it just wasn't the same. Rey and I both wanted to top *Halloween Havoc,* but it just didn't happen. You can't force magic.

It ended up being just an average match. It wasn't bad—I don't think Rey and I could've had a truly awful match. Even our average matches were pretty good.

Rey and I were both pretty disappointed. We knew that we had raised people's expectations with *Halloween Havoc.* When you have a match like that, anything less is simply not going to cut it.

You simply can't duplicate a special match like *Halloween Havoc.* There are so many elements that go into making a match. Every night there are different circumstances. There's no way to guarantee a classic match. That's what makes them special.

CHAPTER 20

WCW's business was booming. The company's success wasn't all based on the nWo. There was also the phenomenal rise of Goldberg.

When Goldberg came out of WCW's training facility, the Power Plant, he was still just plain Bill Goldberg. He had the right attitude toward the business. He was very humble, very respectful, and thankful for the opportunity to be a professional wrestler.

Goldberg became a huge star within months of his wrestling debut. People responded to his badass persona and got very involved in his winning streak.

But as Goldberg got more and more successful, the wrong people started getting into his head. It wasn't long before he began believing his own hype. He started buying into his own record, thinking that he was truly undefeated. He seemed to forget that one hundred other wrestlers had helped to put him over and make him a huge star.

Goldberg has a very good heart. But he was confused by how quickly success came for him. Instead of being humble about how fortunate he was, he started acting like he was doing the business a big favor. He loved being a wrestling Superstar, but he didn't want to do the work that goes along with that.

I'm not saying Goldberg wasn't a major star—he absolutely was. But he was not God's gift to wrestling. He came to the business after his football

GIVING CHAVITO SOME TOUGH LOVE.

career ended, and made himself a pretty good life out of wrestling. I just feel he should've been more appreciative and respectful of the business. Instead, he acted like he could take it or leave it.

No one has the right to come into the wrestling business and behave as if it owes them something. You have to be humble and remember all the people that paved the way. The Rock was as big a star as this business has ever produced, but he always understood that with being a star comes a lot of responsibility. That sense of duty comes from growing up in the business and being surrounded by good teachers and positive role models.

I really want to emphasize that Goldberg the person is great. It's just that as far as business is concerned, I find his attitude to be warped. It's not his fault. He skyrocketed to stardom surrounded by the biggest snake pit in wrestling. Of course he ended up becoming a bit of a snake himself.

Too many of the top guys at WCW walked around with the attitude, "I drew this money, so the rest of you boys owe me." Sorry, but it doesn't work that way. Everybody should be grateful for the living that this business is providing them.

True, the boys need to have respect for the Superstars that are drawing the houses, that are making money for the rest of us. But at the same time,

CHEATING DEATH, STEALING LIFE

the individual that's on top should never forget the people that got him there.

Goldberg had a lot of boys to thank for his success. He went 173-0, which meant just about everybody on the WCW roster had to put him over at one point or another. Somehow, I managed to get out of it. Chavito got jobbed out to Goldberg, but I never did.

Goldberg might have started thinking his doo-doo didn't stink, but his outlook was nothing compared to the guy that ended his undefeated streak, Kevin Nash. Nash didn't give a damn about how much money Goldberg was drawing for WCW—all he was concerned with was being the Number One guy in the company. When he became the company's booker, the first decision he made was to put the title on himself, even though Goldberg's run was far from finished. When he screwed Goldberg for the title, it hurt the business for everybody.

No one has the right to do that. No one has the right to affect how the rest of us feed our families, just because their ego tells them that they need to be the big man. That's bullshit and it still angers me to this day.

It's not that the top guys at WCW didn't deserve the money they made—they drew big houses for a couple of years, and we all reaped the benefits. But they had no right to say, "Fuck everybody else. I don't care what happens to the business as long as I get mine." Maybe that's not exactly how they looked at it, but it's definitely what they did.

Nash and the nWo were killing towns dead for WCW, promising matches and then not delivering. Every night was the same screw-job finish, with all the nWo guys coming in and creating chaos. After a while, the fans simply got tired of it. How many times can you see somebody getting spray-painted? They were insulting the audience, and eventually the audience had enough.

When you insult the intelligence of the fans, you disgrace them. And when somebody is humiliated like that, you lose their business.

I followed my match with Rey Mysterio at *World War III* with a program with Dean. The two of us had the same desire—to tear it up like we did in Japan and ECW.

151

Every time Dean and I got in the ring there was a hunger to do something great. We always wanted to outdo ourselves. We knew that there was an expectation among the serious fans that every time these two guys touched it was going to be something special. And more often than not, it was. With the chemistry we had, we couldn't stink up the joint if we tried.

Dean and I had a good little feud. I spent a lot of time poking fun at his personality, or more precisely, his lack of one. I sat in with the announce team for all of his matches, making wisecracks. "The only respect I have for Malenko," I said as he fought Fit Finlay on *Nitro*, "is that he can keep a straight face when someone tells a joke."

We wrapped things up at *Starrcade*. As usual, we had a high-quality match, though to be honest, it was nothing compared to our ECW classics.

The next night in Baltimore I was told I was going to drop the cruiserweight belt to Ultimo Dragon. He was about to get a major push in Japan, and they wanted him to come with a bunch of titles.

As of that afternoon, our match was scheduled to go thirteen minutes, a pretty good amount of time. A little later it was changed to eight minutes, still a reasonable length to have a good, exciting match that made us both look good. Next we were told, "Okay, you have eleven minutes."

"Well," I said. "That's better than eight minutes."

Finally *Nitro* started. I was standing in the gorilla position, getting ready to go out, when Terry Taylor tapped me on the shoulder. "Sorry, Eddie," he said, "you've got a minute and a half."

A minute and a half! That got me so hot! It showed me just how little respect they had for the cruiserweight title. Terry thought I was angry about losing the title, but that wasn't the case. I didn't give a shit about losing the belt—that's the business. When it's time to give it up, it's time to give it up. What I did care about was that I didn't get the opportunity to go out and do it the right way.

I ran out just after Dragon's entrance and blindsided him with the belt as he walked down the ramp. We hit the ring and I nailed him with a powerbomb and a rolling DDT. Just as we were getting rolling, Dragon locked on the Dragon Sleeper, and that was that. One-two-three, boom. I tapped out, and Dragon was the new Cruiserweight Champion.

I just felt manipulated. It wasn't just me—the entire Cruiserweight Division was taken for granted. As I said, the attitude was, "Just go out there and get it done. We have nWo stuff to get to."

It was just that kind of bullshit that made me very unhappy in WCW. It reached the point where I decided that I didn't want to deal with it anymore.

As always, Mom was a great sounding board. We spoke a lot about how miserable I was. "I can't take it anymore," I said to her. "I want to ask Bischoff for my release."

She was so supportive. She was just concerned that I had something to fall back on. "Don't worry, Mom," I said. "I'll always be able to work in Japan."

"Okay, honey," she said. "I trust you'll make the right decision. I know you'll always do what's best for you and your family."

Having made up my mind to leave WCW once and for all, I started feeling better right away. The next week at *Nitro* I confronted Bischoff in his backstage office. "Eric, I feel like I was on fire and you guys just turned me off," I said. "I'm really unhappy here and I'd like for you to give me my release."

I guess I shouldn't have been surprised when he got hot. "You motherfucker," he swore. "How can you be so damn ungrateful? After all I've done for you, you have the nerve to want out?"

Eric kept cussing at me, calling me all kinds of names. "Forget it," he said. "I'm not going to give you your release. And if you try and go anywhere else, I'll sue you for everything you've got."

I couldn't help being the smartass. "Go ahead!" I said. "I don't have anything!"

Man, he was pissed! Eric reached across his desk for his cup of coffee, but he was so angry and agitated that he hit it off the edge. It flew right at me, spilling all over my pants.

You'd think that would've snapped him out of his rage, but he just kept getting more and more aggressive. For a minute there, I thought it was going to come to blows. I was fully ready to knock him out. That's how heated it got. Fortunately, Bischoff knew better than to fight me. He just stormed out of there, cussing me as he slammed the door behind him.

Of course, from that day on, the gossip was that Eric threw his coffee at me. It's almost become a wrestling legend. But like most legends, it's simply not the whole truth.

A little later on, Bischoff and I sat down and had a less heated conversation. We both apologized and everything was cool. But for all intents and purposes, that was the last real conversation we ever had.

There were times when I felt the reason I was being held back had more to do with my ethnicity than my talents as a wrestler. Wrestling was traditionally a white man's business, from the NWA all the way to Ted Turner's WCW. There were always a handful of ethnic stars—Mexicans and Chicanos, African-Americans and Asians—but we were never allowed to take the next step up the ladder. With the single exception of Ron Simmons, there was never a nonwhite World Champion at WCW.

It felt like there was nothing I could do to get ahead. No matter how talented I was or how hard I worked, eventually I was going to hit that glass ceiling. I tried my hardest, but in my heart I knew it was a battle I wasn't going to win.

Proving that a Chicano can be a top player has made my success in WWE all the sweeter. As a Mexican-American, I really wanted to give something back to my people. They deserve to be acknowledged.

It's just another example of why WWE succeeds where WCW failed. It was definitely one of the reasons I wanted to jump to WWE. I knew that in WWE I'd be able to prove myself based on my merits, not on my ethnic heritage. This company had a great history of minority Superstars, from Pedro Morales to Jimmy "Superfly" Snuka to Rocky Johnson, and, of course, The Rock.

Vince is smart—he understands that one of the things that makes America great is that people of different races and ethnic backgrounds all have a chance to succeed in our society. Wrestling should reflect that. On a more practical level, there's money to be made.

Mexican-Americans are the fastest-growing minority in the United States. Only a fool wouldn't see the financial potential in that. Unfortunately, the powers that be at WCW weren't smart enough to see that. If they had, they might still be in business today.

Since Bischoff refused to give me my release, I was officially trapped in WCW. I started 1998 with a little feud against Booker T, followed by the return of my program with Chavito.

We essentially picked up right where we had left off—I was trying to teach him to be a better wrestler through some good old-fashioned tough love. I would accompany Chavito to his matches, then beat his ass after he lost.

It started with me declaring Chavo Jr. to be a disgrace to the Guerrero name, then beating him in a "Loser Has to Do Whatever the Winner Says" match.

The following week we were down in Panama City, Florida, for *Nitro's* *Spring Breakout* episode. We were hanging out in the bar with Jeff Cohen, a freelance photographer who did a lot of work for WCW. We were talking about the angle, and Cohen came up with the idea that if Chavo lost his match against Booker T, he would have to wear a T-shirt that said "Eddie Guerrero Is My Favorite Wrestler." Everybody cracked up, saying it was a hilarious idea.

That night, Jeff came running up to me backstage. "I did it, Eddie," he said. "I did it!"

He actually went and got a T-shirt made at one of those souvenir booths by the beach. It said "Eddie Guerrero Is My Favorite Wrestler" on the front and "Cheat To Win" on the back, all painted out in really bright, garish colors.

"That's great," I said, and brought the shirt over to Chavo. He took one look and immediately got hot.

"Forget it, man," he said. "I ain't gonna fuckin' wear that."

He thought that if he wore the shirt, he was going to look like a total jack-off. He was genuinely angry, like I was trying to take advantage of him.

"Chavito, you've got to wear it," I said. "It's part of the story. Trust me, bro. You're going to come out smelling like roses at the end."

"No fuckin' way. I ain't wearing this shit."

Chavito wearing his least favorite T-shirt.

At first, I thought he was kidding. He couldn't possibly be so upset over a stupid T-shirt. We went back and forth for a while, and before long, the Guerrero temper started to show itself. Chavo's got the same hot blood that I do, he's just better able to keep it in check. But that day his temper came out in a big way. Chavito started throwing chairs around, knocking over tables, yelling how there was no way he was going to put on "that fuckin' T-shirt."

Chris Jericho was back there, laughing at us. He thought we were joking around. But Chavito was dead serious. He wanted to kick my ass for even suggesting that he wear the shirt.

In the end, he did his job and wore the shirt. The whole point of the gimmick was that he look like a fool. He lost the match against Booker T, so he had to be a man of his word and wear the shirt. But I'm not sure to this day if he's ever forgiven me.

I learned a real lesson about how little regard WCW had for me with that angle. The crowd would go nuts every time Chavo wore his "Eddie

Guerrero Is My Favorite Wrestler" T-shirt, so you'd think they'd say, "Hey, we should sell some of those!"

But they weren't interested in trying to market a midcard attraction like me. The only T-shirts that were printed were the ones we needed Chavo to wear on TV. That showed what they thought of me. They couldn't even be bothered to make money off me.

I felt vindicated when years later, WWE made Los Guerreros T-shirts that said "Cheat To Win." I always knew that was a hell of a good catchphrase. People love that. They come up and say it to me all the time: "Cheat to win, Eddie!"

Night after night, Chavito would get his ass handed to him. I'd stand in his corner with a towel over my head to hide my shame. "I'm trying, Ma," I'd say. "I'm trying!"

I'll admit, my character was pretty vicious. I'd bang Chavo on the head with the microphone—knock, knock, knock—and say, "Hello? Is anybody in there?"

Or I'd tell him how he was embarrassing the entire Guerrero family. I made him apologize to Grandma and to Uncle Mando for "getting him kicked out of the Lowriders Club." That was great, because it was an in-joke for the Chicano fans. I'm sure most Anglos sat there scratching their heads, thinking, "What the hell is a Lowriders Club?"

The stupider I made him look, the angrier Chavito became. He especially hated when I'd throw the towel over my head. He wanted to kick my ass so badly. I had to fight him tooth and nail for months, constantly telling him not to worry, that he'd get his in the end.

"Yeah, okay, whatever," he'd say, but I knew he didn't believe me.

Either he couldn't see it or he just couldn't believe it. He also had a lot of people in his ear, telling him, "Don't do these things. You'll look like an idiot."

I also got heat from his dad and other members of the family. "You're taking it a little bit far, aren't you?" they'd say. I couldn't believe I had to explain myself to them as well as Chavito.

I think that the whole angle touched on some very real feelings. Like any

157

great wrestling angle, there was a tiny bit of truth to the storyline. I really did want to see Chavito develop and grow as a performer.

If nothing else, the program was a good education for him, teaching him to have a little faith.

As the weeks went by, Chavito realized that the angle was working. Before it started, no one knew who he was. But then he started getting recognized, at the airport and on the streets.

Once Chavito got what was going on, he did an amazing job selling the character. Chavito is so bright, so quick-witted. He came up with all kinds of hilarious stuff, like calling me "Little Trooper."

After weeks of abuse, Chavito's character finally snapped. He started challenging everyone in sight—me, the fans at ringside, even "Mean" Gene Okerlund. The crazier Chavo acted, the more the crowd popped for him.

A match was booked—me vs. Chavo at the *Great American Bash,* to be held June 14 in Baltimore. But the new Chavo frightened me. I tried to weasel out of the match, saying that since the Guerreros were now finally proud of him, we didn't have to fight.

The *Great American Bash* was the moment where it was finally time for Chavito to get what was coming to him. It was totally my call—the office didn't want me to do it, figuring they could keep the angle going forever. But I was adamant. "No," I said. "I'm going to put him over. He deserves it."

Considering how long we had been building toward it, in the end, our match at the *Great American Bash* wasn't nearly as memorable as it should've been. For some reason, Chavito and I were both a little off that night. We had flow, but our chemistry just wasn't on the money.

The only thing that made the match somewhat special was Chavo's amazing DDT at the finish. I thought that Chavo should beat me with something spectacular, something to justify all those months of torture I put him through. I suggested that he jump up to the middle of the rope and hit me with a springboard tornado DDT. He wasn't sure he could pull it off, but I had faith in his ability. Sure enough, he landed it perfectly.

PUTTING THE GORY SPECIAL ON CHAVITO AT *THE GREAT AMERICAN BASH*.

hough we'd had what we thought was our blow-off match, WCW's creative team decided to keep my feud with Chavito running for another couple of months.

We did *Nitro* in Tampa a couple of weeks after the Pay-Per-View. Since everybody was going to be in my neck of the woods, I decided to throw a little get-together at my house. A few of the boys came over for a barbecue—Dean, Chris, Fit Finlay, Chavito. Earlier that week, I had taken the family to Busch Gardens. I bought the girls a couple of hobby horses—they were pretty fancy, with stuffed heads and a thing in the ear that, when you pushed it, made the horse whinny and neigh. Sherilyn was crazy about hers; she rode it everywhere she went for weeks!

The kids were running around the backyard with their stick horses. They were so cute! Chavito and I were having some beers, watching the kids playing, and he said, "Now that I'm going crazy, I should start riding out on a stick horse."

THE EDDIE GUERRERO STORY

My eyes just lit up. "That's a great idea, bro," I said. "Will you seriously do that?"

Chavito regretted it immediately. "Um, yeah, I guess so."

But on the night of the show, we forgot to bring the stick horse. Chavito decided to come out dressed as Zorro, with a black shirt and a mask. "You've got to come out with a stick horse," I said. "It'll be great."

"Well, we don't have one," he said, "so I'll just come out like this. It'll be fine."

My friend Art Flores was hanging out backstage with us. "Hey, Tury," I said, "find a toy store and get Chavo a stick horse."

He came back an hour later with a basic hobby horse, not the fancy kind that I got at Busch Gardens. "This is the best I could do," he said.

"That'll be perfect," I said, and went to find Chavo.

"Here you go, Chavito. Now you've got to do it."

"Oh all right," he said, though I could see he wasn't fully convinced it was going to fly.

My match that night was against a cruiserweight named Little Dragon. I was up on the top turnbuckle, getting ready to go for the frog splash, when out came Chavo on his hobby horse. He introduced his pony as Pepe, adding, "You'll have to excuse me. I'm feeling a little horse!"

I had the hardest time keeping a straight face as he came trotting down the rampway on his stick horse. Chavo might not have been all that into it, but he gave one hundred percent to the bit and the people responded.

We got into a tug-of-war with Pepe. Chavito was acting crazy, yelling "Horse thief! Horse thief!" All of a sudden, Dragon came up behind me and rolled me up with a schoolboy—one-two-three! As I stood there enraged, Chavo started chattering about how much he loved his horse, Pepe. I chased him as he galloped up the ramp, riding Pepe into the sunset. When we got to the back, we both completely cracked up! Trying to keep from laughing out there was next to impossible!

The following week, there were "Pepe" signs everywhere. The people loved it. Chavo really didn't want to do it, but the office kept pushing him to come out on his horse again. From that point on, Chavo and Pepe were a team—when Chavo made his entrance, it would actually say on the TV screen, "Chavo Guerrero Jr. *with Pepe.*"

CHEATING DEATH, STEALING LIFE

Poor Chavito! Everybody loved Pepe except him! To Chavo, Pepe was a curse. He had to carry the damn horse everywhere, at the airport and to the arenas. Every now and then, Chavo would say, "Shit, I forgot Pepe!" and we'd have to find the nearest Toys "R" Us. Finally he got smart and gave the ring crew a bunch of Pepes to carry with the rest of the props.

Of course, in classic WCW fashion, the company didn't take advantage of how over Pepe was with the fans. Dean suggested the idea of doing vignettes, like "The Adventures of Chavo and Pepe," but nothing ever came of it. If we'd been in WWE, Vince would totally have known exactly how to market Pepe. He would've made stick horses and sold a million of them!

It was decided that Chavo and I would have our blow-off match at *Bash at the Beach*. Chavo pitched a Hair vs. Hair match to Kevin Sullivan, who thought it was a great idea. Even though we'd been in a program for months, I felt that we were rushing into it. It takes time to build to something as big as a Hair match. As a result, my heart wasn't really into the match. Of course, I wanted to get Chavo over, but I felt that I had accomplished that by putting him over in the *Great American Bash*.

We did do some hilarious stuff to get us to the Pay-Per-View. We started the build on *Thunder*. Chavo—and Pepe—came down to the ring, saying "Heeere, Eddy, Eddy, Eddy," basically us ripping off the commercial where the Taco Bell chihuahua goes looking for Godzilla—"Heeere, Lizard, Lizard, Lizard!"

The rest of the bit was classic *Looney Tunes*, with Chavito impersonating Elmer Fudd: "Be vewy, vewy quiet . . . I'm hunting Eddys." He set up a cardboard box—the "Acme Eddy Trap"—with a stick, twine, and a burrito for bait, then hid outside the ring with a toy bow and arrow. I came down and defused the Acme Eddy Trap, then ran and hid on the other side of the ring. Chavo came back in and lifted up the box to see if he'd caught me. When he saw that I wasn't under there, he hit the punch line: "I think I'm going to need a bigger box."

That's when I came in and attacked him. I threw him outside, lifted up the mats, and gave him a brainbuster right onto the concrete floor. Then I tossed him back in the ring, whacked him across the face with the burrito, then pulled out some scissors and cut off a hank of his hair. Fortunately for Chavo, WCW Head of Security Doug Dillinger ran in to break up the melee.

C havito got his match at *Bash at the Beach* on July 12 in San Diego—two matches, actually. Before we went at it, Chavo took on Stevie Ray—sort of. He came to the ring spraying water with his Super Soaker and an inflatable pool toy around his waist. Chavo reached out to shake Stevie Ray's hand, then fell to the mat in pain. He tapped out to a handshake! "That was for you, Eddy," he said.

Our match started with Chavito biting my ass. We went back and forth, each of us trying to get at the scissors, but always getting caught by referee Charles Robinson. Finally Chavo was distracted and I got him with an inside cradle.

I got out the clippers and a barber's chair, but Chavo took them away and started shaving his own head. That was actually Chavito's idea. I was skeptical. It was a month before his wedding, and I wanted to be sure that he knew what he was doing.

"Don't worry, bro," he said. "It'll grow back."

M emorable as it might be, I don't consider *Bash at the Beach* to be a highlight of my career. My body was as soft as it's ever been in my professional life. I wasn't taking good care of myself. I was drinking pretty heavily, and it showed.

The office wanted me to kick the living shit out of Chavito, to show that I'd had it up to here with his psycho antics. But my love for Chavito trumped any business we were doing. The angle didn't matter—as much as I was supposed to hate him, I simply couldn't beat him up.

After the match, Chavito told me that he finally understood what I'd been telling him all along.

"I've realized that working with you brought out the best in me," he said.

"It wasn't me, bro," I told him. "If you'd worked with Dean Malenko, if you'd worked with Chris Benoit, the same thing would've happened. It's not about me—it's about you."

I meant every word. Chavito is a tremendous person and a wonderful wrestler. It's just a matter of time before he becomes the Superstar that he deserves to be. I'm so proud of him.

CHAPTER 21

Since I'd become a **WCW** employee, my disease began evolving to the point where I was partying harder than ever. I had accepted in my heart that I had gotten as far as I was ever going to get. I really did. My fire had been extinguished. WCW didn't put it out—that's on me. I let them kill my spirit.

Even though I'd accepted it, it still hurt. I was doing anything I could, just to try and block out the pain. I was smoking weed, taking a lot of pills, literally anything I could get my hands on. When someone gave me a pill, I wouldn't even ask what it was. I was doing crazy shit, like cutting up Percocets and snorting them.

Of course, more than anything else, I was drinking. Alcohol is, and always has been, my number one addiction. It's my demon. Booze is the poison that sets my disease in motion. Everything else intensified it, or served as a substitute for it.

It wasn't only booze and dope—my addiction spread to all aspects of my life. Since I'd accepted the idea that I was only in WCW for the money, I started spending like a maniac, with no limits. If there was something I wanted, I bought it. I didn't even think twice about it. I would call my financial adviser and say, "Hey, I want to buy a new car." "Okay," he'd say. "Go for it."

Everything had to be top of the line, the best there was. Not because it meant anything, but because I had the money to do it. I bought a big house. I bought a $55,000 Land Cruiser for Vickie and a TransAm for myself. I bought the boat I'd always dreamed of—a twenty-eight-foot Crownline, a cross between a jet boat and a deck boat. That sucker was a badass.

We ate out every meal. And don't forget, I wasn't just eating, I was drinking as well, so all my bills were basically tripled.

I was constantly buying gifts for my kids, for my family and friends. Vickie and I would get into an argument, and instead of trying to understand what the fight was about, I'd go out and buy her a present—"Look what I got you, honey. See how much I love you?"

Buying presents for Vickie and the girls was a way of washing away my guilt. It wasn't to make them happy, it was to make myself feel better. "Look, honey, I bought you this $5,000 tennis bracelet. I'm not that bad a guy."

It felt good, living a rich man's life. It wasn't just cars and boats and houses and jewelry—I also gave a lot of money away. The Bible teaches us to tithe, to give a percentage of our income back to God. We are just stewards of what God has given us. It is our responsibility to acknowledge His blessings by sharing, by making charitable acts. Tithing doesn't mean giving money to a church—it simply means that you use some of your money to take care of others.

Ultimately, it was all about excess. I thought that if I just did more—of anything—then maybe that would finally give me satisfaction. I was trying to find happiness any way I could, whether it was getting loaded or buying stuff.

In hindsight, my excessive behavior sounds like a nightmare, but in certain ways, I was having a lot of fun. I was actually a pretty happy drunk, laughing and acting crazy. I'd get very affectionate, putting my arm around everyone's shoulder, telling them, "I love you, man."

No question about it, I had some good times. But eventually it reached a point where those good times were few and far between. The constant partying got pretty tiresome. It stopped being a party.

I embarrassed myself more times than I can count, just acting like a complete drunken ass. I would wake up the next day and not remember what I'd

CHEATING DEATH, STEALING LIFE

done. It was like I was two different people—Normal Eddie and Drunk Eddie.

One of the worst moments was when I served as best man at Chavito's wedding. It was such a special day, but my behavior came close to turning it into a nightmare.

Basically, I got wasted and made a scene. Again. Vickie got pissed off because I was so loaded and we ended up having a huge fight, right in front of everybody. When I finally passed out, Tury and my brother-in-law Gilbert carried me out to the car. I was so messed up, I wound up going to the bathroom on myself. My sister and her husband had to clean me up and put me into bed.

That was so damn humiliating. I woke up the next day and everybody was joking about it. "It reminded me of when you were a kid and I used to change your Pampers," Linda said.

I laughed, but inside I was dying. Inside I was hating myself. I didn't want to do these things. I wasn't trying to disgrace myself in front of my family. I just couldn't help myself.

I've asked Chavito for his forgiveness so many times. God bless him, he acts like it was nothing. "Don't worry about it," he says.

It's easy for him to be forgiving—my whole family has always had issues with those types of behaviors. I'm not the first Guerrero to get loaded in front of everybody else and make a scene. It's a natural thing for us. You clean it up and go on.

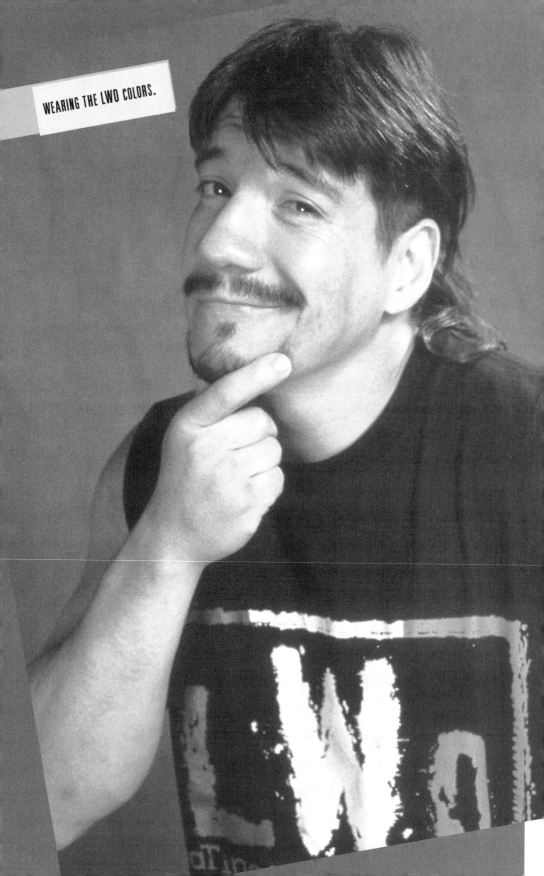

CHAPTER 22

After the Hair vs. Hair match, the angle with Chavo just petered out. He would come to the ring—with Pepe, of course—and interfere in my matches, but it wasn't really going anywhere. It was as if the creative team had no idea what to do with either of our characters, so they just clung to our previous angle.

On August 17, we did *Nitro* in Hartford, Connecticut. Instead of taking on Konnan as scheduled, I walked out to the ring with my luggage and a cup of "coffee."

"Yeah, that's right, unscheduled interview. Hey, Production, don't even think about going to a commercial. If not, I may say my piece on another show. That's right, Eric. So I got your attention now, Eric Bischoff? I can't get it in the back. Huh? I try and go in there and try and talk to you about business and I get screamed at and kicked out. Well, if this is what I got to do to get your attention, Eric Bischoff, then this is what I am going to do. Fire me, do whatever it takes, I could give a you-know-what.

"Eric Bischoff, time in and time out, for one whole year I have been coming here to work just to be mistreated by you, and very much unappreciated, Eric. On the road, on TV, I give you one hundred percent. I give these people my one hundred percent whether they like me or whether they don't. I give you the best show there is and you know it. And you cannot give me the time of day in the back to listen to what I have to say to you, Eric.

"Well, I could give a damn. 'Cause you know what? I don't care anymore. Eric Bischoff, you got a lot of young talent here in WCW and all you do is hold us down for the people you pay a lot of money to. Well, I don't care, Bischoff, anymore. I don't care about nothing anymore. Eric, you have driven me to that. Eric Bischoff, this has nothing to do with you people, this is personal between me and you, Eric. I come to work with my heart and all you do is step on it, and I'm tired of it. You hold me down, you've held me down, and from now on, Eric . . . See, I don't know what it is. I don't know if it's something personal you got against me. Whatever it is, Eric. I don't know. What is it about me that you have against me that you keep me from stepping up the ladder in this profession? What is it about me? I mean, you got me tied down, Eric, in my contract. And I could give—I'm telling you this right now, okay?—and I am saying this for any other guy that wants to come out here and speak his mind that's being held down. If you got the you-know-what, come out here and say it like I am.

"Eric Bischoff, I'm telling you this face-to-face, boy, because I can't get your attention. Wait, not face-to-face, let me say on national television in front of all these people, I'm coming out. And the only reason I haven't come out any sooner is because of two reasons: Chavo Junior—I love you, man, you're my blood and I'll never let that go. You're one of the reasons I haven't said anything about it, what I'm doing tonight. And the other reason is because I have two kids and a wife that I have to support.

"Well, you know what? If losing my dignity means having to put up with WCW, nWo red, black, or white or whatever the hell it is, I don't care. So, Eric Bischoff, I'm telling you this right now. I want out of my contract no matter what it takes, who I got to speak to, or what it is, okay? And let me save you some time, Eric Bischoff. I've thrown the coffee on myself. As far as I'm concerned, Eric Bischoff, you can take this job and shove it up your you-know-what."

CHEATING DEATH, STEALING LIFE

t was a classic example of a worked shoot—an angle that was supposed to appear real, even though it was in fact scripted by the creative team.

It was actually my idea. There was so much gossip on the net, about how I was unhappy at WCW, how I felt like I was being held back. And of course, everybody knew about the meeting I'd had with Bischoff where he "threw" coffee on me. I thought, *Why don't we address all of these things on TV?* I brought the idea to Bischoff, and amazingly, he liked it.

But pulling off a worked shoot is incredibly hard to do. When the segment was done, I couldn't shake the feeling that I'd blown it. I had wanted it to be something different, I wanted it to be a moment of full-on reality in the middle of all the nWo bullshit. But even though there was plenty of truth in what I'd said, there was no way that I could say what I *really* felt. It was still part of a wrestling angle.

Plus I was nervous. Instead of just coming out and speaking my mind, I was worried about sticking to the script. Turner Broadcasting's Standards and Practices Department were adamant that I avoid any swearing, even words like "ass." I know that you shouldn't have to cuss to make a point, but when you're as angry as I was supposed to be, words like that just naturally come out. If I could've said "You can shove it up your ass," it might have made it more realistic. But having to say "Shove it up your you-know-what" just made me sound silly and half-assed.

The speech ended up lacking any real heart. Sure, a lot of my real feelings came out, but I always knew what I was saying wasn't authentic. Even though I threatened to go to WWE if they cut to commercial, I wasn't really saying, "Fuck you, I'm out of here." I didn't really have the option of leaving. I knew I was stuck. I knew I wasn't going to go anywhere.

Hell, it wasn't even real coffee that I threw on myself—it was just a cup of water!

Because I was being so careful, so conscious of not cussing or going too far from what we'd planned, I didn't have true fire in my eyes. I said the words, but I didn't say them with *balls*. And because I didn't believe what I was saying, neither did the fans. It was just another angle.

It's funny, but instead of making me feel like I'd gotten something out of

THE EDDIE GUERRERO STORY

my system, that interview actually made me feel worse about my situation. I think that was the night when I truly gave up inside.

A little historical footnote: At the same time as I was addressing the WCW audience, President Bill Clinton was addressing the American people, apologizing for his relationship with Monica Lewinsky. Clinton didn't really give his all to that speech, either. You might say he also blew his big moment.

My act of rebellion against Bischoff's regime took me off TV for a couple of weeks. A taped match I had with Lizmark Jr. was even edited out of the following *Thunder* in order to fully establish the angle.

I came back so that we could continue the story with a bunch of backstage arguments between Eric and myself. After one fight, he told me that he was sending me to Japan on my daughter's birthday—"You can send her a postcard from Tokyo," he shouted. That took me off TV for *another* few weeks.

I returned to *Nitro* on October 5, in Columbia, South Carolina. I walked out during a match between a couple of Mexican boys, Damien and Hector Garza, holding a mike in my hand.

"One moment, let me talk to you. Relax, just let me talk to you and relax, okay? I got one question for you: What has Eric Bischoff done for you, what has Eric Bischoff done for you? That's exactly what, he hasn't done nothing for you. Just like you and you and me, he's got us wrestling each other week in and week out, right? We're wrestling each other. He never gives us the opportunity to wrestle somebody else, to try to climb the ladder of success, you could say. He doesn't give you any money to where you can get your own rent-a-car, huh? All you guys have to share a rent-a-car, and I'm talking there's five or six guys to one car, three or four guys to one room.

"Who's got all the money? It looks pretty full to me in here tonight, it's rocking and rolling, but who's rolling around in the money? Hey, if you don't have your nose where Eric Bischoff has his nose—Hollywood Hogan—if you ain't part of his clique, then you're not going to make any money. They get

the Lear jets, they get the limos, they get everything. They get to wrestle who-ever they want and when they want, and they're always the main event, and you know what? They probably couldn't even tie your wrestling shoes. So I'm telling you this right now, I can't do nothing by myself, you can't do it by yourself. But we can do it together, united. La Raza, man! I'm talking about what we are—we're Latino! I want you guys to join me, man! LWO—Latino World Order! Together we can do this, we can go against. You want to be part of LWO? You want to be together? Put these on, boys, and follow me!

"Now, Eric Bischoff, I'm telling you one thing, we're going to do what it takes to get our piece of the cake, and you know what you can do, Eric [I gestured 'kiss my ass'], right here!"

A gain, whatever truth there was in my promo—and there was plenty— was diminished by the fact that in the end it was just part of an angle, the start of another World Order stable.

The Latino World Order was Jason Hervey's idea. He was one of Bischoff's buddies, a teen actor who played Fred Savage's older brother on *The Wonder Years*, then went on to work as a sports entertainment producer.

It was initially planned as a stable for Konnan. "We originally wanted this for Konnan," Jason said, "but since he's with the nWo Wolf Pac, we decided to go ahead and give it to you."

Thanks a lot, I thought. But I was in no position to complain about getting Konnan's leftovers. At that point, any storyline was better than none at all.

I suggested keeping the LWO a small crew, with the best of the *luchadors*. But when I was told that I was going to come out during Damien vs. Hector Garza, I knew right there and then that the LWO was going to include the entire Mexican roster.

The angle turned out to be a complete freaking nightmare. Basically, I be-came the Mexican boys' babysitter. I had to act as their interpreter, I had to make sure they were where they were supposed to be. I became the go-between between them and the American boys.

The worst part was dealing with the fact that each and every one of the Mexican boys thought the LWO was going to send them straight to the top. They had no idea it was just another way of jobbing them out.

The Mexican mentality is completely dog-eat-dog. The priority is not to get the angle over, it's to get yourself over. All the Mexican boys did during the LWO interviews was try to steal camera. They would walk in front of me as I was talking, they'd stand on the ropes, all of them trying to draw attention to themselves.

It wasn't personal, it was just the Mexican style. Watch AAA, watch EMLL, and you'll see what they do in the ring. It's all about stealing camera.

I tried to explain it to them, but it was like talking to a wall. "Don't step in front of me," I said. "I'm the leader. You've got to respect me, you've got to back me up. Trust me, you guys will get your spot when the time comes."

But they didn't listen. Either they chose to ignore me or they were too ignorant to understand that they needed to put their selfish behavior aside for the good of the many. Every interview I did degenerated into complete chaos. There was no way for me to get these boys under control. It just about drove me crazy.

Let me just say that this had nothing to do with the Mexican boys' abilities. Most of those guys were tremendous workers. They could wrestle their asses off. It was their psychology that I was battling every week.

The whole thing made me miserable, even more miserable than I'd been in the beginning of the nWo days. I was drinking heavily, not having any fun at all, until one night I decided to change my mentality. *Fuck this,* I thought. *I'm going to get the LWO over.*

I knew no one wanted to see the LWO work, but that just made me more determined to make a go of it. I pushed the idea that the LWO were the pests of WCW. We'd come out, do hit-and-runs, then scatter like cockroaches do when you turn on the light.

We started feuding with Rey Mysterio, trying to force him to join up with us. Of course, Rey didn't want any part of it. He knew that the LWO would turn him into just another pea in the pod, and he was so clearly worth a lot more than that.

On the plus side, I was able to bring in my friend Art Flores to play my bodyguard. Eric wanted somebody like the Mexican-American actor Danny Trejo, who was in *Desperado* and *Heat* and a lot of other films. He's an amazing actor, a total tough guy, covered in prison ink.

I suggested Tury, and Bischoff gave the okay. Tury was very excited about the opportunity. He found a tattoo artist who designed fake ink for him to put on so that he looked like an ex-con badass. He was my unnamed bodyguard, though later on he was given the name "Spyder."

Having Tury around was tremendous. I got to be on the road with my best friend. God, that was so much fun.

Trying to convince Rey Mysterio to join the Latino World Order.

We had a great time, traveling together, partying like madmen.

Art came in and helped me take charge of the Mexican boys. They knew he was a legitimate badass, a real street fighter. He really was the law as far as the LWO was concerned, in the ring and backstage.

Once Art came into the picture, I was able to take a breath and start being me again. I started feeling the fire, trying to think of ways to make the most of my situation.

For the first time in my career, I began getting some significant mike time. I began learning how to express myself by talking about my Latino heritage, by talking about *La Raza*.

Slowly but surely, things progressed to the point where the LWO was

THE EDDIE GUERRERO STORY

being taken seriously by the fans and, more importantly, by Bischoff. What changed things was that the Latin community started getting behind us. The Latin people began coming out to the shows, cheering for the LWO.

Once again, management proved to me how little they cared about me or the other Mexican wrestlers. Even though the LWO was growing in popularity, they couldn't be bothered to sell LWO T-shirts. Again, the only ones they printed were for us to wear on TV. Eventually they did decide to sell some LWO shirts, but only in certain markets, where they knew there was a strong Latin community.

Despite the initial nightmares, things started looking up. The vignettes got funnier and the Mexican boys started showing a little restraint. For the first time, I started thinking that the LWO might not be such a bad thing after all.

But then I went and fucked it all up for everybody.

CHAPTER 23

After *Starrcade,* we were given a very brief Christmas break. My marriage wasn't in big trouble yet, but it was well on its way. Vickie and I were arguing all the time, usually about my partying. She was dealing with it as best she could, but I could see her frustration mounting. Even though my drinking had been a part of our life for as long as either of us could remember, it was clearly growing out of control.

"Let's throw a New Year's Eve party," Vickie suggested. "That can be my turn to have some drinks and enjoy myself."

It was a fun party. All our friends and family came over, and of course everybody got pretty wasted. After everybody had gone home, Vickie and I had a bit of a spat, though to this day, I don't remember what set it off.

Vickie went to bed, but I decided to stay up a while longer. I was feeling pretty hungry and started looking through the kitchen for something to munch on. For some reason, I had an intense craving for eggs. We didn't have any in the fridge, so even though it was three in the morning, I decided to go to the store.

As I was getting into my TransAm, I grabbed a bottle of Renutrient and threw it into the backseat. Renutrient was a legal form of GHB, a drug that promotes fat reduction and muscle building by stimulating growth hormone release. It also gives you a hell of a buzz and makes you pass out. Looking back, I realize I was still feeling upset from my fight with Vickie and thinking very bad thoughts. *I'll show you,* I thought. *I'll hurt myself.*

The store was closed, so I went ahead and drove to the next convenience store up the road. I bought some eggs and a twelve-pack of beer, and then got back in the car.

Before I drove off, I decided to take some of the Renutrient. It's a liquid, taken by the capful. Usually one or two caps would put me down, but God help me, that night I took five good-sized shots.

I blocked that memory for so long. It wasn't until much later that I remembered what I had done. It was a suicide attempt, plain and simple. Maybe I did it subconsciously, but no matter how you slice it, that was what I was doing. I was tired of life and wanted to die.

I had given up believing. I had tried to fill the empty place in my heart with wrestling. I tried to fill it with booze and pills. I was making good money and I was still feeling empty. I was miserable in WCW. I knew I wasn't going to go any higher there, and jumping to WWE hadn't even crossed my mind. I couldn't stop wondering, *Is this it? Is this what I worked my whole life for?*

It didn't help matters that I was constantly fighting with Vickie. I think that night was a culmination of all those bad feelings. The hole inside me had just gotten too large.

I took those five caps knowing that I was going to fall asleep. *If I make it home,* I thought, *then I make it home. If I don't, that's okay too.*

I just didn't care anymore. I just wanted the pain to stop.

I wasn't thinking about Vickie or the kids. I was being selfish, thinking only of myself. I wasn't knowingly trying to commit suicide, but it was clearly going on deep inside my subconscious. Why else would I do something like that?

I started driving, heading down Highway 54. I pushed down on the gas pedal and felt the power of my TransAm—*Vrooom! Here we go!*

The next thing I knew, there were doctors all around me, holding my leg. As my eyes opened, the first thing they said was, "What are you on?"

"What?" I had no idea where I was or what was going on.

"You've been in a car accident," one of the doctors told me. "You're in the emergency room. Your leg is in very bad shape and we need authorization to start surgery on you."

I sat up and looked at my leg. "Oh wow," I said. "I'm pretty fucked up."

The doctor looked straight at me. "Yep," he said, "you sure are."

And then I passed out.

I woke up again as the doctors were trying to work on me. I freaked out and started trying to fight them off, but they grabbed my arms and held me down.

Again they asked me, "What are you on?"

"Alcohol," I told them.

"No, you're on more than that. What are you on? Tell us what you're on."

They kept pushing and finally I said, "Renutrient."

"What's that?"

"GHB."

"Okay," the doctor said. "Can you give us any contact information so that we can call your family?"

I managed to give them our phone number before going unconscious again.

I was in and out of consciousness for a couple of days. I remember opening my eyes and seeing Shaul by the bed, with tears streaming down her little face. I knew I was in bad shape—they don't allow little kids into the intensive care unit unless they think the person isn't going to survive.

My family all came to the hospital the afternoon after the accident. My brothers and sisters all flew in from their respective homes. My mom had just flown home to El Paso after spending the holidays with us in Tampa—she literally got to Texas, then turned around and flew back to Florida. All my friends, like Dean and Tury, came to see me. Our family pastor came and prayed over me.

When I finally came to, the police told me what had happened. I had fallen asleep at the wheel—obviously—while going upwards of 130 miles per hour. I came to a curve in the road but didn't make it. The car went off the embankment into a ditch and just started rolling. The embankment basically acted like a ramp, sending the car into the air, soaring up over some trees. They knew this because they found parts of the car in the treetops, which weren't all mangled like they would've been if the car had hit them.

The car flipped so many times it was flattened like a pancake. It looked

179

like a Coke can after somebody stomped on it. Luckily for me, I shot out through the T-top as the car started rolling. I must've flown a hundred feet or so before landing in the gravel on the roadside. Vickie thinks an angel pulled me out through the T-top, because had I stayed in the car, there is no way on earth that I'd have lived.

The cops came to the scene and started dealing with the traffic situation. They saw me lying there and just assumed I was dead. Fortunately for me, a lady who had pulled over to volunteer her help saw me moving. They called for an air evac—a helicopter ambulance—and immediately flew me to St. Joseph's Hospital.

My injuries were pretty brutal. I'd fractured my collarbone and compressed a few discs in my spine. I had severe scrapes all over my body from the gravel and broken glass—Vickie was still pulling little pieces of glass out of my back a month later. I was bruised and swollen all over from the trauma.

Both of my legs were a complete mess. I'd broken my right hip socket and shredded my left calf. A piece of glass had severed the nerves and ligaments so badly that there was no way the doctors could reattach them. Instead, they just pulled the skin over the wound and sewed it up. They literally removed a pound of my calf.

The worst injury I'd sustained was a badly lacerated liver. When Vickie first got to the hospital, the doctor pulled her aside. "We suggest you call your family," he told her, "because we don't believe he's going to make it through the next two nights."

By the grace of God, somehow I didn't hit my head. My brother Mando jokes that it was because of my dad's training. He taught all the Guerreros to tuck and roll whenever we fall. I guess it was instinctive. Even when I was shooting a hundred feet out of a flying car, I still managed to tuck and roll and protect my head.

I only found these things out after all was said and done. A lot of what happened—in the accident, in the hospital afterward—remains a mystery to me. I suppose I could've asked more questions, but I don't think I ever really wanted to know all the details.

All things considered, I was very fortunate. My hip socket broke cleanly, so they didn't have to repair it surgically. All I had to do was give it time to mend and it'd be all right.

I wasn't so lucky with my other leg injuries. After performing reconstructive surgery on my calf and thigh, the doctor told Vickie that he doubted I would ever walk again. "What does he do for a living?" he asked.

"He's a professional wrestler."

"Oh no, he'll never wrestle again," the doctor replied. "That's certain. He'll have to find another career. That is, if he makes it."

Within a couple of days it became clear I was going to survive. My liver showed definite signs of healing and it looked like I was out of the woods. The doctors told me that my physical condition was a huge factor in my ability to heal. A normal thirty-six-year-old, without my level of physical activity, would've probably been crippled for life.

Still, the doctors were all pretty surprised. They would come into my room and tell me how fortunate I was. "You're a lucky, lucky man," they said.

Yeah, right, I thought. *Sure I am.*

While I was in the hospital, the doctors had me on morphine drip all day long. I was able to push a button and get a dose every seven minutes. And believe me, I pushed that button every time.

Obviously I couldn't do that after I went home, so I started taking a lot of pills. Anything to stop the hurting. How could I do the physical therapy if I was in terrible pain? I had to dull the pain before I could begin learning to walk again.

But as a result of having so much painkiller in me, I was pretty much in a fog. I was like the walking dead—only I couldn't walk!

I started physical therapy about a month after the accident. My whole body hurt, like I'd taken the worst bump ever. I was in pain all the time, on the inside. My hip socket was still in the process of healing, but I couldn't wait anymore.

The physical therapy was as frustrating and painful as anything I'd ever experienced. I didn't want to be there and behaved like a real asshole. They were poking and pushing at me, and all I wanted was to go home and take more painkillers.

I eventually got my legs working again. My hip healed. It was painful, but I was able to get through it. The physical therapists were shocked at how quickly I started walking again. Still, they didn't think I should even consider wrestling. "No," I said, "I'm going to wrestle."

"At least wait a year," they said. But I couldn't put it off that long. I needed to get back to work.

I was in a pit of despair, but still determined to push myself back into shape. I knew that if I was ever going to get back in the ring, I was going to need to do some serious training. I probably would never come close to the condition I was in before the accident, but at least I'd be able to wrestle.

When I started getting back into shape, I couldn't believe how hard it was. My legs were working, my body was just about healed, but I didn't have the same strength that I used to. I couldn't even curl five pounds without it hurting. But I was persistent, spending all day, every day, in the gym. Slowly but surely, I got my strength back. After five weeks, I was back to where I was before the accident.

I was on painkillers almost all the time. I was taking Vicodin, OxyContin, anything I could get. I wasn't getting high—I was using them to get through life. Along with the pills, I was drinking pretty much all the time. Anything to dull the pain.

Most people, when they've taken that much painkiller, can barely walk, let alone hit the gym and train. But it was normal to me. I was driven to keep going.

Once my body was back in some semblance of shape, I went back to the ring. Steve Keirn—a great wrestler who was a star in the AWA and went on to WWE fame as Doink the Clown—had taken over Dean Malenko's wrestling school, and he invited me to come on down and work out. I'd get in the ring with whoever was there.

Other than my close circle of friends—Tury, Dean, Chris—not many people knew the extent of my injuries. In this business, no one talks about getting hurt. You get injured and you just keep going.

Being a wrestler gave me the ability to deal with my injuries in a way that most people couldn't. I've been wrestling with injuries my entire life. Even though what had happened to me was far beyond the normal wrestling injury, I didn't let myself go there in my mind. To me, it was another injury.

I was running on pure instinct. Even though I was feeling pretty down, wrestling is my way of life. It's how I support my family. I don't know any other way. Since the day I was born, wrestling has sustained me and my family. It's the way my father fed me; it's the way I feed my kids.

More importantly, wrestling is my greatest release. It's been such a blessing for me. I can step into the ring and let it all go—all my anger, all my frustration, all my pain. Whoosh! Everything just comes out of me. It's a beautiful feeling, a gift.

I honestly can't describe what goes on in my head when I'm out there. People who don't wrestle can't possibly understand it. When I'm in the ring, I don't feel any pain. I'm in another world out there.

When I'm backstage, I walk around like Slowpoke Rodriguez. My lids are heavy, my head hangs low, my shoulders are slumped. But the second I go through that curtain I become Speedy Gonzalez. The adrenaline starts pumping and I just go to a different place in my head. My energy picks right up, everything starts clicking, and I feel like a million bucks. The shift from one persona to the other is instantaneous. It's almost as if I'm two different people—Superman and Clark Kent.

To me, wrestling is therapy. No matter how bad my personal situation is, when I step into the ring, all my troubles disappear. My baggage stays in the back where it belongs.

After the accident, I started to see myself as bulletproof. I wrecked my car, came within an inch of killing myself, and I was still here. In my mind I felt nothing could stop me.

At the same time, there was part of me that felt guilty for being alive. I still feel that way sometimes, especially when I hear about other wrestlers that were in the same boat that I've been in, but didn't make it. The emotions hit me hard. I understand that my survival is by the grace of God, but it's still very difficult to accept.

My brother Mando asked me, "Did you see a light or a tunnel or anything?"

There was no light, no out-of-body experience. That made me question my relationship with God. I wondered that if I had died, was I going to heaven? I thought that maybe God had left me here because I wasn't saved. Maybe He knew that I hadn't really made that choice in my heart and He was still giving me another opportunity.

Things between Vickie and me began improving a bit. At first, we were both still scared by the idea that I almost died. Then it was simply that we were spending more time together. It was great to be able to be around Vickie and the kids. Even though I wasn't completely there, I was still around more than I'd ever been.

But it turned out to be a false peace. Just because things had chilled out and we weren't at each other's throats all the time didn't mean the issues between us had gone away. They just went into hibernation for a few months.

Physically, everything healed with time—my hip, my ribs, my liver. My spirit was another story. That hole inside me was still empty.

I knew I needed to change my life. But knowing you've got to change doesn't mean you're going to do it. It's meaningless unless you actually take steps to make those alterations.

I had so many questions about my own behavior. Why am I doing these things? Why am I trying to hurt myself? Why do I keep hurting my loved ones?

With all that was going on, I never once considered therapy, let alone going into rehab. I didn't think there was anything wrong with me. I just thought I was making bad decisions. I thought I had no willpower. I think I probably didn't want to know if there was anything wrong with me.

I just wasn't there yet. I still hadn't reached rock bottom.

In the spring, WCW did a show in Orlando, so I drove down to talk with them about my comeback. Kevin Nash had the book at the time. "I know it's only been a few months," I said, "but I'm ready. Can I please start working again?"

I've got to admit, Kevin was cool. He totally put me over. "Sure, Eddie," he said. "Nobody with a wrestling show would ever have a problem having you as part of it," he said, paying me a nice compliment.

But the truth was we both knew that there was a good possibility that things were going to be different, that I wasn't going to be the same wrestler I was before the accident. I knew I'd fucked up with the car accident. I just wanted the chance to come back and earn my spot again. I wasn't done. I didn't want my career to end like that.

On June 21, 1999, I flew to New Orleans for my return to WCW. Despite having been told that I'd never wrestle again, I honestly didn't think of it as being that big of a deal. I was just going back to work.

I was obviously pretty nervous. I'd seen it so many times—a wrestler would take time off due to injury, and when they came back they just weren't the same.

There's no mercy in this business. If you can't produce, the fans can tell. It doesn't matter how much they love or respect you, they'll turn their back on you if you can't deliver in the ring. Like it or not, they're going to compare you to the person you were. *Does he still have what it takes?*

Kevin used the car accident as a way of getting me over. I walked out and the crowd seemed genuinely glad to see me. They chanted, "Eddy! Eddy!" even though I was a heel the last time I was on TV.

I got my heat back pretty quickly. I gave an interview, talking about how lucky I was to be alive and how pumped I was to be back. Juventud Guerrera came down and gave me a hug, then offered his hand in friendship. I refused, letting him know that I hadn't forgotten how the LWO called it quits. As Juvi tried to explain, I slapped him right across the face, setting up our match.

It was an okay match. I remember watching it later and thinking, *I'm not down.*

For better or worse, I've made a lot of comebacks, and if there's one thing that I've learned, it's that you've got to come back right. You can't come back out of shape. If you don't, you're never going to be able to get back to where you were.

I knew the boys were going to test me, to see if I still had what it took. You can't just come back and expect to be treated the same way you were before you left. You have to remind people who you are in the ring. Sure, there was going to be some ring rust, but I was determined to work at the same level I was at before the accident.

That first night, I realized that I had a lot of work left to do, but at least I was back.

THE EDDIE GUERRERO STORY

HITTING PERRY SATURN WITH THE FROG SPLASH.

CHAPTER 24

I had renegotiated my deal just before my accident. To his credit, Eric Bischoff honored our agreement, even when it wasn't certain that I'd ever be able to wrestle again. A lot of bosses would've taken the opportunity to cut and run.

All the usual promises were made—"You're so great," Bischoff told me. "We're definitely going to find more for you to do on the show." I knew enough to take that with a grain of salt, but since Eric was also offering more money than I had ever made before, I agreed to go with it.

Eric and I might have had our differences when it came to business, but when push came to shove, he showed himself to be a real nice guy. After my accident, he looked out for me, calling frequently to see how I was doing.

Most importantly, he called Vickie to tell her he was going to send me my new contract and to make sure that I signed it. That way I'd continue to get paid while I recuperated. I didn't realize it at the time, but I was selling my soul.

The first angle I was in upon returning to the active roster had me going to war with the masked *luchadors*. We did a hilarious vignette where I claimed one of them had stolen my wallet. I forced

187

Doug Dillenger to make a lineup so I could unmask a few of them. Of course, they all had their backs to the camera, which meant that I got to do all the "serious" acting work. There were some funny moments, like when I took Ciclope's mask off and got all freaked out: "Oh my God! Were you in a fire or something? Put it back on!"

The masked boys started running in to interfere in all my matches. I had just beaten Psicosis, when La Parka and Villano V came down and started kicking my ass. All of a sudden, Rey Mysterio came out. I'm sure the fans figured he was going to join in the beatdown, but instead, he helped save me.

I returned the favor a couple of weeks later by running in with a chair to save Rey from Vampiro and the rappers Insane Clown Posse.

I got to admit I wasn't thrilled to see Vampiro on the WCW roster when I came back. I knew him from back in Mexico and he was one of the most two-faced guys I've ever had the displeasure of working with. He'd shake your hand and say, "I'm so thankful, it's an honor to work with you," then badmouth you behind your back. You could never believe half the shit he said. Maybe some of it was true, maybe it wasn't. To this day, I still don't know when that guy was being honest.

In a lot of ways, Insane Clown Posse were more professional than Vampiro. They were huge wrestling fans and as a result, they were very respectful and appreciative that any wrestler would take them seriously.

"Anything you want to do, Eddy," they'd say, then honestly work to the best of their abilities to get the match over. They were definitely easier to work with than Vamp. He'd be all agreeable before the match, but as soon as you got in the ring with him, he'd start trying to put himself over at the expense of everyone else and the match. A lot of that has to do with where he came from. He was a major star in Mexico, drawing huge houses wherever he went. Then he came to WCW and instantly assumed he was going to do the same thing.

Gimmicks—like putting movie stars and rappers on the roster, or pretending to be a scary punk-rock vampire—will get you only so far. They'll be a big draw at first, but in the end, if they don't know how to wrestle, it's going to fall off. That's the nature of the beast, the first law of wrestling—when all is said and done, you have to be able to wrestle.

I've got to give Vampiro his due—it was a good gimmick. In his time, he really drew. He made a lot of money for the boys in Mexico. But ultimately, the people saw through the gimmick and realized that he just wasn't a great wrestler.

Before long, the thrill of being back at work wore off and all the old frustrations came back to haunt me. Once again, I felt like I was just running in place.

Things were not going well for the company. WWE was blowing WCW out of the water on every level, from ratings to the overall quality of the product. No matter how much money Bischoff threw at the problems—and there were plenty—it was pretty clear that nothing was going to fix things except a complete overhaul.

In September, Eric was "reassigned" by the Turner Broadcasting bigwigs—a fancy way of saying he was fired. A month later, WWE writers Vince Russo and Ed Ferrara—two guys who had helped Vince McMahon create the hugely successful Attitude Era—were hired by our new boss, Turner Executive Vice President Bill Busch, to come in and turn things around.

When the boys heard Russo and Ferrara were jumping to WCW, we were all thrilled. It reenergized the boys. We all felt it was just the shot in the arm we needed to get back in the fight. For the first time in ages, people started feeling positive. "Things are finally going to change," we all said.

The buzz went through the grapevine that I was one of the people Russo and Ferrara felt hadn't been used to the company's best advantage. I swear, when I heard that, I just about got a hard-on! I felt the old fire coming back to me. I started thinking, *Hey, maybe there is a chance for me here in WCW.*

We were doing *Nitro* in Philadelphia when Russo and Ferrara showed up for their first day of work. Over the course of the day, they pulled each of the boys aside to introduce themselves and lay out what they had in mind for them.

Right off the bat, they told me that they felt WCW's biggest mistake was underutilizing guys like Chris, Dean, and myself. I'd heard that a million times before, but this time I really believed it. I genuinely felt a sense of hope that I'd never felt before in WCW.

I liked how self-assured they seemed, like they knew exactly what they wanted to accomplish. They were very confident about their ability to change the company's creative direction. It really was an exciting time, like Russo and Ferrara were bringing new life to the company.

The first thing they did was attempt to bring WWE's professional style to WCW. I can't overstate how much I learned from Ed. He started guiding me with my interviews, working with me on things like not looking at the camera. He taught me how to cheat toward the camera, but to still talk to the person I was supposed to be talking to. No one had ever told me that before!

Russo and Ferrara tried to turn *Nitro* into WCW's own version of *Raw*. I was made part of a new stable called the Filthy Animals, alongside Rey, Konnan, and Billy Kidman. The idea was that we'd be WCW's version of D-Generation X. We weren't babyfaces or heels, we were somewhere in the middle. On one hand we were supposed to be cool street-smart tough guys, and on the other, sometimes we were thugs doing things like stealing Doug Dillenger's wallet.

I was the misfit member of the Filthy Animals. One thing I've never been is hip. I didn't dress cool, I wasn't up on hip-hop style. The only reason I was part of the group was because Konnan wanted me in there. He pitched it to Vince Russo, who said, "Okay, run with it."

I really enjoyed being a part of the Filthy Animals. Carlos—Konnan—was a friend, and Rey is like my little brother. It was nice to feel a little bit accepted for a change, even though I knew that I didn't really fit in.

Meanwhile, Dean and Chris had become part of their own stable, the Revolution, with Shane Douglas and Perry Saturn. Our two factions went to war, and though it might not have produced anything special as far as the product was concerned, I at least got to surround myself with my best friends in the business.

CHAPTER 25

'd been taking a ton of painkillers since the accident. By October, it was clear even to me that my addiction was spinning out of control. I decided to be a man and quit cold turkey. I didn't know that quitting drugs like that was actually very dangerous.

The hardest thing about kicking was that I couldn't sleep. After five nights without any sleep, I started freaking out.

"I've got to get some sleep," I pleaded. "Give me one cap of Renutrient."

I was begging Vickie. "Please. I'm going crazy."

"All right," she said reluctantly, "I'll give you a cap."

Vickie was a classic co-dependent spouse, believing in her heart that she was helping me. She'd let me have enough so that I'd fall asleep, but that was it.

Well, if there's one thing a drug addict knows, it's how to manipulate people. I asked for a second cap. "C'mon, Vickie," I said, "give me another one. Please, it's the only way I'll ever fall asleep!"

After a few minutes of begging, Vickie relented and let me have another dose. But when she turned her back, I quickly snuck another cap.

What I didn't know was that kicking the painkillers had done a number on my body. The shock to my system was too much. I crashed, and crashed hard.

I was in bed, and all of a sudden, I had to piss more than I ever had in my life. I got up and started for the bathroom, but it felt like my muscles had turned to jelly. I couldn't move my legs; it was like they were just gone. I was all messed up. It was weird—my mind was there, but my body was someplace else.

Somehow, I made it to the bathroom. I had to sit on the toilet to piss, but then I couldn't get up again. When I tried to stand, I fell on the bathroom floor. I felt as if I were sinking down into a long tunnel. No matter how much I reached, I couldn't pull myself up. I got so scared, I started yelling for Vickie to come help me.

She ran in and helped me back into bed. The next thing I remember, Vickie was trying to wake me up. I heard her, but it was like I was dreaming. I was in a big hole, screaming for help, but I couldn't get out. It was this dark, black pit that I couldn't pull myself out of. It was like a grave! I could see the rim, but I couldn't get out. I was howling, "Help me! Help me!"

Vickie didn't know what to do. She called our neighbor, who told her to dial 911. "I can't," Vickie said. "He'll get in trouble at work."

"That doesn't matter," our neighbor said. "If you don't get him help right away, he could die."

Vickie dialed 911 and told them that she needed an ambulance. By the time the EMTs got to the house, I had started having some kind of seizure. I was swallowing my own tongue. They started working on me, but I kept fighting them off. I was begging for help, yet pushing them away at the same time.

Somehow they managed to hold me down and get restraints on my arms and legs, just so they could put me into the ambulance. I was fighting them every step of the way. I was sure that this was it. I was going to die in that tunnel.

I was still freaking out as they wheeled me into the emergency room. The gurney was jumping up and down on the floor. They called for an orderly, who literally sat on top of me while they attached an IV to my arm. They needed to flush my system and get my heart pumping again.

My entire system had started to shut down. It was as if my body just crashed from the shock. The Renutrient set off a chain reaction that caused my body to give out, to say, "That's it. No more."

When I woke up, I was strapped down in a hospital bed with a respirator tube down my throat. My lungs had collapsed in the ambulance—they simply stopped working. When I got to the hospital, the first thing they did was put me on a respirator.

My entire body was still shaking. The doctor was there with Vickie. "You need to relax," the doctor said. "You need to calm down."

No matter how hard I tried, I couldn't stop shaking and fighting the restraints. All I wanted to do was pull that respirator out of my mouth, but I was still strapped down to the bed.

After two days, they told me they were going to take off the restraints. "Whatever you do," the doctor said, "don't pull out the respirator."

Of course, the second my hands were freed, I yanked the tube from my throat. The doctor wasn't happy, but luckily, I didn't do any harm to myself.

Once I was fully stabilized they sent in a psychiatrist, who asked me questions to find out if I was suicidal. After I assured them it was an accident, I was told that I could go home. "You need serious rest," the doctor explained. "At least two weeks' worth."

I went home on Sunday afternoon. That night, Vickie helped me pack my bag, and the next morning I flew to where we were doing *Nitro*.

I knew I should've listened to the doctor, but I had to keep working. I couldn't risk having that taken away from me. I looked horrible, but I managed to keep my overdose covered up. I didn't tell anybody what had happened. Obviously, I wasn't at one hundred percent, but I managed to get through my match without anybody being the wiser.

THE FILTHY ANIMALS.
FROM LEFT: ME, KONNAN, TORRIE WILSON, AND BILLY KIDMAN.

CHAPTER 26

R usso and Ferrara were under the misconception that gimmicks and bad comedy vignettes were the answer to WCW's problems. *Nitro* became even more of a mess than it had been in Bischoff's final days, as Russo and Ferrara tried to pop ratings with an endless series of stupid angles, swerves, and what they thought wrestling fans wanted to see most—gimmick matches.

For whatever reason, those guys were total marks for a Pole match. They'd put anything on top of a pole—piñatas, brass knuckles, a crowbar, a leather jacket, Buff Bagwell's mother. My personal Pole match fiasco had the Revolution locking Billy Kidman's girlfriend, Torrie Wilson, in a shark cage. Then Perry Saturn challenged me to a match, with the key to the cage on top of the pole.

I was supposed to save Torrie by grabbing the key and winning the match. But the finish was a total mess. I had put on too much baby oil before the match, and the combination of baby oil and sweat all over my arms and chest made it impossible to climb up the damn pole! Every time I tried to get up there, *whoosh,* I'd slide right down. *Oh shit,* I thought, *what am I going to do now?*

CHRISTMAS WITH MY GIRLS, 1999.

The other Filthy Animals started panicking and tried to help me. I pushed Konnan off. "Don't worry, I've got it!" I unintentionally piefaced Billy Kidman. "Fuck off! I can do it!"

Finally I leapt for the key, and thank God, I didn't miss. I would've been so screwed! That was one of those do-or-die moments when you do whatever it takes to make the match work.

By this point, I had figured out what was becoming obvious to everybody—Russo and Ferrara had no idea how to save WCW. The backstage politics might have improved under their reign, but the product continued to suck.

Once again, I began to get disillusioned with my life in WCW. I worried

CHEATING DEATH, STEALING LIFE

that my career was sliding down the toilet with the rest of the company. I decided to take some time off to deal with an injury that had been bothering me for a while. I had bone chips in my right elbow that needed to be surgically removed. It had reached the point where I no longer had any choice. My elbow had gotten so swollen, I couldn't straighten out my arm.

I left WCW after Thanksgiving, little knowing that I wouldn't have to worry about Russo and Ferrara—or WCW—for much longer.

I had started seeing a pain specialist after my OD, in an effort to curb my addiction to the pain pills. He put me on methadone—synthetic heroin. The idea was that they get my system stable, then gradually taper off the dosage until I could safely kick altogether. The pain specialist also put me on Resterol, to help me sleep.

Christmas week came along, and so Vickie, the girls, and I flew to El Paso to spend the holiday with my family. As usual, the alcohol was flowing. Mando and I were partying the hardest, drinking vodka together. I was pounding them down and at the same time popping my methadone. We stayed up a while after everyone else had gone to sleep, and eventually I decided to go to bed.

But Mando couldn't sleep. As he was walking around the house, he heard a noise, like someone gasping for air. He looked in my bedroom and saw that the noise was coming from me. I couldn't breathe. Not only was I unconscious, I was blue from head to toe from lack of oxygen.

Mando freaked out and started shaking me, trying to wake me up. The average person takes about twelve breaths per minute—I was down to three or four. Mando started giving me mouth-to-mouth, trying to get me breathing again. By this time, the whole house was awake. My sister Linda called 911 and got an ambulance.

I woke up again to the familiar scene of paramedics looking down at me, asking me questions. They couldn't take me to the hospital, because I wouldn't give them permission in my semicoherent state.

Finally my mom took over. She backed up everybody and asked me to go to the hospital. "Please, Ewis," she said, caressing my face. "Please. For me."

"Okay, Mom," I said. "I'll do it for you."

When I arrived at the hospital, the doctor said I was in very serious condition, more serious than what the EMTs had initially thought.

Linda and Mando and my mom were gathered around me, telling me not to stop breathing. Vickie was also there, but standing at a distance.

"I am breathing," I said, but it clearly wasn't enough.

The doctor started shooting me up with a huge needle. I felt something ice-cold shoot through my veins. I looked at him and said, "What the fuck are you doing to me?"

"It's adrenaline," he explained. "Your lungs are collapsing and we need to get you breathing."

"I'm not that bad," I said, still in denial.

"Oh yes you are," the doctor said as he injected the adrenaline into me.

Thank God, that shot snapped me out of it. My breathing became constant, my color came back. I'd survived again.

After I'd stabilized, Dr. Moreno, the family physician and a good friend, came to visit me. He tried to talk to me, to find out what I was doing to myself. Again, I was in denial. "I'm fine," I told him. "Really."

They released me from the hospital the next day. When I got back to the house, everybody was hot at me.

"How dare you," Linda fumed. "In our mother's house!"

I understood where they were coming from. I was so ashamed to have put my whole family through such an ordeal. I wanted to change my ways so badly!

Like a fool, I went to my room and flushed all my pills down the toilet. Of course, I started jonesing an hour later and we had to call the doctor to prescribe something to get me through, to take away the bite.

Once things settled down to some level of normality, I sat down on the couch with Mando. "When we were talking last night," he said, "you kept telling me you were tired. 'I'm tired of all this shit,' you kept saying. What are you tired of, bro?"

I thought about it for a while, but I couldn't answer him. I honestly didn't know.

CHAPTER 27

I was home healing up from my elbow surgery when I got the word that Vince Russo had quit. Apparently management was not happy with the changes he'd made, and he'd decided to bail out rather than become part of a booking committee led by Kevin Sullivan.

My friends all told me how bad things were backstage. Everybody was miserable, walking around like the living dead. Nobody's heart was in it anymore.

The fact that Kevin Sullivan had the book was not a good thing for me, Chris, and Dean. He actually told Dean, Perry, and Shane Douglas that "they were the largest waste of money the company had and they would never draw a dime." That pretty much said it all about his mind-set toward us.

Worse, there was personal animosity between Kevin and Chris that didn't exactly put any of us in a good spot. There weren't any issues between Kevin and myself, but Chris was my family, and what you did to him, you did to me and Dean as well. I'm not saying Kevin would've acted on those personal feelings—I just know we didn't feel safe.

To his credit, Bill Busch decided that Chris should be the WCW World Champion. Either he was smart enough to know that Chris was the best wrestler in the company, or he was trying to extend an olive branch to the boys. Sullivan agreed to give Benoit the title at the next Pay-Per-View—*Souled Out*—though who knows what he planned for Benoit after that.

At *Souled Out*, Chris Benoit finally won the WCW World Heavyweight Championship that he'd deserved for so long. But Sullivan booked the finish so that his opponent, Sid Vicious, had his foot under the ropes, either as a way of setting up a rematch or as insurance in case he wanted to get the belt off Chris anytime in the future.

The next night was my first day back from the elbow surgery. We were doing *Nitro* at Ohio State, in Columbus, Ohio, and I had literally just walked into the arena when Chris and Dean approached me and said they were going to ask for their releases. "Are you in?" they asked.

"Of course," I said.

I had wanted out since asking Bischoff for my release two years earlier. Now I knew that I didn't stand a chance of getting ahead with Sullivan as the head of the booking committee. I was already fed up, and without the head booker on my side, things were only going to get worse. I was happy for the chance to finally get the hell out, once and for all.

We basically gave management an ultimatum. "We're not comfortable with the current situation," we said. "We cannot work under the structure that you have set up."

"Anybody that's not happy should come ask for their release," Busch said, "and we'll give it to you."

We were all sent home, with the exception of Benoit. He was the new champ, after all. But Chris wasn't going to let himself be used like that. He told Bill Busch that if the rest of us were going, so was he. Being the professional that he is, he agreed to drop the title to anyone they wanted that night on *Nitro*. "Don't bother," he was told. "Just go home."

"You got it," Chris said. He handed his title belt to referee Nick Patrick, and we all walked out of the building together.

By the middle of the week, enough people had whispered in Busch's ear that none of us were ever going to make it in WWE that he decided to officially let us go. There was a problem, however. A clause in our contracts said that we couldn't work for any other company for at least six months. Obviously we tried to get them to take that out, but they were adamant. They'd let us go, but they weren't about to let us go earn our livings in WWE.

Fortunately, we had some ammunition in our pockets that forced WCW to give us full releases. When we said we wanted out, one of the WCW road agents got pissed off and threatened to "slice our throats." He was just talking out of anger, but it allowed us to go to Turner's Human Resources Department and say, "Look, one of your employees threatened to kill us if we left. Either take out the no-compete stipulation in our contracts or we'll sue."

Needless to say, Chris, Dean, Perry, and I were all given full unconditional releases. We were officially free agents.

The very next day, I was playing golf when Dean called. "Hey, man, we've got to go up north to meet with Vince McMahon." I ran straight home, changed clothes, and headed to the airport.

It was a great meeting. Vince told us how much he admired the fact that we were willing to give up all that money for the chance to go and wrestle with our hearts again. All we asked for was a chance—to be ourselves, to be able to advance in the company—and he said he would absolutely give us that opportunity. God bless him, his word has been true. Vince has given us every opportunity to get ourselves over.

As it turned out, we got away from WCW at exactly the right time. One year later, they went under, allowing Vince to buy the pieces of the company that were left. I believe our leaving was the first nail in the coffin. That's what started their final downfall. Whether they liked to admit it or not, wrestlers like myself, Dean, and Chris were the backbone of the company.

I was talking to Jimmy Hart not long after and he joked that after we left, they had to cancel *WCW Saturday Night* because it was all based around us. Of course, that was the problem in a nutshell—we were seen as the stars of the meaningless *WCW Saturday Night* show as opposed to *Nitro*.

We were all really excited to be WWE Superstars, and even a little bit scared. Though we didn't know what Vince was planning to do with us, we were all keyed up for new challenges. Coming to WWE was like a breath of fresh air. Our hearts had been broken so many times, and all of a sudden, we had hope again.

When it feels like everything you worked for your entire life has been taken from you, it just squeezes the spirit right out of you. You can't help but lose your faith.

Starting out at WWE, I think we all felt that we had a second chance. Sure, we were a little intimidated because we didn't know everybody and we didn't know if they were going to accept us, but we were definitely happy to be there.

It was obvious from the moment we arrived in Pittsburgh that WWE was a completely different world than what we'd grown used to. The atmosphere was the exact opposite of WCW, just completely organized and professional. It was incredible. We all knew WWE was the best wrestling company in the world, but it was still unbelievably exciting to experience it firsthand. We felt like we'd reached the top of the business. It's like going from college football to the NFL, just a whole different league.

As with any time I do something new, I went in there very timid. I was watching every step I made. I just wanted to please, to make everybody happy. Any worries I might have had about how we would be treated by the locker room were quickly resolved. Everybody seemed genuinely glad to see us. I don't think anybody saw us as a threat. If anything, they saw our arrival as being good for everybody's business. Mick Foley, who I'd known slightly from ECW, was especially nice. He really made an effort to make us feel comfortable.

WWE kayfabed our debut beautifully—hardly anyone knew we were going to be there. *Raw* kicked off with Al Snow & Steve Blackman vs. the New Age Outlaws. As the match started, Dean, Chris, Perry, and I took seats in the front row. The second we walked out, we could feel the buzz spreading around the crowd, like, "What the hell are these guys doing here?"

We immediately felt the huge difference between *Raw* and *Nitro*. *Raw* is bigger than life. The houses were always sold out, and the atmosphere was electric. I think the *Nitro* crowds weren't as easily excited because like the wrestlers, they'd also had the thrill beaten out of them over the years.

Not long into the match, Road Dogg got thrown over the railing into our laps. He took a swing at Chris, so we jumped the rail and attacked. Perry suplexed Billy Gunn, then I delivered the frog splash, while Malenko suplexed Road Dogg, setting up Benoit's diving head butt.

The crowd just went crazy. It felt so good. We had no idea how the WWE fans were going to react to us. Fortunately, they seemed as excited to see us as we were to be there.

As we laid the boots to the New Age Outlaws, the announcer—and then man in charge of WWE Talent Relations—Jim "J.R." Ross, gave us our name: we were the Radicalz.

Backstage, Cactus Jack asked us how it felt to look out into the stands and see a paying crowd. That was a bit of an inside joke. WCW's business had gotten so lousy, they were forced to paper the houses—give away free tickets—just so there wouldn't be thousands of empty seats showing up on the TV broadcasts. Perry said what we all were thinking: "I haven't had this much fun in a long time."

We did a number of vignettes, with Cactus introducing us around to various folks, including D'Lo Brown, who also used a frog splash as finisher. "Nice move," we said to each other.

Sometimes when people imitate you, it's a form of flattery, but there are times when somebody doing my moves really upsets me. Fortunately, God has blessed me with enough talent that one move doesn't make me. I don't have to win with the frog splash every time. Don't get me wrong—it's important to have a dramatic finishing move, it helps a match out tremendously. But I'm cool with other people doing their own version of the frog splash. D'Lo does it one way, Rob Van Dam does it his own way. It's the same movement, but done in a different style by each of us.

The show ended with the four of us helping Cactus put the beatdown on Triple H. I think the immediate plan was to get Chris into the main-event picture. I know Vince had wanted to get his hands on Chris for a long time. He admired Benoit's pure wrestling talents and thought he could make him a star.

I was perfectly okay with that. First, I believed that Chris deserved to be a top-tier player. I also didn't think I had the right to walk into a new job thinking I was going to be the star of the show, right from the get-go. I knew I needed to prove myself.

THE RADICALZ PUTTING THE BEATDOWN ON TRIPLE H.

My second night in WWE wasn't nearly as much fun as my first. We were doing *SmackDown!* in Detroit, at the Joe Louis Arena. The

CHEATING DEATH, STEALING LIFE

show was all geared upon the events of the previous night's *Raw*. In order to win contracts with WWE, the Radicalz had to fight D-Generation X in a series of three matches — Malenko vs. X-Pac, Benoit vs. Triple H, and Saturn & myself vs. the New Age Outlaws. If the Radicalz won two out of the three, we'd get contracts.

The whole show hinged upon us going over. Dean lost to X-Pac in the first of the three matches, so the plan was for Chris, Perry, and myself to win the next two matches.

Perry and I were having it out with the Outlaws. When I went for the frog splash on Billy Gunn, I unconsciously went to protect my right elbow, the one I'd only just had surgery on. As a result, I landed wrong and popped my left elbow out of its socket. It was so loud you could actually hear it on TV.

The pain was unbelievable! I literally couldn't move. I didn't know what to do. I couldn't communicate to Perry or Billy what was going on. "Cover me," I said to Road Dogg through clenched teeth. He didn't know what to do either, so he got on top of me — 1-2-3!

Looking back, I know that I had panicked. I should've rolled out and let Perry come in and do the finish that we had planned. But I was in such pain,

THE EDDIE GUERRERO STORY

my mind went blank. When I got to the back, I immediately started apologizing. "I'm so sorry! I just wasn't thinking!"

"Don't worry," Vince said. "We'll fix it."

I was still in my wrestling gear when the ambulance came. The only way I could relieve some of the pain was to hold my arm up over my head.

The EMTs put me on the gurney, my arm propped up over my head, but as they tried to slide into the ambulance, it just wouldn't go in. The EMTs started trying to force it in, jerking me all over the place, making the incredible pain in my elbow even worse. I got so hot! I got off the gurney and said, "C'mon, just get the freakin' thing in there, already!"

They finally managed to get it into the ambulance. I climbed in the back, lay down on the gurney, and off we went to the hospital.

We arrived at the hospital and the EMTs tried to pull me out on the gurney. Of course, the thing was stuck in the ambulance. They started trying to pull it out of there, jerking me around again. "Stop! Stop!" I screamed, and hopped out of the back of the ambulance into the freezing cold and snow. I started walking into the hospital, in my tights, my arm over my head, when a nurse came out and stopped me.

"We can't let you into the hospital like this," she said.

"What?"

"Regulations says we've got to bring you in in a wheelchair or a gurney."

Man, I got so angry! I'm standing there, freezing my balls off, in terrible pain, and they're talking to me about regulations! Not only that, the doctor that wheeled me into the hospital had the nerve to lean over and ask, "Is all this wrestling stuff really real?"

Finally they decided to allow me into the emergency room. Now, this was Detroit, after all. It was a busy emergency room. There were people going in there for gunshot wounds, stab wounds. All I had was a dislocated elbow.

It took about an hour before they got to me. The first thing they did was shoot me up with morphine to ease the pain some. But with my tolerance for pain medication, it didn't have the slightest effect. They hit me with another dose of morphine, but even that didn't knock me out.

The doctor explained that because my muscles had all tightened up, they weren't going to be able to just pop my elbow back into its socket. They were going to have to put me out in order to relax my muscles enough for them to fix it. I was given anesthesia and, finally, I went unconscious.

When I came to, Vince and his daughter, Stephanie, were standing over the bed. "Don't worry, Eddie," Vince said. "We'll use it. We'll get it over. You'll be okay."

Thank God, I thought. So many thoughts had been racing through my head. I was afraid that I had burned my bridges. *I screwed up in my first WWE match. Now what am I going to do?*

But Vince was great. He's been in this business long enough to understand that sometimes, stuff happens. When it does, you try to make the best of it and keep moving forward.

By the time I got out of there, it was four in the morning. I went back to the hotel, packed my stuff, and flew home to Tampa on the first flight out.

CHAPTER 28

I ended up not missing a single show due to my injury. Instead, I came out with my arm in a sling. And hidden inside my sling was the gimmick that ended up helping me to get over in WWE—a lead pipe. It's ironic, but dislocating my elbow turned out to be a blessing in disguise.

On the next *Raw*, the Radicalz turned heel. We put the boots to Mick Foley and hooked up with the McMahon-Helmsley Era. I explained to Michael Cole that Cactus's mistake was thinking we'd put friendship before business.

Right away, Chris was put into a main-event role, working with people like The Rock. As for Dean, Perry, and myself, we began feuding with Too Cool and Rikishi. Since I couldn't yet wrestle, I was working in more of a classic managerial capacity. I interfered in just about every Radicalz match, using my lead pipe to cheat to win.

I wasn't bothered about working in the midcard. What was important was that I was going to get an opportunity to elevate myself. That's all I wanted. I can't speak for Dean or Perry, but I don't think any of us were expecting to come in at the top, right from the very beginning. All I was concerned with was having a chance to move myself up in the business.

I got my my first official WWE win by "forfeit"—sort of. First I helped Perry and Dean beat Too Cool by taking out Scotty 2 Hotty with my trusty lead pipe. Then when Rikishi came down to make the save, I took him out for good measure. As they loaded him into an ambulance, I started yelling at ring announcer Tony Chimel, demanding that he announce me as the winner against Rikishi "by forfeit." Referee Mike Sparks raised my hand up and man, I celebrated like I'd just won the World Championship—"I did it! I did it!" Perry and Dean joined in the festivities, hugging me, then carrying me out on their shoulders.

On February 21, 2000, *Raw* hit Atlanta, the home turf of WCW. We did a sold-out show at the Georgia Dome, which is to WCW what Madison Square Garden is to WWE—the home arena. It was extremely surreal, performing at a place I'd played so many times before, only this time, everything was different.

Rikishi and I had a No DQ match, which he won by nailing me with a metal crutch. I've wrestled hundreds of people, taken hundreds of finishing moves, but I'd never been given the Stinkface before. I learned pretty quickly that there's not much you can do to protect yourself when Rikishi plants his big butt on your face—you just close your eyes, hold your breath, and pray that it doesn't last too long!

I was lucky—Rikishi liked me. When he's working with someone he doesn't get along with, he can really lay it in good. Fortunately for me, he was always very professional whenever we had a match together.

As it turned out, I probably shouldn't have been wrestling yet. It was just five weeks after I'd injured my elbow, but I put a lot of pressure on myself to get back in the ring as quickly as possible. The office actually encouraged me to take it easy for a few weeks longer, but I really wanted to get back to it. It was so frustrating, watching everybody wrestle, knowing that all I could do was swing a lead pipe. I wanted to show the WWE fans what I could do.

It was decided that I wasn't ready to wrestle just yet, but I was definitely kept busy. I spent the weeks leading up to my first *WrestleMania* assisting

my fellow Radicalz, interfering in matches against such opponents as Tazz, Jericho, Chyna, Edge & Christian, Test & Val Venis, and The Rock.

On March 13, Dean became the first Radical to wear WWE gold when he beat Essa Rios for the Light Heavyweight title.

Since Essa was accompanied by Lita, it was only fair that I help out in Dean's corner. Before the match, we were told that they wanted Lita to hit me with a huracanrana, which I would reverse into a powerbomb onto the mats outside the ring. I knew it was going to be a bad bump, and that there was no real safe way to protect her.

I tried to get out of doing it, but unfortunately, no one seemed especially concerned that it would be a problem. "Figure it out," we were told.

Before we went out, I asked Lita, "Are you sure you want to do this?"

"No, no," she said, "I'll do it."

God bless her, she was a trouper. She wasn't thinking about herself—she was thinking about the business.

The time came to do the move. I was on the outside. Lita came off the top, but I caught her before she could finish the move. I tried to lay her down flat, but the angle was slightly awkward and the force of the landing separated her shoulder.

I felt so horrible about that. By the grace of God, very few people have gotten hurt working with me. One of the first things my dad taught me was how to take care of people. "When you get in the ring with someone," he said, "they're giving you their body. It's your job to keep them safe."

I returned to the active roster two weeks before *WrestleMania*. Perry, Dean, and myself took on Too Cool & Rikishi. Once again, I got a Stinkface for my trouble. The following week on *Raw*, I teamed with Benoit for a match against Chris Jericho & Chyna. As the Chrises fought in the ring, Chyna and I went at it on the outside. Dean and Perry ran down to help out, followed by Too Cool. A big brawl ensued, setting up my first *WrestleMania* match. It would be Chyna & Too Cool vs. the Radicalz.

After the match, I was told that there was a natural chemistry between Chyna and myself. When they suggested that I work with her, I wasn't worried that it would damage my standing as a wrestler. My goal was to take whatever they gave me and run with it. That's the attitude I try to have all the time, to take whatever they put in front of me and do the best that I can with it. To grab it and make it bigger than life.

I think a lot of boys wanted to steer clear of working with Chyna. Nobody wanted to play second fiddle to a woman, even if she was The Ninth Wonder of the World. But I knew I could get away with it. In fact, I was pretty sure that I could use the angle to take another step and get myself over.

WrestleMania 2000 was an unbelievable experience. I was so happy to be there. It's the biggest event in our business, the Super Bowl of wrestling.

When I was in WCW, I honestly didn't watch much WWE. I was a team player. But every now and then I'd tune into Raw or one of their Pay-Per-Views, just to see what they were up to. Obviously, the differences were huge—WWE was just so much more exciting and interesting than what we were doing in WCW.

But like all wrestling fans, I always watched WrestleMania. It didn't matter which wrestling promotion you liked best, whether it was WWE, WCW, or ECW. If you love wrestling, you watch WrestleMania.

My first WrestleMania appearance wasn't exactly a five-star classic. Probably the most memorable thing about our match was Chyna's wardrobe malfunction. I was going for a powerbomb, but she escaped—splitting her pants in the process—then hit me with a powerbomb of her own. Her butt was hanging out as she grabbed my cojones and pressed me into a chokeslam for the pin.

I wasn't especially shocked when there was trouble with Chyna's costume. She was having problems with it before the show, so I kind of knew something like that was going to happen. Usually that kind of thing is funny, but not at WrestleMania. On such a big night, the atmosphere is very intense, and everyone is just too focused to see the humor in anything. Afterward, sure, but during the show, it's all business.

The next night's Raw—at the Staples Center in Los Angeles—was much more significant for me, careerwise. I cut a promo on Chyna before my

European Championship match against her friend Chris Jericho. "Take it easy, Mamacita," I said. "I know you're here really 'cause you want some Latino Heat. I mean, let's face it, last night you were practically coming out of your pants at the sight of me!"

The crowd went crazy when I referred to myself as Latino Heat. Right away, I knew I had something. Later on, Jack Lanza—one of the WWE road agents—came over to me and said, "All that 'Mamacita' and 'Latino Heat' stuff was great. You should run with that."

Vince thought the same thing. God bless him, he's the master of seeing the crowd's response to something relatively small, then making it bigger than life. Before I knew it, I was known as Latino Heat.

The match was also pretty eventful. Jericho hit me with a drop toehold, sending me flying into referee Tim White. While he was knocked out, Chris nailed me with a double powerbomb and a Lionsault. He pinned me—the crowd counted "One! Two! Three!"—but Tim was still down. Chyna went to check on him, and seeing he was still unconscious, she dropped down and counted me out. She raised Jericho's arm in victory, but then surprised him with a lowblow and a DDT. Chyna dragged me on top of Jericho and woke up White, who hit the three count.

Chyna handed me my first WWE title belt, then threw her arms around me as the crowd booed and jeered. Later on in the show, we got into an orange lowrider and left the building. The Latino Heat Era had officially begun!

CHAPTER 29

first got the idea for Latino Heat when I saw the movie *The Birdcage.* I loved Hank Azaria's character, Agador, the flaming houseboy. At one point in the film he asks Robin Williams's character why he won't let him perform in his show. He says something like, "Are you afraid of my Guatemalan heat?" I just thought that was hilarious!

In the beginning, Latino Heat was the guy that thinks he's God's gift to women, even though he really isn't. I know I'm not a particularly handsome guy, and that's what made it a clever character.

I had been thinking about this character for a long time, even before my car accident. I knew I wanted to create a character that reflected *La Raza,* my Chicano heritage. It would be based on the barrio guys that I grew up with, my buds in El Paso.

I'm so proud of *La Raza.* I'm proud of my culture, of lowriders and Chicanics and Tejano music. I know who we are. I know the truth.

With the emergence of Latino Heat, the time had finally come for me to show that side of myself.

Chyna and I pulled into *SmackDown!* the next night in San Jose, driving a sexy lowrider, then went out to the ring for an interview.

"Why you did what you did, Mami?" I asked her.

215

"I really couldn't resist your Latino Heat," she replied.

"You truly are The Ninth Wonder of the World," I said, doing my job, which was putting Chyna over. Of course, I had to get a little something for myself in there. I noted that all my ancestors were proud of me—Cortez, Don Quixote, Pancho Villa, adding, "And now there's Eddie!"

Just then, Y2J ran out. We exchanged blows, ending with him giving me a powerbomb. Fortunately for Chris, the refs all came to the ring to break it up before I could get my revenge.

I retained the European Championship—with Chyna's help—in a match with Jericho the following week on *Raw*. He did burn me with a good line before the match. "I think the Taco Bell chihuahua has more Latino Heat than you," he said, "but at least the chihuahua's bitch is housebroken!"

"In order to be a good leader," "my dad used to say, "first you have to be a good follower."

That was wise advice. Throughout my career, I managed to draw heat

CHEATING DEATH, STEALING LIFE

onto myself by doing a good job as somebody else's sidekick—first El Hijo del Santo, then Art Barr, and then Chyna.

The Latino Heat & Mamacita angle was very fulfilling for me. It was a wonderful chance for me to show how versatile I can be. Vince knew I could work in the ring, but he had no idea I could do vignettes. I wanted the creative team to see that there were lots of ways that they could use me. I wanted them to know that I could be funny or mean or tough or even sweet. The more I could do, the more opportunities I'd have.

I was perfectly comfortable with Latino Heat being a comic character. I had no problem being completely goofy. Making people laugh doesn't make you any less tough.

Fortunately, I was blessed with a lot of great material for Latino Heat to work with. I declared myself a true European Champion, because after all, I was of Spanish descent. When I said that, J.R. got off a funny line— "I thought he was from El Paso!"

My character also started studying for the GED—the high school equivalency diploma. At first, I was a little unsure about it, but I was determined to take whatever they gave me and make it work.

This is a show, I told myself. *This is not who I really am.*

Wrestling walks a very fine line. People get confused about what's real and what isn't. The idea that there were people who thought Chyna and I were actually a couple still baffles me. People didn't think David Schwimmer and Jennifer Aniston are a real couple just because Ross and Rachel were.

It's important to remember what is reality and what isn't. I have to be okay with who I really am in order for me to play my character. So I have to play a guy that's getting his GED. What's wrong with that?

As I studied for my test, Chyna and I started feuding with Essa Rios and Lita. I knew that the angle was more about getting the two women over than it was about pushing Essa and myself. They were getting ready to separate Lita from Essa, and they felt that working with Chyna would help develop her character. The fact that Essa and I could put on some good wrestling matches was just gravy.

Essa and I had our big match at the *Backlash* Pay-Per-View in

Washington, D.C. Chyna and I came to the show after attending my prom—
I had, after all, just passed my GED. We drove to the ring in a lowrider, then
I popped the trunk and took off my tuxedo. Most of it, at least—I actually
wrestled in tuxedo pants and a bow tie!

The match ended with me hitting an airplane spin into a neckbreaker on
Essa for the pin. After the three count, Essa dropkicked me into Chyna. Then
Lita came into the ring and stripped off Mamacita's prom dress, leaving her
standing in the middle of the ring in her bra and panties.

I know there are stories floating around about how I was in pretty bad
shape during that period of my life. There's some truth there, but I want to be
perfectly clear about one thing—I was never less than professional when it
came to business. I was perfectly functional and able to get into the ring and
have a good match. The office wouldn't have tolerated me if I wasn't.

Still, I wasn't doing a lot of serious wrestling during that period. My heat
was usually on Chyna. She was a big part of the WWE image at that time,
one of the biggest Superstars of the Attitude Era. I knew that she was the
main attraction and I was the second banana. My job was to get her over.

218

I'd do the work, then let Chyna come in for the finish and claim the spotlight. I just played my part, which was to complement Chyna. It wasn't a problem for me—I'm very good at working to accentuate somebody's strengths without making myself weak.

After our feud with Essa and Lita, Chyna and I went to war with Perry and Dean, resulting in a Triple-Threat match at *Judgment Day* in Louisville. We were all a bit worried going into the Pay-Per-View. None of us were especially comfortable doing the Triple Threat. Figuring out what to do with three people in there can be difficult.

It's like watching a complicated movie—there's so much going on, it's hard to grasp the big picture. That's the problem with Triple-Threat matches—sometimes there's just too much going on. You've got to make sure to space out the action. You don't want to give the audience too much to eat at one time, or else you'll lose them.

I've gotten used to three-way matches, though personally, I don't really enjoy them very much. I've had some good ones, but I still find them to be a bit of a struggle.

As it turned out, *Judgment Day* wound up being a pretty good match. I retained my European Championship when Chyna decked Saturn with the belt, then smashed a vase of flowers over Malenko's head, allowing me to roll Dean up for the three count.

Joanie Laurer—who played the character Chyna—is a really nice person. In the beginning, we actually had a lot of fun working together. Unfortunately, she began having to cope with some heavy personal problems, and it reached a point where she became hard to deal with. As human beings, sometimes we can't help but carry what is happening in our personal lives into our work.

I felt for her, but I also wanted to keep my nose out of it. I did my best to stay neutral. Whenever anybody tried to talk to me about Joanie's issues, I just kept my mouth shut. It wasn't my place to discuss other people's personal business.

Besides, I was having major problems in my own life. I'm sure I was stressing Joanie out as much as she was stressing me. For her part, I think she began to have trouble dealing with me and my issues with drugs. She began worrying about how reliable I was and if my issues were going to put her in jeopardy.

We decided that we'd both be happier if we split up, but the office was dead set against it. As far as they were concerned, Latino Heat & Mamacita was a winning combination. In fact, Chyna and I were doing so well that we began turning babyface. It was the fans that made that happen—they responded to us in a positive way, so it was only natural that we become good guys.

To show just how babyface we became, I teamed up with Rikishi for a *SmackDown!* match against Chris Benoit & Val Venis. There was a big brawl at the end, when T&A ran down and interfered, leading to a DQ for Chris and Val. After the ring cleared, Chyna and I had to do the Too Cool dance segment with Scotty 2 Hotty, Grandmaster Sexay, and Rikishi. I hated it, but it was something every babyface had to do at one point or another. I'm a team player—they told me to dance, I danced.

I dropped the European Championship to Perry Saturn at *Fully Loaded* in Dallas, then started a program with Intercontinental Champion Val Venis & Trish Stratus to take us into *SummerSlam*. Mick Foley—in his role as Commissioner Foley—declared an Intercontinental Mixed Tag match for the Pay-Per-View. The stipulation was that if either Chyna or myself pinned either Val or Trish, they'd win the Intercontinental Championship. Of course, Chyna ended up the winner, the first female Intercontinental Champion.

I know a lot of the boys would've been frustrated by that, seeing a woman beat them for a major title, but I didn't let it get to me. My job was to put Chyna over, in any way possible. If Chyna wasn't in the spotlight at the finish of a match, then I wasn't doing my job. The good part was that because I had to use her in that way, I rarely took a straight fall. That ended up getting me over.

To be honest, I wasn't really focused on myself at the time. Things in my life had gotten so out of whack, my wrestling career was basically on cruise control.

CHAPTER 30

The Chyna angle wasn't easy on Vickie. People would come up to her in the street and ask her how she could put up with my cheating on her with Chyna. Come on, that's just ridiculous. It's amazing to me how a lot of people can't separate the show from reality. And these are the same people that talk about how wrestling is fake! Make up your minds!

It got worse as things heated up between Mamacita and myself, with more directly sexual overtones coming into the storyline. That was very difficult for Vickie to deal with. To show my respect for her, I was adamant that there would be no actual contact between Chyna and me. In all the time we worked together, I never kissed her, not once.

A lot of Vickie's feelings had to do with the tension that was going on in our marriage at the time. Our relationship had degenerated into total chaos. All we ever did was fight. We were constantly at each other's throats.

Even when I was home, I wasn't home. I was out getting drunk or trying to score drugs, hanging out with my friends and my various connections. And when I was there, I was high out of my mind.

Vickie, bless her heart, did the best she could. I was a hard man to live with. But eventually it reached the point where she couldn't stand to be around me. She would find things to do that would keep her out of the house, because when we were there together, it was just miserable.

One weekend Vickie was with the kids in El Paso. While they were away,

I got a call from my brother Hector. In the middle of the phone call, I just passed out. Hector got worried and called the police to come to the house and check on me. I woke up to hear a policeman knocking on the back door, shining his flashlight in the window to see if I was alive.

That's how I was living. I was wasted around the clock. I was trying to kill the pain, though I couldn't put my finger on where the pain was coming from. I was unsatisfied by life. I simply wasn't happy. There was an emptiness inside me. No matter what I tried, nothing could fill the void in my heart. Not alcohol, not pills, not even my family.

The only time I felt alive was when I was in the ring. Even though I was messed up most of the time, when it came time to work I was still able to deliver, night after night after night.

Wrestling is the easy part of my life. When the bell rings, I become a different person. It's the same to this day—I walk through that curtain and I'm somebody else. All my troubles go away.

In those days, *Raw* was still on the USA Network. Every summer USA would broadcast the U.S. Open tennis tournament, forcing *Raw* to go live on the air at 11 P.M. for two weeks in a row. That was very difficult for me. My body is set to go a certain time of day, and having to wrestle at midnight really threw me off.

As luck would have it, that night saw Chyna and me getting mixed up in the top storyline of the time, the ongoing soap opera between Triple H, Stephanie McMahon, and Kurt Angle. The upshot was I was booked in a match against Triple H.

Simply put, it wasn't a great match. I was so disappointed in myself. Here it was, the chance to work with Triple H, one of the best wrestlers in the world, and I didn't have what it takes to give him my heart.

It forced me to take a long, hard look at myself. I realized that my body and mind were simply not in top condition. When you're addicted to drugs and alcohol, it can't help but affect you physically.

I think it was right around then that the office began to suspect that something was going on with me. They might not have realized how bad off I was, but they definitely started to grasp that something wasn't right.

There were clues, of course. When I dislocated my elbow that first week in WWE, the doctors shot four cc's of morphine into me and all it did was give me a headache. Then they shot another four cc's and it still didn't knock me out. "Wow," the doctor said, "this guy's got a really high tolerance."

Nobody wanted to ask, "Well, why does he have such a high tolerance?" I think my issues were kind of an open secret throughout the business. Everybody knew, but no one wanted to talk about it.

The following week on *Raw*—which was again live at 11 P.M.— Commissioner Foley booked a Triple-Threat match between Chyna, Kurt, and myself, with the Intercontinental Championship on the line.

The match ended with Kurt hitting Chyna with the belt. I dropkicked him, then suplexed him out of the ring. Chyna was laid out in the middle of the ring, so I went to check on her. When I leaned over and hugged her, referee Jack Doan saw me on top of her and counted 1-2-3, making me the new Intercontinental Champion.

Obviously, Chyna was not amused. "I was just trying to protect you," I told her. "I don't know what happened!"

I tried to give her back the title belt, saying, "Mami, you mean everything to me! This belt doesn't mean nothing compared to what you mean to me. You're the world! *Eres todo!* You're everything, I promise! Please forgive me!"

"You deserve it more anyway," said Chyna.

As we hugged, they showed me grinning over her shoulder, letting the audience know that I was actually pretty happy to be the Intercontinental Champion.

That was a significant moment for Latino Heat. It started my character's move away from being Chyna's sidekick to getting a bit of the glory for myself.

While I've learned over my career that titles aren't always a big deal, winning the Intercontinental Championship was still pretty exciting. It's a transitional title, to help a wrestler move up from one level to the next. It also means that you're one step away from being the WWE Champion.

But I couldn't really enjoy being the Intercontinental Champion. I was in a very bad state of mind at the time. I wasn't focused on my wrestling career— I was just trying to survive.

223

The tension between Latino Heat and his Mamacita increased when Chyna posed nude for *Playboy*. As a hot-blooded Latin lover, my character did not want the world to see his woman in all her glory.

WWE went out to Phoenix to do two nights of TV in a row. After we finished *Raw*, I went back to my hotel. Late that night, I got a phone call: "We want you to fly to Los Angeles first thing tomorrow morning to tape a vignette at the Playboy Mansion."

The Playboy Mansion! Every guy's dream! I was pretty excited, even though I knew it was going to be an extra-long day of travel and work.

The vignette had me going to be the mansion to talk Mr. Hefner out of publishing my Mamacita's naked pictures. Most of the bit was me trying to muscle my way past the security guards. "Look, *ese* Lurch, just do your job, okay? Go get me a Pepsi, go call Mr. Hefner, okay? And there won't be a problem between me and you, all right?"

"Look, sir, you're going to have to leave," the guard said.

"Maybe you don't understand who I am, *ese*. You're talking to the WWE Intercontinental Champion, okay?"

Eventually a second guard showed up and forced me to leave the premises before the authorities arrived. And that was pretty much that.

Unfortunately, I didn't get to hang around to see what happens at the Playboy Mansion when the sun goes down. I didn't see a thing—no parties, no girls, no grotto. I taped my vignette, then hopped on the next flight back to Phoenix to tape *SmackDown!*

Latino Heat started getting more and more heelish, which I was pretty pleased about. I tried to straighten things out with Chyna by proposing to her. The crowd was very much against it. They started chanting, "Just say no!"

Chyna accepted my marriage proposal, kicking off the beginning of the end of our on-screen relationship. In a weird way, the storyline reflected my actual marriage, with my behavior becoming more erratic and Chyna getting fed up with my lies and unreliability.

A match against Right To Censor's Val Venis & the Goodfather got under way when footage of me coming out of the shower came on the TitanTron.

"Keep it warm, baby," I said. "I'll be right back!"

Then one of the Goodfather's ex-hos—who later became WWE Women's Champion Victoria—peeked out from behind the shower curtain: *"Yo quiero Eddie Guerrero!"*

At the other end of the shower curtain, Mandy—another former ho—stuck her head out from the other side: "Bye, Eddie!"

Needless to say, Chyna was not happy. The crowd was pretty amused, however—they gave me a total babyface "Eddie! Eddie!" chant.

As Chyna and I stood there distracted, Goodfather & Val Venis proceeded to beat me down. RTC leader Steven Richards started kicking Chyna's ass, but Billy Gunn ran in for the save.

Later in the parking garage, I tried to explain my infidelity to Chyna. She didn't want to hear it and threw her engagement ring at me.

"I'm nothing without you," I cried.

"You already are nothing, Eddie!" said Chyna, driving off.

I dropped down on my knees to look for the ring when Billy Gunn approached.

"You dumb bastard," says Billy. "You've just lost the best thing in your life over what, two cheap-ass hos? Hey, I'll tell you what. Why don't you pick this cheap-ass ring up, take it back to the pawn shop, and get your twenty bucks back, because I promise you that is as close as you will ever get to her, as long as I'm around. *Comprende, ese?*"

"*Comprendo,*" I replied, then smashed a bottle over his head.

Poor Billy! It was his first day back after an injury. Even though the bottle was gimmicked—what's known in the stunt business as "candy glass"—I still managed to cut him open pretty badly. Not exactly a great way to get welcomed back to work!

Even though I was partying hard, I was not out chasing girls. My affair was with drugs and alcohol, not with women.

I'm not the kind of guy that draws women to himself. And I'm not really very good at pursuing them, either.

More than that, I was very happy with what I had at home. No woman has ever turned me on or given me as much pleasure as my wife.

I got so nervous when I was told that I had to get into a shower with two beautiful women, mostly because of what was going on between me and Vickie. I knew it wasn't going to make things easier. The first thing I did was call home and tell Vickie what was going to happen. I asked her, "Are you okay with this?"

There was so much tension between us, I didn't want to do anything that would hurt her in the slightest way. God bless her, she was very supportive. "Yes, I understand it's just business," she said.

Even though Vickie understood it was just work, there was so much stress in our lives that having this extra pressure just added to the chaos. Our neighbors, the people at our church, would come up to her and say, "Did you see what Eddie did? I can't believe he did that!"

All they wanted to do was stir the shit. It really angered me. First people say wrestling is fake, which insults my profession and how I make a living for my family. Then they turn around and act like they seriously believe what goes on on the show. Where is the line drawn? I'm damned if I do and damned if I don't!

Things actually got worse the following week. I had to kiss Miss Kitty, who was dressed up as Chyna—Chynette, they called her. That was the first and only time I ever kissed another woman on TV.

That one actually caused a lot of shit at home. The problem wasn't that I was kissing someone. Vickie knew me well enough to know that I wasn't out there cheating on her. It was more about the fact that she had no faith in me anymore. I had lied to her so often, how could she believe anything I told her?

I had lied to her because I didn't want to get in trouble, or because she wouldn't understand what I had to do to get the drugs I needed. I wasn't doing these things to hurt her—I was sick. I was doing what I needed to do to survive.

I'm sure there are plenty of people out there who will think I'm full of it, that I was lying to Vickie to protect myself. But anyone with the disease of addiction will understand what I'm talking about. You do whatever it takes to feed your addiction, even though deep down you know that you're hurting and deceiving the people you care about the most.

The Radicalz got back together for *Survivor Series*, where we took on Chyna, Billy Gunn, Road Dogg & K-Kwik.

It was nice to get back together with those guys, even for just a short while. One thing about Dean and Chris and Perry—when it came to work, it was always a pleasure being in the ring with them.

We had a match on *Raw*, the Radicalz against Billy, Chyna, The Rock, and Stone Cold Steve Austin. It ended with Stone Cold stomping a mudhole into me, setting up a singles match the next night on *SmackDown!*

I had first met Steve in Japan, right before he was let go by WCW. We did some drinking together and I liked him a lot. I thought he was a tremendous person. No matter how successful he got, he always treated me right.

Getting the opportunity to work with someone of his and The Rock's caliber is always exciting and a real honor. It felt good that no matter how messed up my personal life was, I was still held in high esteem professionally.

I dropped the Intercontinental Championship to Billy Gunn in November. When the Christmas holiday break came along, I took a few much-needed weeks off TV. I had been dealing with an injured hamstring for months, pretty much the entire time I was working with Billy. Because I was compensating for that injury, I ended up doing further damage to my left leg. I pulled my groin and hurt my knee, all on the same leg.

I returned to action in February and immediately went into a program with Chris Jericho over the Intercontinental title. It led to a Fatal Four Way at *No Way Out*—me, Jericho, X-Pac, and Chris Benoit.

If Triple-Threat matches are hard, then Fatal Four Ways are just about impossible. The four of us were at a total loss as far as how to make it work. We simply couldn't get the psychology of the match down. We were all kind of bewildered, like, "How do we do this?"

227

THE EDDIE GUERRERO STORY

DEAN MALENKO AND PERRY SATURN HELP ME CELEBRATE MY WWE EUROPEAN CHAMPION-SHIP WIN AT *WRESTLEMANIA X-SEVEN.*

We didn't get a chance to lay things out before we went out there. Every time we tried to connect, one of us was busy doing an interview. We literally sat down five minutes before the match, talked a bit, then went out there and winged it.

All things considered, it was a very good, fast-paced match. Fortunately, the four of us were all comfortable together in the ring. We all had a good chemistry, which allowed us to pull it off without a hitch.

WrestleMania X-Seven—at the Houston Astrodome—was a much better event for me than the previous WrestleMania. I had the opportunity to work against Test, with the European Championship on the line.

Because it was a singles match—as opposed to the three-man team match I worked the previous year—it meant much more to me on a personal level. They actually gave us a decent amount of time, eight minutes or so, which I was thankful to have.

Test and I had been working together for a few weeks, feeling each other

CHEATING DEATH, STEALING LIFE

out, and we'd developed a nice chemistry. For the finish, Perry and Dean interfered, giving me the chance to nail Test with the European title belt and get the pin.

Winning a title—any title—at *WrestleMania* is special. Everybody is watching and it's guaranteed to go down in the history books. Winning the European Championship at *WrestleMania* felt like a reward, a pat on the back.

Always being funny!

It was a good week. Vickie joined me in Houston and we actually had a great time together. Getting four days to ourselves was so rare, and we took full advantage of our time together. We bonded in a way that we hadn't in a long time.

Of course, I was still partying, but it was nice to have her join me for a change. It was very comfortable, the two of us having a few beers and a few laughs together.

I promised Vickie, "After *WrestleMania*, I'm going to slow down on the drugs and the drinking."

She was so looking forward to it. I think we both saw that *WrestleMania* week as a kind of last hurrah. I could enjoy partying without any guilt, because when it was over, I was going to really make an effort to change my behavior.

I was sincere, too. I wanted to stop what I was doing. I really did. I cut back on the drinking for a couple of months, but before long, I was partying as hard as ever.

Eventually I reached a point where I gave up trying to be sober. I accepted it. *This is the way I am,* I thought. *There's nothing I can do to change it.*

THE EDDIE GUERRERO STORY

WITH MY BUDDY CHRIS BENOIT.

CHAPTER 31

"**W**e need to talk," Vickie said one day as I came home from the road. She sat me down and told me that she couldn't take living with me anymore and that she wanted a divorce.

I begged her to stay with me. "Don't give up," I pleaded. "Let's work through this."

But she'd had enough. My behavior had reached such a level of toxicity that it finally poisoned her against me.

It wasn't just Vickie that was having issues with my behavior. My friends were also starting to worry.

When it came to business, I was sure to never come to work while I was messed up, but getting wasted every night takes its toll on you. I was constantly hungover, my attitude was getting more and more negative. I wasn't myself, and people were beginning to notice.

Dean, Chris, Perry, and I had traveled together through our first couple of months in WWE. After a while, we decided to split up. Four guys in a car can be pretty tough, plus I think Dean and Perry had grown tired of babysitting me.

Chris and I continued to ride together. God bless him,

231

he always looked out for me. He's such a good friend. He would do pretty much all of the driving, mostly because he was so afraid of me falling asleep at the wheel. I'd sit in the passenger seat, with a couple bottles of wine, while he stayed up all night getting us from one town to the next. On those rare occasions when I did drive, Chris wouldn't sleep so he could keep an eye on me. The only times he would crash out in the car, it was out of pure exhaustion.

Chris gave me so much love, but I've learned that that's not necessarily a good thing. The people who took care of me didn't know it, but they were enabling me. They were rescuing me from the consequences of my addiction. In a sense, that only supported my dysfunctional behavior. They didn't realize what they were doing—they believed in their hearts that they were looking out for my best interests. But by protecting me, they allowed me to continue acting out my self-destructive behavior.

With my drinking and drugging plainly getting out of hand, Dean and Chris talked among themselves and decided the only way to help me was to intervene. It had reached the point where they were more worried about my life than they were about management finding out that I had a problem. What good would having a job do me if I wasn't alive to do it?

They didn't know what to do—they only knew that they had to do something. They decided to speak to Jim Ross, let him know of their concerns. They weren't stooging me out to the boss—they were genuinely worried about my health and my safety.

As far as I can remember, they never approached me to discuss their fears. On the other hand, it's very possible that they did and I simply don't remember. I was pretty far gone at that time, getting more and more loaded every night.

I first heard that they had spoken to J.R. when I saw the UPN TV special about my life. I had no idea that they had done that. I'll be honest, it hurt me deeply. Not so much that they felt that they had to go to J.R., but that even after I got sober, they still hadn't told me.

When I asked Dean about it, he told me why they felt they had to do what they did. "I wouldn't be able to live with myself if I would've found you dead in a hotel room," he said. "And there's no doubt in my mind that that's the path you were on."

CHEATING DEATH, STEALING LIFE

t started like any other day. I walked into the building and before I even made it to the dressing room, I was told that J.R. wanted me to meet with him and Bruce Pritchard. Bruce was one of the top guys in the Talent Relations Department.

They told me that they were both very concerned. "We're not here to judge you," J.R. said. "We're trying to help you."

I was infuriated. All I could think was, *Hey, you try working with the kind of hamstring injury I've been dealing with.*

I had been telling myself that the pills were to help with my hamstring, but the truth was that the pain they were killing was mental. If I took a pill, then I wouldn't feel sad that I wasn't near my family, that my marriage was falling apart, that my kids barely knew me. Having an injury just allowed me to justify my addiction.

My meeting with J.R. and Bruce didn't really force me to rethink my bad habits. I hadn't confronted my addiction yet. Instead, I took their words to be a threat—straighten up or you're out on your ass.

A week later, everything in my world came crashing down on me. *Raw* was being broadcast out of Minneapolis. I'd had an especially rough weekend. I ran out of pills and started jonesing badly. No matter how much I drank, it didn't help. I made calls to all of my connections but came up dry. I knew one of Vickie's friends had some codeine and some Valium, so I called her and begged her to let me have a few pills. "Please don't tell Vickie," I asked her. "I'll get a lot of heat if she knew I came over to get pills."

"Don't worry, Eddie. I won't say anything."

Of course, she got on the phone the second I drove off. That was all it took to stir the shit between Vickie and myself. She actually started thinking that I went over to her friend's place for other reasons. Needless to say, we had a huge fight. I went to my bedroom, knocked back a bunch of pills with hard liquor, and crashed out hard.

The next morning, I literally couldn't get up. Even though Vickie was fed up with me, she was still thinking responsibly. She packed my bags for TV, got me out of bed, and drove me to the airport.

God, I was a mess. I could barely stand up. I was stumbling as Vickie tried to get me to my gate. I actually fell down the escalator, twisting my ankle and scratching the hell out of my shoulder in the process. Fortunately, a security guard recognized me and helped Vickie get me up again.

I ended up missing my flight to Minneapolis. Considering the shape I was in, the last thing I needed was to try and reschedule a flight. Luckily, I knew some people from the airline, and they worked with Vickie to book me onto a new flight.

Vickie was barely talking to me through all of this. Once I had a new ticket, they stuck me in a wheelchair and rolled me to the gate. Vickie just left me there, but I was so out of it, I barely noticed. I just sat there, passed out in the wheelchair, waiting for my flight.

Four hours later, the flight attendant shook me awake and got me onto the plane. When we landed in Minneapolis, I was still completely messed up. "Sober up, Eddie," I said to myself. "You can't go to work like this."

When I got to the building, I looked and felt like shit. The Dudley Boyz saw me coming in and helped get me to the dressing room. Chris and Dean came over and told me just to stay where I was and hopefully no one from the office would see what kind of condition I was in.

Of course, word got around that I was all messed up. Chris and Dean went to bat for me with J.R., but there was nothing they could do. J.R. is a good, compassionate man, but he's also a businessman. He told me I had a choice: either go to rehab or lose my job.

I was so afraid of not being able to provide for my family. "Okay," I said. "Yeah. No problem. I'll go to rehab."

J.R. said that the office would take care of everything. They would put me into the best addiction treatment center in the country—Talbott Recovery Campus in Atlanta.

But I didn't want to go to Talbott. Not only was it far from home, I knew that it was a long program. I wanted to get into a twenty-eight-day program in Florida, so I could stay close to Vickie and the kids.

I started crying, saying, "I don't want to be away from my kids for four months."

"Sorry, Eddie, but we've got to send you to Talbott. It's the best."

"Please," I sobbed, "I'm trying to keep my family together. My wife is divorcing me."

"Well, do you blame her?" J.R. said. "You're a fucking drug addict."

That was the single most hurtful thing anyone has ever said to me. The reason it hurt so much is because I knew it was the truth.

I was still in pretty bad shape when I arrived back in Florida. When I called Vickie to tell her what had happened with J.R., she told me not to come home. The scene at the airport was the last straw. She'd been on her last legs for a long time and she was through. "If you come back here," she said, "then I'm leaving."

I stood there in the Tampa airport, feeling more alone than I'd ever felt before. It was easily one of the toughest days of my life. Five days later, things got even harder.

NOTHING'S BETTER THAN SPENDING TIME WITH MY BEAUTIFUL DAUGHTERS.

CHAPTER 32

Talbott Recovery Campus is one of the leading rehab facilities in the world. TRC treats chemical dependency as a chronic, relapsing disease that affects people on a number of levels—physically, emotionally, socially, and spiritually. It's considered the treatment center of choice for addicted professionals such as lawyers, businessmen, and doctors.

The people at Talbott were very beautiful. So loving and so giving. They work there because they genuinely want to help. Obviously that's their job and they get paid well for doing it, but there's a lot of love in that place.

As for the other patients, it was like anywhere else—there were people I loved, people I couldn't stand, people who I knew were full of shit.

They came from all walks of life. The disease of addiction does not discriminate. There were doctors and lawyers, athletes and housewives. There were even a few therapists who were themselves suffering from addiction.

The first thing that happens after checking into Talbott is a complete detoxification. They can't help you until your body is fully clean from drugs and alcohol.

237

It's like being in a hospital. There are doctors and nurses keeping an eye on you, checking your blood pressure to make sure you don't have a heart attack while you're coming down. Most people don't realize it, but quitting drugs and alcohol can be very dangerous. If you're not careful, you can die from the shock.

Detox was one of the scariest and most painful experiences of my life, both physically and emotionally. I found the mental pain much harder to take than the physical. They were able to help me come down from the substances I'd been putting into my body, using various medicines to get all that shit out of my system. Unfortunately, there wasn't much they could do to ease the intense emotional agony that goes along with detoxing.

After detox, I was moved into the rehabilitation side of the campus. It's essentially a dormitory, an apartment complex. I was put into a two-bedroom apartment with three other people—two to each room.

From that point on, I worked around the clock with a team of five therapists, led by an amazing man named Jim Weigel. God bless his soul, I still speak to him to this day.

More than anything else, TRC reminded me of college. They told me that I needed an education, so that I could fully understand and accept what was going on in my life. At first I didn't believe I actually had a disease. "You're sick," they told me. "Sure I am," I replied.

What I came to understand was that alcoholism is a very real thing. Alcoholics like me can't process liquor the same way other people can. It changes our chemistry and behavior. It deforms our decision making. It makes us chemically insane. We can't make rational decisions.

When they told me that I was chemically insane, I thought they were the crazy ones. Then I learned that one of the definitions of insanity is doing the same things and expecting different results. Look at the facts—I crash my car and I keep drinking. I OD two times and I keep drugging. That's just not sane thinking.

The team at TRC did a great job teaching me about what I'm battling, making me knowledgeable about what was going on with me. Before that, I honestly had no idea.

When I wasn't studying, a great deal of my time was spent in very intense therapy sessions. It was the first time that I'd ever done therapy, and nothing could have prepared me for how difficult it would be. No joke—therapy was one of the hardest things I've ever done in my life.

I hated therapy. Deep inside, I didn't want to change. I wanted the pain to stop, but I didn't want to stop partying. I wanted the chaos to stop, but I didn't want to stop drinking. I wanted the best of both worlds.

Really, I just wanted to be like everybody else. Why shouldn't I be able to enjoy a glass of wine or a cold beer on a sunny day? I had to come to the understanding that I'm not like everybody. I am powerless over alcohol. That's who I am. It's one thing to say it, it's another to believe it. You can wish it was different, but that won't change the facts.

Rehab is like an emotional roller-coaster ride, with so many ups and downs. You find out things about yourself that you don't want to accept. Basically all you're doing is looking at yourself. That's what therapy is. It doesn't offer a miracle cure. It gives you the ammunition to fix whatever is wrong with yourself.

Of course, it's a lot easier said than done. You just can't make those changes overnight. It takes a lot of therapy and a lot of hard work.

Like most rehab centers, TRC utilized the 12-step program to help patients conquer their addiction. The 12 steps were originated by Alcoholics Anonymous to serve as the spiritual foundation for recovery from the effects of alcoholism. Since then, the program has been used to help addicts of all kinds.

The 12-step program is more than just a way to stop drinking. It's actually a guide toward a new way of life. The essence of the 12 steps is to accept the fact that you have a problem with drugs and alcohol and that you're powerless to stop yourself. Only by allowing God into your life can you hope to regain some control.

Simply put, you've got to have faith in God and you've got to have faith in yourself.

One of the hardest things I had to do in TRC was to ask my family to write me letters, describing just what it was like being around me. It's a way of making you realize just how ugly your behavior has been, and how that behavior has affected others.

It was important that they were completely honest, no matter how hard it was for me to take. Basically you're giving everybody license to tell you how much of a fuck-up you are, how you've been a nightmare to be around, how you've made their lives miserable. It gives them a chance to let out all the anger and bad feelings they have toward you.

Obviously I asked Vickie to write me, though God help me, I almost wish I hadn't. I also asked my mom and my brothers and sisters. God bless her, Mom couldn't do it. She couldn't express her pain and sadness and disappointment toward me. My brothers and sisters, on the other hand, really let me have it.

The hardest letters to take were the ones my kids wrote to me. It hurt so bad, hearing what these two beautiful girls thought of me. They told me that they loved me, but that they lived in fear of me. That's a terrible thing for a father to hear—that his children are afraid of him.

They told me that they didn't understand what was going on. Shaul's letter said that it made her sad when Vickie told her we were going to divorce, but "I'm glad that you guys aren't going to be fighting anymore." It broke my heart, the idea that she had to see her mommy and daddy fighting all the time.

Those letters were like a wake-up call, a big-ass blow to my face that made me start to see things more clearly. They helped me to look at myself and what I'd done to the people I love most. I honestly didn't know any of these things. It was almost as if I was blind to what was going on around me.

Until that point, I didn't truly understand how my disease affected the people around me. It's almost like a cold—eventually everyone around you is going to get sick. That's exactly what happened. My disease spread until everybody in my house was also sick.

One of the goals of therapy is to break down your defenses to get to the core of your pain. They start peeling away at you, like an onion's layers.

A lot of my therapy dealt with my childhood, my relationship to my parents. I can honestly say I had a wonderful childhood. There was so much love in my house.

What I began to understand was how I had been in the spotlight my entire life. I was Gory Guerrero's son. I was Chavo Guerrero's brother. I was Mando Guerrero's brother. I was Hector Guerrero's brother.

There was a lot of pressure on me to live up to the legacy they had created. I've been living in the shadow of these legendary wrestlers for all my life. From the minute I started wrestling, people would say, "Is he as good as his brothers? Is he as good as his dad?" I've had to deal with that since I was nine years old.

From the moment I came out of my mom's womb, it's been all about wrestling. I have always identified myself with wrestling—the reason I'm so good at it is because that's all I know. I was lousy at living life because I didn't know how to do it.

I've tried so hard to please my family, to live up to the standards they set. But let me be perfectly clear about one thing. They didn't put the pressure on me—I did that myself. I created that burden on my own.

No matter what happens in your life, you have the ultimate responsibility for your decisions. You should never blame your choices on anyone else.

I've seen plenty of people come from the hardest times life has to offer and make it through just fine. Then there are people who blame every aspect of their life on their parents, on their jobs, on everything else around them. That's bull, plain and simple. The fact of the matter is that they don't want to look at themselves. Too many people go into therapy and think all they have to do is say, "My parents did this to me, that's why I did what I did." That's stupid. You have to be responsible for your own life.

Therapy helped me to confront my issues. I didn't know how to look inside and see what I was going through, what I was living.

I was living with an enormous amount of stress, and drugs and alcohol helped me to dull the pain. But they couldn't help me deal with the pressure. All they did was cover up the hurt.

Once I began to understand my issues, I was able to start dealing with them. The only way you can move on with your life is by confronting your obstacles. You can't ignore them. You might get away with it for a little while, but they will always come back and beat you down again. When you confront a problem, you might fall on your ass, it might knock you down a couple more times, but sooner or later God gives you the strength and the wisdom to overcome it.

That's why I love God so much. It's only through knowing Him, through His power and His grace, that I've been able to learn to live with myself. In some ways I still have not forgiven myself. But only through the wisdom that I find in God and in the Bible do I find the strength to overcome the adversities in my life.

Nothing in my experience has taught me as much as Scripture. There have been plenty of people that have given me great advice, but of course, that's just another way that God speaks to you—through other people.

Though Talbott is a secular facility, it was the place where I began to reconnect with Jesus Christ. Working through the 12 steps helped me come closer to my beliefs that I had from a long time ago. I accepted Jesus Christ in my heart when I was ten years old. Through all the ups and downs of my life, I never gave up on that relationship.

When I first started getting sober, I came to a realization. The pain inside me wasn't about the business. It wasn't about my family. What was destroying me was that I had drifted away from Christ. The emptiness I was feeling was my separation from God. That's the true definition of sin. Sin is not about doing something bad, it's about losing your touch with God.

The only times in my life that I've truly felt at peace came through knowing Jesus Christ. That's my testimony. Christ's love is the only thing that gives me any release from the pain that I feel inside. As much as I love my kids and my wife, as much as I love this business, they simply don't compare to the love and peace that I receive through Jesus Christ.

I realized that if I was ever going to get sober, I was going to have to restore my relationship with Him. It was only then that I began to come out of the dark place where I had been for so long.

It was a long summer, maybe the longest of my life. There were times when it felt like I was never going to get out, that I was going to be trapped in this prison forever. Not that it was anything like prison—it was actually very nice. But in a lot of ways, it felt as if I was serving a life sentence in there. I thought I'd never see my family again.

I tried to keep my hope alive. The main thing that kept me going was the idea that if I could make it through, then maybe I'd have a chance to work things out with Vickie. I thought that if she saw what I was willing to go through to get better, then she'd come back to me.

I didn't want to lose my family. Of course, I didn't realize that I already had.

All I ever thought about was getting out of there. From the time I first walked in, all the way to the day I left, the only thing I cared about was leaving.

243

THE EDDIE GUERRERO STORY

While I was allowed phone calls to the outside, I pretty much cut myself off from the world during my stay at Talbott.

I talked to people—like my brothers and some of my friends—when they called, but I wasn't reaching out to anybody myself. I was very embarrassed about where I was. It felt like everybody was pointing their finger at me, judging me, and I didn't want to deal with it. I talked to as few people as I could. The only people I would talk to were the people that were with me at rehab.

One morning in early September, I was between classes and stopped by the common area. There were these crazy images on the TV, the Twin Towers were in flames. I thought it was a movie, I didn't exactly understand what was going on. Then someone told me it was real. Everybody started freaking out, saying that they had to get out of there, that they had to go home. Everybody saw it as an excuse to go home.

The staff gathered everyone together and calmed us down. "Nobody is going home," they told us. The therapists were careful not to let the disaster distract people from their personal issues. Like everybody else, we were in a state of shock. But also like everybody else, once we knew our families were safe, we went back about our business.

I called Vickie to make sure that everybody was okay. She was very cold to me. Her anger hadn't faded over the time that I was at Talbott. She told me the kids were all right and got off the phone as fast as she could.

Had I not been in rehab, I'd have been trapped in Houston with the rest of WWE.

But I was already trapped.

Things progressed over the course of my stay. I started getting a little bit more freedom. They began getting me ready to go into the real world. They don't just say, "Okay, it's been four months," then throw you out there. They do everything they can to prepare you for the rest of your life.

After a couple of months, I was given the first of two weekend leaves from the Talbott campus. As much as I wanted to get out of there, when the moment came to walk out the gate I was terrified to leave. It's easy to stay clean in rehab. But when you hit the real world, all your old habits come rushing back to the surface. It's up to you to take what you've learned in rehab and control your urges.

It was a total shock to the system, walking out of a place where I was being educated about my disease, where everybody was supporting me and loving me, into the harsh light of the real world. The real world didn't give a shit about me. Society didn't care that I have a disease. In the real world, I was a drug addict and a drunk.

Rehab was the first time in my life that I started to live with my emotions instead of trying to numb them with drugs and alcohol. That might be the most important lesson of the entire experience. I needed to feel my feelings. I couldn't cover them up anymore. I couldn't hide from them.

There was a moment toward the end of my stay where I began to feel grateful for the experience. I really started to believe that I could do it, that I could live a sober life.

But when it was finally time for me to go, I was as scared as I'd ever been in my entire life. I had spent four months dreaming of the day I could get out of there and when the time finally came, I didn't want to leave.

I had gotten comfortable in Talbott. As difficult as the rehab process was, it was still a safer, warmer environment than what was waiting for me outside. I didn't want to go out into the world and deal with everything that had been going on while I was inside—my financial situation, the divorce, learning to live alone, coming back to work and proving myself.

I was so scared. I really didn't know if I could do my job and stay sober. I didn't believe I could.

Rehab taught me a lot about myself. It taught me a lot about what I needed to do to stay sober. It's important to understand—rehab does not get you sober. If they teach you anything there, it's that. Rehab doesn't keep you clean. All it does is give you a foundation for staying sober. You have to go to meetings, you have to constantly look at what's going on inside you, you have to work.

Unfortunately, it actually wasn't until much later that those ideas began to sink in. Despite all my hard work, when I left Talbot, I still hadn't fully acknowledged the truth.

CHAPTER 33

We're all human. We make mistakes even when we don't want to.

Looking back, it's amazing how self-destructive I was. I didn't like myself very much at all. At the same time, I had an instinct for self-preservation. Every time I hit a bump in the road, I came back stronger. I never said, "Okay, I'm down and I'm staying here." I always got back up. Of course, then I'd fall down even harder than the last time.

I was inside Talbott when I first learned how much money I owed the government.

When it rains, it pours, I thought when I found out just how bad my financial situation had become. When I hit bottom, I truly hit bottom.

It shouldn't have come as such a surprise. I hadn't been smart with my money. It was another aspect of my life that I hadn't been able to control.

Simply put, I had been spending a lot more than I was making. You can only do that for so long before the weight of your debt catches up to you.

It turned out that my financial adviser at the time wasn't looking out for me the way I thought he was. He was supposed to guide me on how to manage my money, but in fact, he was just another enabler. I would call him and say, "Can I buy this?" "Sure, Eddie. Go ahead." I liked him because he always said yes.

I'm not blaming anyone but myself. I wasn't attentive to my money. But as it turned out, neither was my financial manager. Not only did he allow me to piss away my money, he wasn't making sure I was filing my taxes properly.

As an independent contractor, I'm responsible for paying all my own taxes. When most people get their paycheck, the government has already taken their bite. Me, I've got to pay it myself, every quarter, like any self-employed businessman. And that doesn't include all my other work-related expenses—food and lodging and rental cars.

I admit it—I was irresponsible. I wasn't aware of what I was doing. I was paying the IRS, just not the full amounts that I was supposed to be paying. If I owed ten dollars, I'd send them six. I'd get behind one quarter and say to myself, *Okay, I'll make it up in the next quarter.* So then I owed for the next quarter, plus a little more.

Before long the interest and penalties accumulated to the point where it was impossible to get caught up. I owed close to six figures in penalties alone, not counting my regular quarterly taxes.

I can't blame anyone for what happened. Messing up my taxes was on me. I was not responsible for my own affairs. Nobody screwed me. I screwed myself.

I knew I was going to be audited, so I decided to get in front of the situation. I contacted the government as soon as I got out of Talbott. "I'm sorry, but I fell behind on my taxes. Tell me what I owe you so that I can begin paying it off."

The government didn't give me one break. I didn't just lose everything, I put myself in the hole for years to come. I didn't just go flat broke, I went into debt. Big-time.

My overhead was so high, there was no way for me to afford that lifestyle anymore. In addition to the back taxes, I owed money on the family house and everything else I'd bought—I'd been living on my credit for so long, I didn't own anything outright.

I had no choice but to file for Chapter 7 bankruptcy. When you're unable to pay your debts, the law provides for a plan that allows you to resolve those debts through the liquidation of your assets, which are then divided among your creditors.

I did what I had to do. I sold the house and the boat. Vickie's truck got repoed.

Filing bankruptcy didn't include the money that I owed the government, but otherwise, it enabled me to wipe the slate clean. Of course, my credit was wiped clean as well, but it gave me a chance to start fresh.

The first thing I did after getting out of rehab was rent an apartment in Tampa. Two bedrooms—one for me, one for the kids. I literally had nothing but the clothes on my back and in my bags.

Other than hotel rooms, I had never lived alone in my life. I was always protected. First, at home, by my parents. If I visited my brothers, they'd take care of me. When I went to college in New Mexico, I stayed in the dorms. When I went to Mexico City to wrestle, I lived with my cousin. After that, I got married and lived with Vickie and the kids.

My first night living alone in that apartment was nerve-wracking. At about three in the morning, I called Tury. "I can't sleep here, man," I said.

"Come on over," he replied, doing what he always did—extending his love and hospitality, no questions asked.

I went back to my apartment the next morning. I hated being there. It made me feel so alone. I spent as little time there as I could, constantly finding some excuse to go out. I'd go to the store for toilet paper or dishwashing soap or some snacks. But my mind was so preoccupied, I'd just walk around the store and come home with nothing. If I did buy something, it wasn't what I'd gone out for in the first place. I simply couldn't think straight.

I was in a state of total despair. I was lonely without my family. I was in so much pain inside, it hurt just to breathe. It reached the point where I didn't think I could take it much longer. I didn't want to live anymore.

It was awful. I suffered from terrible anxiety, with full-blown panic attacks, especially at night. The sun would go down and I'd just lose it. Talk about scared stiff—I literally couldn't move. I would sit in the middle of the room and stare at my front door, terrified that there was something on the other side waiting to get me. I knew that if I went outside my door, something bad was going to happen to me.

As soon as the sun came up, I'd start feeling better. I could handle the daytime. It was just in the night that I couldn't live with my demons.

Considering how despondent I'd become, my relapse was probably inevitable. It finally happened on my birthday. *I'm going to get drunk because I want to get drunk,* I said to myself. *Nobody's going to tell me whether I can get drunk or not.*

Tury and I share the same birthday, so I decided we should celebrate together. "I'm going to have a drink tonight," I said.

"Don't do it, man," he said.

I was fed up with being sober. "Why not? Everybody else can, why can't I?"

"Because you can't," Tury said. "You'll lose your job."

He tried so hard to convince me not to drink. Finally I said, "Look, I'm going to have a drink. Do you want to come with me or not?"

"All right," he said. "I can't stop you. I just hope you know what you're doing."

We went to a local bar and had a few drinks—I had a couple of shots of tequila and a beer. "Okay," I thought. "That's enough."

I honestly felt that I'd proven my point, that I could go out and have a few drinks, the same as anyone else. The next night I called my brother Hector and told him to meet me at another bar in my neighborhood. *What the hell,* I figured. *Another drink won't kill me.*

We ended up getting so loaded, the bartender had to call the cops just to get us out of there. Fortunately, one of the police officers recognized me and took pity. He looked at my driver's license and drove us home. The only problem was that my driver's license had my old address—he dropped us off right in front of Vickie's house!

Vickie came outside and saw Hector and me, wasted on her front lawn. Oh boy, she got hot! She allowed me inside to sleep it off in my old office while she called Tury to come get me. God, was she pissed! She wouldn't let Hector in the house—she left him out there, passed out in a lawn chair.

Tury came over and took Hector and me back to my apartment. When we woke up the next day, neither of us had any idea what had gone down until Tury called and told us. He was as angry as Vickie was. He reamed us pretty good.

By that point, it didn't matter what Tury or Vickie or anyone said. I didn't listen. I honestly didn't care anymore.

I spent the next day drinking by myself until Tury took me back to his place and put me into bed. In the morning, he came in and tried to get me up. "Promise me you'll go to the gym today," he said, but I couldn't move. I could hardly breathe. The alcohol had worn off and now the pain inside me was a million times worse than when I'd started drinking three days earlier.

It was almost like I had the flu. I was in such agony, I literally couldn't move. It hurt to breathe and my legs were so weak that I didn't have the energy to get out of bed. When I closed my eyes to sleep, I couldn't.

That morning was the first time I clearly thought, *I want to die.* I didn't want to live anymore. I had given up hope in everything—in God, in myself—and just wanted my life to stop.

Even though I knew it wasn't a good idea, I picked up the phone and called Vickie. "Please help me," I pleaded. "I can't take this. Please come and help me."

"No, Eddie," she said. "I can't help you anymore."

Boom! She hung up on me.

When I got off the phone, I decided I had to get out of the apartment. It took everything I had, every ounce of strength, just to get out of bed. I got in my truck and started driving. I had no idea where I was going, I just knew I had to keep moving. I was in so much pain, crying my eyes out behind the wheel.

As I was driving, my cell phone rang—it was my brother Mando. He heard me crying and asked, "What's going on?"

"I can't do this anymore," I wept. "I can't go another day living in this pain. It hurts to breathe."

"What do you mean? Are you having a heart attack?"

"No, it's not that. I just can't take any more of this pain."

Mando was genuinely afraid that I was going to kill myself. "Don't do anything stupid," he said.

As I drove past the church my family used to go to, something inside me told me to stop and go in. I walked inside and asked for Pastor Phair. He saw the look on my face and immediately brought me into his office to talk.

I just released everything, asking him a million questions: "If I believe in God, why are these things happening? Why is Vickie divorcing me? Why do I have so much pain?"

Pastor Phair suggested that maybe I needed to reconnect with God. I knew immediately that he was right. My despair wasn't just about the fact that I was doing all these bad things; it was that inside my soul I had separated myself from God. That's the definition of sin—separation from God. The farther I got from Him, the more painful it was for me.

I got down on my knees and begged the Lord for forgiveness. I told Him that I didn't want to drink anymore; I didn't want to get high anymore. "I don't want to live like this," I prayed. "I don't want to feel the pain that I'm feeling. I want to change my life."

The act of praising God, of thanking Him for His gifts and for His mercy, was such a release. I immediately began feeling a little better. Pastor Phair gave me a Bible and showed me some verses to say out loud in times of despair. I started reading Psalm 51, which says, *Have mercy upon me, O God, according to thy loving kindness: according unto the multitude of thy tender mercies blot out my transgressions.*

Walking out of the church, I could feel the difference in me. Some of my pain had been released. For the first time in a long while, I had some hope.

From that moment on, I understood that God was the only way out for me. Nothing else would do. I had to focus on my spirit, on my relationship with God. Jesus Christ is the only one that can take away the pain, that can give me peace and fulfill me inside.

When I got home, I called Jim Weisel, my therapist from rehab. "Go to an AA meeting," he told me, "and get yourself a sponsor."

I did as I was told. I went to the nearest meeting and asked the most approachable-looking person there if he'd be my sponsor. Bob turned out to be a huge blessing in my life. He made himself totally accessible to me. I can't say enough positive things about him. He was a big part of my recovery. His help was crucial in the early days of my sobriety.

For the next couple of weeks, I worked hard to maintain my sobriety. I focused on God, reading my Bible, listening to Christian music. My heart's desire was truly not to drink anymore.

Meanwhile, I also tried to focus on getting ready to go back to work. WWE was sending me to Heartland Wrestling Association in Cincinnati to get into shape before coming back to the main roster.

It was a little embarrassing, like having to go to the minor leagues after having played in the World Series. It turned out that the boys at HWA were actually very understanding. They weren't judgmental at all. If anything, they opened themselves up to me, shared their own fears and experiences with me.

My old friend Brian Adams was there, working as a trainer. He was an enormous help to me. It was great to have somebody there that I could open my heart to. We talked a lot and worked out together in the ring. Brian's a good friend. He saw me going through all kinds of shit and was totally there for me emotionally.

It was hard getting my groove back, getting into shape again. The desire was there, no question, but getting my body back into condition turned out to be pretty difficult.

I pretty much kept to myself. If I wasn't training, then I was in a quiet corner, reading my Bible. I was determined to stay on the straight and narrow, once and for all.

But there was still a little part of me that couldn't help wanting alcohol. I started thinking, *Now that my heart is true, now that I don't want to do these terrible things to get messed up, I can have a glass of wine like a normal person.*

This is how I know that addiction is truly a disease. I was serious about changing my life. I truly was. But when the craving came over me, there was not a damn thing I could do about it. I had promised the Lord that I wasn't going to drink, but I simply could not stop myself. I went to the package store and got myself a bottle of red wine.

No one's going to know, I figured. *Just one glass and that'll be that.* I went back to my apartment, poured myself a glass, and took a sip. I'll never forget that feeling—it started in my fingers and went right down to my toes. It was *ecstasy.*

I finished the glass and decided, *Okay, just one more.* Before I knew it, I had finished the bottle. I was feeling good, so why not get another couple of bottles and have a few more drinks before I go to bed?

I went to my local bar, where a number of people recognized me and started buying rounds. I did nine straight tequila shots—*ding, ding, ding, ding, ding, ding, ding, ding, ding.* Part of it was just pure ego. I was showing off, like, *Hey, I'm Eddie Guerrero, watch me go!*

From there, it's all pretty much a blank. I ended up heading to another local joint with a couple of guys. I must've started buying rounds for everybody, because I left my credit card there. I eventually woke up in these guys' apartment and all I wanted to do was go home. They helped me into my truck and drove me right to the gate of my community. "Don't worry," I told them, "I've got it from here."

They left me there, trying to enter the PIN code to open the gate. But I was such a mess, I couldn't get it right. *Screw this,* I thought, *I'll just open the gate with my truck.*

I stepped on the gas and started trying to drive my truck through the gate. It didn't budge—I had the indentations on my bumper for months after that.

The community security force called the police. They got me out of my truck and tried to give me a sobriety test.

"Hey, look," I admitted, "I just can't do it, okay?"

I was just totally gone. When they started handcuffing me, I started pleading, "C'mon, man! I'm a WWE wrestler! I'll get you free tickets! Please, dude, don't arrest me."

But there was no getting out of it. I was so screwed up and I'd made such a scene that they had to take me in. When we got to the jail, it was just totally ridiculous—there were cops asking me for my autograph even as they were booking me and taking my fingerprints. Finally they put me in a cell by myself and I fell right to sleep.

When I woke up, I had no clue where I was. All I knew was that I was lying on a cold, hard slab of concrete. I looked around and saw the toilet and realized I was in jail. Then I looked down at what I had been using as a pillow. It was the toilet roll. A dirty, disgusting toilet roll that had been pissed on and God knows what else. That's when it really hit me.

Look how far I've come down, I thought. *I'm in jail, lying on the floor, with a pissed roll of toilet paper as a pillow.*

I was mad. I mean, really hot. I looked up at God and said, "You knew my intentions. All I wanted to do was have a glass of wine just like a normal person. Why can't I do that? Why did You let this happen to me? Why?"

Then it hit me like a Mack truck. God was telling me, "You can't do this anymore. I don't want you to do this anymore." I wasn't hearing His voice,

CHEATING DEATH, STEALING LIFE

but I could feel it in my heart. "You're not going to live a perfect life, but I want this one thing from you, Eddie. I don't want you to drink anymore. I need you to get this right, that way I can work on the rest of you. This is the one sacrifice I want from you, Eddie. You can't do this anymore."

Finally I understood. We're saved by grace, not by our words. You don't accept Jesus Christ as your savior and say, "Okay, now I can go do what I want." That's not the way it works. If you truly accept Him in your heart, then your heart's desire is to do the right thing by Him. That's what having Christ in your heart is all about.

Okay, I thought. *I can't do this anymore. I've proved it to myself. Right here, right now. Everything changes.*

After all that time, after all the drinking and all the drugs, after losing my family, losing all my money, I had finally hit bottom. I knew I was going to get fired from WWE. I knew it. I could've fallen farther economically. I could've wound up in the street. But it didn't matter. I had reached the lowest point in my life, but with the Lord's help, I was going to pull myself back up.

I was locked up for about eight hours. They've got to make sure you're sober before you're allowed to post bail. My bail was $1,000—double the usual amount, because I had caused property damage.

When I called Vickie to tell her I'd spent the night in jail, she really lit into me: "You worthless piece of shit!" She had no mercy at that point. I tried to lie to her about what had happened, telling her I had gotten into a fight. What I didn't realize was that the media had already gotten ahold of the story. There was my mugshot, right on the front page of the sports section. When you see that picture, the look on my face is more surprised than anything else, like, "Wow, how did *this* happen?" I know that it's a newspaper's business to cover the news, but I really felt that they jobbed me out. They didn't consider my family's feelings, they didn't consider how the story was going to affect my children.

As we spoke, Vickie was sitting there, reading the newspaper with my picture in it.

"Oh really?" she said. "You got into a fight?"

Even though we had made plans to get together for Thanksgiving, I knew that my getting arrested was the final nail in the coffin. There was no way we were ever going to reconcile our relationship. I had put her through too much for her to ever consider taking me back.

That night I got a call from Johnny "Ace" Laurinaitis, who was J.R.'s assistant, now WWE's Executive Vice President of Talent Relations. "Hey, you screwed up," he said in that raspy voice of his. "Well, we all screw up. I don't know what's going to happen, but for now, just shake it off and move on."

The next day, Johnny called and said J.R. wanted to speak to me. J.R. got on the phone and man, was he pissed! He gave me a serious ass-chewing, telling me that I was "an embarrassment." That hurt. That hurt a lot.

"Do I still have my job?" I asked.

"Yes, but if you do this again, you're gone. You hear me?"

I flew to Cincinnati the next afternoon to work out at HWA. I checked into my hotel and that's when I got the call. As soon as I saw Johnny's name on the caller ID, I knew I was fired.

"Eddie," he said, "I've got some bad news. J.R. and I just spoke to Vince. We told him what went on with you and he made the decision to fire you."

I starting begging, "Come on, Johnny, wrestling is the only thing I've got left. Please don't take this away from me."

"Vince was clear on this, Eddie. What kind of an example is he setting for the rest of the boys if he doesn't discipline you? I'm sorry, but this is how it's got to be."

I took getting fired pretty hard. I was so upset, I called my mom in El Paso. I could hear in her voice that she was scared for me, like I might try killing myself. It took my brother Chavo to snap me out of it. He called and really let me have it.

"Hey, man, what the fuck's the matter with you? Stop being such an asshole. Think of Mom, think of your kids. Don't be so fucking selfish."

I got hot. "Fuck you, man, I just lost my job!"

"Yeah, so? Wrestling isn't everything. Is Vince everything? Is he? No, he isn't. So stop acting like such a baby and figure out what you're going to do next."

Chavo was right—the time had come to stop feeling sorry for myself and move on.

CHAPTER 34

There was no more bottom left to sink to. I had lost everything—my family, my job, my money, my dignity. The only good thing that came out of the whole business was that I was truly done drinking.

In a way, getting fired was a kind of release. There was one less thing for me to constantly worry about! On the other hand, working for WWE was my sole source of income. Without wrestling, I had no way of earning a living.

I was freaking out, wondering how on earth I was going to support my kids. Bob offered me some words that really had a lot of influence in helping me stay sober.

"You know, Eddie," Bob said. "God doesn't have any grandkids. We're all His children. Your kids are His children just as much as you are. One way or another, God is going to provide for your kids, whether it's through you or Vickie or one of your family members. It might even be through another man."

That last part really got to me. "No way," I said. "I don't want anybody supporting my kids except me."

"Well, before you can help your kids," Bob said, "you've got to get Eddie right."

Bob's words focused me, helped push me forward to straighten up my life and do the right thing by my children. It showed me the way toward what I needed to do.

Word of my situation spread throughout the business. It wasn't long before I started getting calls from independent promotions looking to hire me. I don't think they cared what kind of shape I was in. I had name value from being in WWE, and that was enough to put asses into seats.

The first person to reach out to me was a promoter named Jac Sabboth, from Impact Championship Wrestling in New York. He offered to fly me up to New York City to work a match at the Elks Lodge in Queens—the old ECW Madhouse of Extreme.

It was very humbling. I needed to check within myself to see what I really wanted. Did I want to keep wrestling? I thought so, but the only way to find out was to get back to it. The best way to prove it to myself was by getting back to the indies.

Working the indies is the real deal. You're not wrestling in front of twenty thousand people; you're wrestling for two or three hundred. In order to put your body on the line for that many people, you've got to really love what you do.

I was very nervous when I arrived at Elks Lodge, but the other wrestlers made me feel very welcome. They were all extremely respectful, coming over to meet me and tell me that my work was part of what had inspired them to get into the business.

Jac Sabboth shook my hand and told me that he'd booked me in an ICW World Title match against the current champ, a terrific young wrestler named Low Ki. "Would you mind going to a draw?" he asked.

I had a better idea. "Why don't you let me put him over?"

Jac's jaw just dropped. "Just give me a good amount of time," I added, "and let me call the match my way."

"That would be amazing," he said, looking like a kid in a candy store.

He ran over and told Low Ki. I swear, both of those guys had sparkles in their eyes, they were so excited.

Basically, I knew I was going to be working independents for a while. Most guys, after being in WWE or WCW or ECW, come into the indies with the attitude of "Oh, I can't job to one of your guys. I was a big star." I've always believed you can put somebody over and still get yourself over if you do it right. As long as the people get a great match, that's what they remember.

When I walked out to the ring, the place went crazy. The ICW crowd weren't your average fans either. These were die-hard wrestling people, the people who read the Internet and exchange tapes and support indie promotions. They knew exactly what had been going on in my life the past few months and they still gave me a standing ovation when I came out. They valued me for my talent, for what I could do in the ring. I felt so appreciated.

As I stood there, taking in all the love, I thought, *Maybe I still want to do this. I think I want to wrestle.*

I went to the indies searching for my heart. When I lost my job with WWE I had to ask myself what I wanted out of life. I'd been in so much pain for so long. I had to decide if wrestling would bring me happiness.

All these questions were running through my mind: Is this it? Is this how I'm going to finish off my career? Am I going to work the indies wishing I had another opportunity in WWE, or am I going to accept it and do the best I can? Should I move on from wrestling and start looking for another way of life? If I do, how will I provide for myself and my kids? My head was spinning. I really didn't know the answers.

Putting over Low Ki opened up the floodgates. Before I knew it, every indie promoter in the country was calling me. They wanted Eddie Guerrero to put their boys over, and that was fine by me. As long as they met my conditions and paid me what I wanted. If I was going to work in the indies, I was going to be smart about it.

One of my first indie bookings had me wrestling in front of twenty-five people in some school gym. The match was the drizzling shits, and when I came back, I was livid! I was so pissed off, I started throwing chairs around, cursing, the works. Then I thought, *Hey, who cares? There were only twenty-five people out there. Who gives a shit?*

But then it hit me. Who gives a shit? *I give a shit!* I don't care if there are twenty-five people or twenty-five thousand—I only want to give my best out there.

That's when I knew I still had the fire. That's when I knew I still wanted it. From that point on, I had one goal, to be the best wrestler I could be. *Okay, Eddie,* I thought. *Let's go to work.*

Over the next few weeks I made a real effort to get myself into top shape. Money was tight, so I had to adjust my diet. Tuna, rice cakes, oatmeal, that's pretty much all I was eating. Plus, without Vickie there, I had to cook for myself. A can of tuna, some fat-free mayo, a couple of rice cakes and boom, here I go. Low fat and instant protein.

Eating that way helped me lose all the weight I had gained while I was in rehab. Rehab was the first time since I was a little kid that I wasn't working out, so when I came out of there, I was a little heavier than I needed to be.

Since I was only working a couple of days a week, I suddenly had a lot of time on my hands. My friend Steve Keirn opened up his gym to me, Steve Keirn's School of Hard Knocks. I would do weight training, then get in the ring with whoever was around. There were some good kids training there, guys like Lex Lovett and Steve Madison. I worked out with a young worker named Kid Romeo; my buddy Brian Adams would come by and wrestle with me. All these people just opened their hearts to me. They were a great blessing in my life.

I would get in the ring and not leave for hours. I would do Iron Man matches, wrestling nonstop until I blew myself up. That way there was no chance of me getting exhausted in a regular match. I also began studying my favorite wrestler, Chris Benoit. I wanted to learn from him, to try and capture some of his intensity and apply it to my own style.

I was like Rocky Balboa. I had the eye of the tiger! I became completely focused—on my Bible, on my sobriety, and on getting myself into peak condition to wrestle. I'd work out in the morning, go to an AA meeting, go home and eat some tuna and rice cakes, go to another meeting, then go back to the ring at night.

I encountered so much kindness during those days. People were incredibly supportive of me, and I'll always be grateful for that. A good example was after I did a couple of matches for the Independent Wrestling Association, Mid-South promotion. First I had a great three-way match with CM Punk and Rey Mysterio in Indianapolis. I became the IWA Mid-South World Heavyweight Champion that night, then dropped the title back to CM Punk the next night. He was IWA's top star and I had no problem putting him over.

I ended up getting stuck in Chicago after the match. I had eight hours to kill before my flight and all the hotels were full. CM Punk opened up his house to me, inviting me to crash at the place he shared with another worker, Ace Steel. We hung out at their pad, talking about wrestling and life in the business, and then they drove me to the airport. Their hospitality made me feel so good. They didn't care about my past mistakes. They welcomed me into their home as a fellow wrestler, as part of the family.

There are some tremendous talents out there, wonderful wrestlers that have not had the chance to be seen by the majority of fans. I was so impressed by some of these young workers, people like Low Ki and Chris Daniels and CM Punk. These guys are so talented, such phenomenal athletes. I was amazed by their high flying and their love of the business.

One of the best things about my time in the indies was that I was blessed with a chance to work with a bunch of young Latino wrestlers, guys like Xavier and Amazing Red and the SATs—Joel and Jose Maximo. I formed a real bond with those guys. To this day, they call me to talk about the business, to talk about the Lord.

Some time later, after I'd gone back to WWE, Xavier sent me a very moving letter, telling me how seeing the things that I've gone through and witnessing to him was helping him get through some tough times of his own. He also gave me a Christian book that really impacted my outlook, *The Purpose-Driven Life* by Rick Warren. It teaches about why we were created, what we're really here for. It teaches about getting out of oneself and serving others. The fact that Xavier thought to send this book to me really touched my heart.

Going to the indies was truly a blessing. It reminded me that I still had a lot left to prove. More importantly, it allowed me to humble myself and give a little something back to the business that I loved so much, the business that's fed me since the day I was born.

In March, I heard from my dear friend Black Cat. He was still working for New Japan and wanted to know how I'd feel about coming over and working there. He knew that my past history with the promotion, as well as my successes in the States, would make me a hell of a draw over there.

I was all set to leave for Japan when I got a call from John Laurinaitis. We'd stayed in touch over the months since I'd been let go, and he was always incredibly supportive.

"I heard you're going to New Japan," Johnny said. "Do me a favor, don't sign anything."

"Why not?" I asked.

"We're thinking about bringing you back," he said.

"What do you mean 'thinking'?"

"Look, just don't sign anything," Johnny said. "Give us an opportunity to talk to you when you get back."

I was blown away. Nothing happens in the wrestling business without WWE knowing about it. They must have gotten word that I was doing well in the indies. I'm sure they'd heard that I was sticking to my sobriety, or else they never would've given me a second chance.

But in my heart, I really didn't know if it was time for me to go back to WWE. I thought I should work another year of indies, really get grounded with my sobriety. Obviously I wanted to go back—I was just questioning whether I was ready. After all, I had only been truly sober for six months.

Those thoughts ran through my brain during the entire Japanese tour. I worked an eleven-day tournament, *Hyper Battle 2002*. I was part of Team 2000—with Koji Kanemoto, Jado, Gedo, and the new Black Tiger—going up against Team New Japan, which was Jushin Thunder Liger, El Samurai, Minoru Tanaka, Masayuki Naruse, and Masahiro Kakihara.

Being in Japan this time was so different from my previous experiences there. Japan was a place where I had done some of the most serious partying of my life. Now I was sober, spending my off time keeping to myself, reading my Bible.

For the most part, it was a successful tour for me. It allowed me to fine-tune everything that I had been working on in the indies—my wrestling skills, my overall conditioning. It helped add fuel to my fire. If I was going to go back to WWE, then I needed to be Black Tiger again.

Still, I wasn't really happy in Japan. My last few nights helped me make my decision about going back into WWE. To this day, I think that was the closest I have ever come to relapsing. Being so far away from home simply wasn't good for me. The walls started closing in and I began feeling terrible stress and anxiety. Thank God Black Cat was there. He helped me through it, talking to me and giving me a lot of positive energy.

When I came home, my decision was made. I weighed my worries about returning to WWE, and the good far outweighed the bad. I called Johnny Ace and we got things rolling. "Here's the deal," he said. "We're willing to wipe the slate clean and give you another chance."

He explained that they weren't offering me the same deal I'd had before. Instead they were going to offer the basic contract they'd give any new wrestler. That was fine by me. I had no trouble coming back and starting from scratch. I understood that I needed to prove myself.

There was one minor hitch. I still had a few indie bookings left on my plate. J.R. was great about that. "Don't worry about it," he said. "Be true to your word, finish your commitments, and then we'll get you back into the mix."

My last indie commitment before returning to WWE was with Ring of Honor, at the former ECW Arena in Philadelphia. It was a very special night, easily one of the best moments of my entire career.

The crowd was going wild from the second my match began—it was me and Amazing Red against the SATs. I swear, the ovation started during Red's introduction and never let up.

After the match, the entire ROH roster came out of the dressing room and clapped for me, wishing me their best. Even though Red and I had just gone over, the Maximo brothers took the mike to tell me how much they loved and respected me.

It was extremely moving. The fans were on their feet the whole time, cheering me with "Thank you, Eddie!" and "We'll miss you!" It was the exact opposite of the old ECW attitude of "You Sold Out!" They were actually happy for me, that I was going back to WWE.

I got on the stick and told everybody just how much the evening meant to me. "I will always have my brothers and sisters," I said, "but this is my other family, the wrestlers in the locker rooms and the fans."

It's so true that God works in mysterious ways. The ECW Arena in Philadelphia was where I started my run in the United States, and here I was, starting out all over again. Standing in the ring, feeling all the incredible love from the fans and my fellow wrestlers, I felt that God had truly answered my prayers. He was giving me a second chance.

CHAPTER 35

I had a lot of time to think in the months after I got fired, and looking back at my career, I realized that I had always given one hundred percent to every job I'd ever had—with one exception.

I was satisfied with my run in Mexico, not so much because of what I did there, but because I gave it everything I had at that time. When I left New Japan, I was content because I knew I had given my heart to what I did there. Leaving WCW was demoralizing for so many reasons, but I knew I had given the best I had to give while I was there.

The only exception to the rule was with WWE. I knew that as far as WWE was concerned, I had not given the job my full heart and soul. To be honest, I didn't have much heart to give. I was in survival mode from the day I got there. It was a struggle just doing whatever I could to get by. With everything that was going on in my personal life, there was no way I could fully give myself to my work.

Not that I didn't accomplish things—God had certainly blessed me in WWE. But the cold hard truth was that I was complacent for most of the time I was there. I was happy right where I was and it was okay if I didn't achieve more. That's a dangerous attitude.

So I prayed for the opportunity to go back to WWE and give my heart. I wouldn't make the same mistake I'd made before. This time I'd give it my all.

My first day back on the WWE roster was April 1, in Albany's Pepsi Arena. It was wild how much the business had changed in the year since I'd left. First WCW went under and was bought by WWE. Then Vince came up with the idea of the brand extension, of turning *Raw* and *SmackDown!* into two distinct products, each with their own roster and style. By the time I came back, *Raw* and *SmackDown!* were two completely separate shows and all the ex-WCW workers had been folded into the roster.

It was a strange day. I could feel everybody's eyes on me, watching my every move. People came over and said, "Good to see you back," but for the most part, I could feel a hesitation as far as talking to me. They must have sensed that I was in a quiet mood and responded in kind.

Of course, my immediate circle of friends—Chris and Dean—were glad to see me. Paul Heyman made a point of welcoming me back with open arms. He seemed genuinely happy that I was there. And as always, Vince was incredibly kind and gracious to me.

"Let's wipe the slate clean," he said, shaking my hand.

I was thrown into the storyline mix right away, making my surprise return by frog splashing Rob Van Dam after his Intercontinental Championship defense against Booker T.

I had never wrestled Rob before. All I knew was that he is a hell of a worker, one of the most gifted athletes ever to work in this business. That night, we had a talk after the show. "Trust me," I told him. "I'm going to put you over."

Rob and I started working together at house shows. We had a particularly great match one weekend in Denver. I knew everybody was watching to see if I could still go. Well, we went out there and just tore the house down. We were doing false finish after false finish, and the crowd was just eating it up.

Finally Rob hit me with a Five Star frog splash and went for the cover. The ref started counting, "One! Two!"—*and I kicked out!* We'd done so many false finishes, I guess I was just caught up in the heat of the moment.

When I realized what I'd done, I grabbed Rob and pulled him back down on top of me. "Sorry about that," I said, as the ref counted to three.

There was clearly some chemistry there, but it took us a little while to find our groove. I needed to gain Rob's confidence, and once that happened I felt comfortable going out and working my psychology. From that point on, we were unstoppable. When the chemistry between two wrestlers is right, there's nothing better.

I got right back into the swing of things. I won the Intercontinental Championship from Rob just three weeks after my return. It was the office's way of sending me a message: *We believe in you.*

On May 27, we went up to Chris Benoit's hometown, Edmonton, Alberta, Canada, to do *Raw.* I was just chilling out backstage, wondering what I was going to do that night. When the agents put up the sheet—listing the lineup for the show—I saw that Rob and I were going to be the main event. My eyes lit up, but then I noticed that next to our names, it said "Ladder match."

"Oh, great," I said. "Thanks for telling me in advance, guys."

I immediately flashed back to my Ladder match in WCW with X-Pac. It wasn't the shits, but it sure wasn't a classic. The problem was that we had no idea what we were doing out there. I promised myself that this time, I'd be more prepared.

Of course, Rob and I were both kept busy all day and never really got a chance to sit down and work out what we were going to do out there. Before I knew it, it was showtime. I got worried and spoke to Benoit. "Chris, what do I do? I'm not really comfortable doing this match."

"Just be Black Tiger," he said. "Just do what you do best and you'll be fine."

All of a sudden, I heard my music and that was that. I didn't have time to think about it anymore. As I was going through gorilla, people were barking stuff at me—"Don't forget the finish! You've got twenty minutes!"—but I could barely hear them.

I walked through the curtain, thinking, *Just go balls-out and whatever happens, happens.* As nervous as I was, I knew this was a big opportunity. I was determined to show that when called upon to main-event, I could deliver.

Rob and I started out slow, using old-school psychology and really letting it build. Too often, a Ladder match is just a bunch of crazy high spots with the ladder. The psychology of a Ladder match should be exactly the same as any other match. You have to take your time and make the crowd want to see it escalate. The more you build, the more you make them want to see you go up the ladder, the better it is. Every step should mean something.

We made a point of wearing each other down before bringing the ladder into the mix. For example, I wrapped Rob's leg around the ring post, then smashed his knee with a chair, the psychology being that if I damaged his leg, it'd be harder for him to climb the ladder.

That night, I learned the secret to a good Ladder match. You have to be willing to put your body on the line. You've got to give yourself completely, and you have to do it with a clear head. If you hesitate, you're going to get hurt. The only way to go is balls-out.

There is no way to make a ladder not hurt. How can you? It's fourteen feet of steel. All you can do is take it. You protect yourself as best you can—putting your hand up or tucking your shoulder in—but the bottom line is that you're still taking the blow.

Before the match, Pat Patterson had reminded me, "Don't stop during the commercial break. Just keep going." As the match progressed, everybody's advice was running through my head. I did what everybody had told me. I just kept going.

Even when things went wrong out there, I didn't stop. The ladder broke twice. Referee Earl Hebner kept telling me different times, so I thought we were in break when we weren't. I busted my inner lip in the middle of the match when Rob laid the ladder on top of me, then did one of his patented split-legged moonsaults onto me. One of the steps hit me right in the mouth—boom! I thought I lost my teeth!

The worst thing to go wrong was when some fan decided to hop over the barricade and interfere in the match. I've got no explanation for why he did it other than he must've been crazy. Though that kind of thing has happened to me so many times, this time it was different—if I hadn't seen him coming, there's a good chance he could've broken my neck.

I was starting to climb the ladder when I saw this guy coming at me out of the corner of my eye. He was wearing a jersey like the kind Crash Holly—

God rest his soul—used to wear. I honestly had no idea what was going on. My first thought was, *What the hell is Crash doing running in on this match? Did the office send him?*

Thank God I spotted him, because I was able to leap off the ladder just as he flung himself into it. I landed on my feet and realized that it wasn't Crash, it wasn't one of the boys, it was some idiot fan!

Okay, it's on, I thought, and got ready to deck the guy. Fortunately Earl Hebner ran over and grabbed him. I quickly pulled my punch, so as not to hit Earl. The guy was lucky, because if that punch had connected, I would've hurt him.

Before I knew it, security had hustled the guy out of there and I went back to the business at hand. My mind was so focused on the match, I didn't have time to stop and think about what had happened. Even with an interruption like that, I just kept going.

My favorite thing about a Ladder match is that it allows me to express myself in new ways, to use my imagination to try moves that no one has ever tried before. The more things went wrong, the more Rob and I were able to improvise.

For example, nobody had ever attempted a shootover sunset powerbomb from a ladder. It had been done off the ropes, but never from the top of a ladder. I called it to Rob in the ring. God bless him, he's crazy. "Come on," he said, "let's do it."

Things just kept popping into my head. I laid Rob down under the ladder, then did a rolling senton off the top. That move was definitely a one-time deal—there was just no way for me to protect him, and as light as I am, the law of gravity meant that my weight just about killed poor Rob!

For the finish, Rob put the ladder into the corner and climbed up for a Five Star frog splash. Unfortunately, one of the hinges was broken and it went out from under him. I covered by going up to the top rope for a frog splash of my own. Rob nailed me with an overhead kick, sending me out to the mats, giving him a chance to climb the ladder and pull down the Intercontinental belt.

After the match ended, Stone Cold Steve Austin ran down and stomped a mudhole into me, followed by a big brawl between Steve, Benoit, Ric Flair,

THE EDDIE GUERRERO STORY

Arn Anderson, and myself. Through it all, I was plagued with disappointment about the match. I couldn't understand why the fans were cheering so loudly. I just figured they were happy Rob won the belt back.

When I got to the back, everyone was clapping. Stephanie McMahon came over and gave me a hug. "That's the Eddie we know and love," she said.

C'mon, I thought. *It wasn't that great.*

I had to watch that match over and over again before I agreed that it was actually pretty damn exciting. But on that night, I hadn't yet reached a place where I could believe anything good about myself. I couldn't accept that anything I did was worthy of people's compliments.

Later that week, I spoke to my sponsor, Bob, and my grandsponsor, Bill. "All this good stuff is happening too quickly," I said. "I don't get it."

"Well, Eddie," Bill drawled in his thick Florida accent, "if you don't want to be on top of the ladder, that's fine. God will put somebody else there."

I thought about that for a few minutes. "No," I said finally. "I want to be there. I definitely want to be there."

CHAPTER 36

When I first came out of rehab, my therapist told me not to get my hopes up for getting Vickie back. "I know you have it in your mind that you're going to go home and make things better," he said. "I just want you to know that it's probably not going to happen."

Sure enough, it played out just like he said. I begged Vickie for another chance, but she wasn't interested. "I don't love you anymore," she told me. "We're done."

I couldn't accept it. "That's not true," I said. "You still love me. I know you do."

"No, Eddie. I don't."

I heard the words, but I refused to believe them. I wanted Vickie back so badly that it hurt. For the life of me, I couldn't understand why she'd stopped loving me—I never stopped loving her.

ME AND VICKIE.

My beautiful daughters, Shaul, Sherilyn, and Kaylie.

I tried to forget Vickie, I truly did. I asked God to relieve me of the pain I was feeling. "If Vickie is not supposed to be in my life," I prayed, "then please, God, take this burden away from me."

But God never relinquished. He never let my love for Vickie go away. I know now that it was for a reason. God had a plan for us.

Over time I came to understand that if I truly loved Vickie, I had to be willing to let her go. I had to want what was best for her, even if it broke my heart. I had to accept whatever she needed to do to be happy, even if that meant that we couldn't be together, even if it meant her being with another man.

I had to be willing to lose her.

Once I accepted that fact, I was able to start moving on with my life. I distracted myself as best I could by spending a lot of time at the gym and attending regular AA meetings.

Vickie and I basically stopped speaking altogether. When we did talk, it just ended up in an argument. It got to the point where we literally couldn't face each other. All discussion had to be done through our lawyers.

CHEATING DEATH, STEALING LIFE

Though our divorce hadn't been made official, Vickie and I both jumped the gun and started seeing other people. I'd begun dating a woman I'd met in the program, Tara. She was so great for me at that time. There were some rough patches that I couldn't have gotten through without her.

Tara and I moved in together while I was working in the indies, and not long afterward, she told me that she was pregnant. At first, I didn't know how to feel about it. I was filled with joy, of course, because children are a blessing. But I wasn't sure I was ready to start a new family. After all, I was only recently sober. I was getting used to my new career as an independent wrestler. And I wasn't even divorced from Vickie.

Tara and I ended up separating long before our child was born. Our split was completely mutual—it simply wasn't working between us. While our relationship wasn't successful, Tara and I did do one wonderful thing together—our daughter, Kaylie Marie. She's so beautiful. I consider her a genuine blessing in my life.

Since then Tara and I have put our personal issues aside and devoted ourselves to the thing we have in common—the love of Kaylie.

One of the promises I made to myself at rehab was that when I finally got sober, I was going to get closer to my girls. That was a major priority for me. I didn't want Shaul and Sherilyn to be scared of me anymore. I love them so much and hated the idea that their love for me was being overwhelmed by fear.

Even with all the bickering and all the fighting, Vickie never used the kids as a wedge between us. Whatever our difficulties were, she never denied me my rights as a dad. She was always open to my seeing the girls. She was completely understanding about my schedule and the fact that I was working so hard to get my life together.

Before Vickie and I separated, I had never really spent much time alone with my daughters. Vickie was always there. Learning how to be with them was really rough at first. I discovered that I didn't have a clue how to take care of them. I was constantly calling Vickie, asking, "What do I do?"

But as time went on, I learned to be a good dad, how to mind them and

make sure they were happy and safe. I also became their friend. I would take them to the playground. We'd run around, play tag, play hide-and-seek, and it would get my mind away from my troubles. It was awesome. I hadn't realized how shallow our relationship used to be before I got sober, but I quickly learned what amazing people Shaul and Sherilyn are. I started to appreciate them as more than just my kids.

Spending that time together, just the three of us, created a really tight bond that continues to this day.

Little by little, Vickie and I started communicating again. Our relationship was complicated—some days it was smooth, other times it was pretty rocky.

She told me later that she'd been keeping tabs on me via the Internet. At first, she was just going online to see whether or not I was working, but she confessed to me that she really just wanted to see what I was up to. Vickie might not have loved me anymore, but that didn't mean she had stopped caring about me.

Vickie and I began having wonderful phone conversations. Pretty soon, she asked me out to lunch. Slowly but surely, we became friends again.

"No matter what happens," I said, "let's be truthful with each other."

Vickie and I were brutally frank with each other, and believe me, it was no picnic. We laid out all our dirty laundry, all our garbage. We told each other the truth, and the truth hurt. A lot.

But being honest with each other was the only way we could heal.

Though we had revealed certain hard facts to each other, we discovered that we were still willing to love each other. Despite all the bad stuff that had gone on between us, we wanted to be together.

It didn't happen overnight. At first I had a hard time trusting Vickie when she told me she still had feelings for me. She'd been telling me the complete opposite for so long.

Wait a minute, I thought. *She's been telling me for almost two years that she wanted nothing to do with me, that she didn't love me, and now she's changed her mind?*

I had just gotten used to the idea of Vickie not loving me. I didn't like it, but I accepted it. Just thinking about getting back with her was a huge risk. I had gotten comfortable being alone. I was okay being a bachelor. Then all of a sudden, she was asking me not to believe it. I didn't know what the hell to think anymore!

What I didn't understand was that Vickie had fallen in love with a different me.

Lunches turned into dinners and before long, my wife and I were dating again. We always kept it open, so if things didn't work out, there wouldn't be any new hang-ups. We tried to be very mature about it all.

It was actually very romantic. I took Vickie on real dates, like we were a couple of teenagers. I remember how one night we went to the movies—*Mr. Deeds,* with Adam Sandler. We were holding hands, laughing at the movie, and I turned and looked at her profile. Even though it was dark, her face was full of light, smiling and laughing. *Wow,* I thought. *I love this woman. Thank you, God.*

One evening after we had been dating for a month or two, Vickie said, "You don't have to go home tonight."

"No," I replied. "I do. I don't want to give the kids the wrong message. We don't know what's going to be with us yet."

Vickie respected me. She knew I was going through all these anxieties.

"Anything you need," she told me. "We'll just take our time. Tonight, why don't you sleep on the couch?"

That seemed like a good compromise. That night I went to the girls' room and saw both my kids sleeping in their beds. I started crying so hard, it was something I'd missed so much. Sure, the girls would come stay with me, but that wasn't their home. Their home was with Vickie.

"Thank you, God," I prayed, "for letting me see them asleep in their own beds again. Thank you for letting me be here."

God really guided us, as far as making the kids comfortable with the idea of me and Vickie getting back together. We broke it to them slowly. When we first started seeing each other, we told them not to get the wrong idea. On one hand, they really wanted to see their mommy and daddy together, and on the other, they were scared it would go down like it had in the past. "I love you both," Shaul said, "and I like seeing you guys together. I just don't want to see you fighting like you used to."

We promised that if it didn't work out, we would do everything in our power to keep it civil. Shaul and Sherilyn were just little girls, but they'd already seen so much ugliness and sorrow. I didn't want to hurt them again.

Over the next six months or so, Vickie and I began to take the idea of our relationship seriously.

Once we got out all the bad feelings, all the hurt and anger and misgivings, we were able to start taking stock of what was good about us. We remembered how much pleasure we took in each other. Having a powerful physical connection definitely helped the healing. There was so much passion there. No matter what else had gone down, there was still a spark between us. The fire was still hot.

Vickie had also gone above and beyond in her efforts to understand my sobriety. She began going to AA meetings, where she learned all about my disease. She realized that I was afflicted with the illness of addiction, that the horrible things I'd done over the years weren't in any way personal. Just as important was that Vickie came to understand her own role in my sickness. She learned how she'd enabled me and that she had to change her behavior as well.

In a way, Vickie had gotten sick just from being around me. Addiction is like a cold—if you hang around with somebody that has it, you're going to get sick too. She didn't have the disease of addiction, but she was codependent and had to heal from that.

Having Vickie's support made such a big difference to my life. Some of my other family members didn't fully understand my disease. They didn't believe it was real. Their attitude was, if you drink too much, then stop drinking. But Vickie was totally behind me. "Do whatever you've got to do to stay sober," she'd say. "I'm here for you."

Meanwhile, our divorce was still being processed. Luckily, these things don't happen quickly. Vickie got a call saying that the papers had been drawn up and all they needed was our signatures for it to be a done deal.

She called and told me, asking, "What do I do?"

"That's up to you," I said. "If you want to sign them, then that's what we'll do."

The divorce was Vickie's choice, not mine. She had to be the one that called it off. She decided to call her lawyer and say, "We're not going to do it."

Our family was mending.

Vickie and I first started seeing each other just after I had signed another half a year's lease on my apartment. That was a blessing because it allowed us time to figure out what we wanted to do. There was no rush to decide whether or not to live together again.

But after eight months, we truly felt ready to be together again, to be married. We sat the girls down and explained that we were going to get back together. They didn't know how to react, but I could see from the looks on

My wonderful family, together again after Vickie and I renewed our vows.

their faces that they were scared. They had seen us go through so much, I couldn't blame them for being a little frightened.

The four of us moved into a bright and cheery new apartment in the same complex where Vickie and the kids were already living. Before we moved in, we blessed the apartment—we prayed over the house, anointed it with oil in Jesus' name. It felt like a fresh start.

CHEATING DEATH, STEALING LIFE

I was so full of joy about my family reuniting. I wanted to do something special to celebrate our second chance, so I spoke to Pastor Phair. He suggested that Vickie and I renew our vows. He also thought that we should confess to each other, make a public apology as a way of putting our past behind us.

Renewing our vows meant so much to me. In a way, it meant more to me than my actual marriage. It was for real this time. Not that it wasn't real before, it was just that we had grown up so much since then. We were one hundred times closer than we were when we first got married.

When we told the girls that we were planning to renew our wedding vows, they were so happy. They were literally glowing. I could tell that they weren't scared anymore.

We decided to do it on the beach at Sand Key, up near Clearwater. It was an intimate little gathering, just me and Vickie, Shaul and Sherilyn, Pastor Phair, and a few special people, including my brother Hector and my sponsor, Bob.

It was a truly beautiful day. I apologized for all the pain that I'd caused Vickie over the years. She, in turn, confessed that she was sorry for all the things that she'd said and done to hurt me. It meant so much to me, that Vickie was willing to admit that in front of other people.

Then we renewed our wedding vows. I want to renew our vows over and over again, every couple of years. It's a great way of reinforcing the reasons why we're married. Just because we said our vows once doesn't mean they don't bear repeating.

It's also very romantic. One of the many things I've learned over the past few years is that marriage does not mean the death of romance. If anything, it is the exact opposite. Marriage means life. Two lives become one, connected. Vickie and I see to it that we romance each other now. I take great pleasure in giving her my love and affection, wherever and whenever.

My kids are always rolling their eyes because I'm so publicly affectionate with my wife. They see Mommy and Daddy kissing and holding hands and they go, "Oh, Dad!"

But inside, I know they love it.

VICKIE BACKSTAGE AT
MADISON SQUARE GARDEN.

I am crazy in love with my wife. I just look at her and it makes me smile.

I believe in my heart that God wanted us to have another chance. That's why our divorce didn't pan out. People get divorced overnight, but that didn't happen for us. Our divorce took forever.

God worked it out so that we're back together. But it's not in any way, shape, or form the same relationship. We're both completely different people. When we renewed our vows, I married a different Vickie and she married a different Eddie. We're closer now than we ever were before.

I've never loved a woman like I do Vickie. She's the sexiest woman in the world to me. Her eyes, her smile, her body. Her walk, her giggle, her smile. Her touch, her smell. The way she plays with me, the way she consoles me, the way she loves me.

It takes a very strong woman to live the wrestling life. Sometimes I think that Vickie's got a harder job than I do. She takes care of me, she takes care of the girls, she runs the household. She goes above and beyond to make sure that I'm able to do my job, from packing my things to organizing my travel arrangements. For all intents and purposes, she's my road manager as well as my wife and best friend. She makes every day so much easier.

I'm so blessed to have Vickie in my life. I truly believe that my relationship with her is a gift from God. When you love somebody so deeply, so passionately, so unconditionally, it has to come from God.

CHEATING DEATH, STEALING LIFE

CHAPTER 37

I'd been back in WWE for just a few months, but Stone Cold Steve Austin—the star of the show, the top guy—decided that he wanted to work with me.

Steve had been supportive from the moment I came back to WWE. He liked my attitude, the aggressiveness I had in the ring. "That's what I need," he told me.

I felt so honored that Steve thought so highly of me. I was blown away to have the opportunity to work with somebody of his stature.

Vince came to me and told me that Steve and I were going to start our program by filming a vignette in a bar. "Are you all right with that?"

I wasn't totally sure how I felt about going into a bar, but I wasn't going to blow the chance to work with Steve. "Sure, Vince," I said. "No problem at all."

I went in there with my walls up. I hadn't been in a bar since I got sober. When the time came to shoot my scene, I was given a fake beer bottle. "No, no," Vince said. "Put a real beer in his hand."

Vince looked me straight in the eye. "That's not a problem, is it?"

"No problem, Vince." I could smell the beer as I held the Rolling Rock bottle in my hand. I wasn't tempted to drink it, but it set my nerves on edge just the same. I was more scared than anything else. It was like holding fire in my hand.

Of course, when it came time for me to smash the bottle over Steve's head, we exchanged the Rolling Rock for a fake bottle. Even though it was sugar glass, it still cut Steve up.

After the vignette aired, my therapist called and he was livid. "That was a mean thing to do," he said. "How could you let them do that to you?"

I know that's what most people would think. But I was in the real world. Vince was getting ready to give me the opportunity to headline the show with Stone Cold Steve Austin. He couldn't put me in a spot like that and then have me relapse. He needed to know where I was at.

I didn't see it as unfair, I saw it as a test. And as my employer, Vince had every right to do it. In fact, if I had been in his shoes, I would've done the exact same thing. When you're the main event, when you're headlining, it's not only you and whoever you're working with that's on the line. It's the whole company.

What if I wasn't ready? What if I was given this opportunity, then went out and got drunk and didn't show up? Then the question would've been why was I put in that spot in the first place. So I didn't blame Vince at all. I was just thankful to be there.

Unfortunately, Steve was going through some tough personal times and decided to leave WWE before we could truly get our program under way. I did get to work a few house shows with him, which was a great thrill for me. It was so exciting being in the ring with a wrestler of his caliber.

WWE's road agents saw our house show matches, and the reports got back to Vince of how good they were. No matter what else happened, those two weeks with Steve gave me a chance to prove myself. It was like a test for things to come.

I admit, I was a little disappointed when Steve left. I felt we'd missed a great opportunity. Our feud could've been something special. I called him not long after he left WWE, just to express my gratitude for considering me. "Thank you for letting me be a part of your life like that," I said. "If there's ever anything that I can do for you, I'll be there."

I'll always be indebted to Steve. In a way, it was his wanting to work with me that opened the door for Vince to look at me as a potential main eventer. He might never have thought of me in that light if it wasn't for Steve.

With Steve gone, I was left without a program. I ended up challenging Ric Flair to a match at *King of the Ring*.

I admire Ric so much. He's been one of my heroes for as long as I can remember. In many ways, I've tried to model my career after his, my own wrestling psychology. To work with one of your idols is a great honor.

Even at his age, Ric is an amazing athlete. He can still go. He's just tremendous. In all the years I've been watching him work, I've never seen Ric weak in his game. He has always been strong.

If God blesses me to go as long as he has, I'd love to still be wrestling when I'm Ric's age. But there is only one Ric Flair. It would be very arrogant to even think of myself in that light. If I have the blessing of God to make it that long, I still won't be in Ric's league.

I was determined to have a tremendous match with Ric at the Pay-Per-View. I wanted us to go out there and tear down the house.

But when the time came, I blew it. I was too tense to give him a great match. Even though we'd worked together a number of times, I was still eager to prove myself to him. That happens to everybody that steps into the ring with Ric. We all want to impress him, to get him to say, "What a great worker, what a talent." Everybody wants to hear Ric say that about them, because there's no higher compliment.

I wish I could've relaxed and just been myself. I tried too hard and it wasn't a particularly good match. I should have gone out there and worked the style I'm good at instead of trying to do things to impress him. I should've just gone out there and been Eddie.

If God ever gives me the opportunity to wrestle Ric again, I'll make sure I do it right. I'll just go out there and let him lead. I'll let him be Ric Flair.

Vince must've thought I was doing well because I kept getting to work with WWE's biggest stars.

On July 22, I was given a shot at The Rock's Undisputed Title. The match was made after I interrupted The Rock's interview with a promo of my own.

"I got two little girls, *ese,* and they worship the ground that their father walks on," I said, in full Latino Heat swagger. "They idolize me, man. The other night when I walked in their room to say good night, for them to show their father the respect that he deserves, I saw something very disturbing. I looked at their wall and not only did they have a picture of me, but right next to that picture was a poster of *El Rey de Scorpion, ese.* The Rock. Mr. Big Shot, the movie star man. You know what, man? In my heart, I knew I had to teach my little girls a lesson. I got your poster and I ripped it up and I burned it! They ran after me, going 'Daddy? *Por qué? Por qué?* Why did you rip that poster?' Shut up! Don't disrespect me!"

Rocky cut me off, mocking me in his own inimitable way, comparing me to Cheech and Chong. Well, that just got me hotter!

"You're jealous of me, man," I said. "You know and all these *gavachos* know that I'm the better wrestler, homes. I'm more good-looking. The People's Champion? *Orale, ese,* let me tell you something. I got the hottest haircut going on in America today. Nobody can wear the mullet like I do. I mean, come on, this should be called the People's Mullet!"

"Well, let The Rock say this," he replied. "With a haircut like that and a face like that, it looks like Billy Ray Cyrus went ahead and had sex with a retarded hyena!"

He proceeded to sing "La Bamba," with the words changed to make more fun of me. That was it—I challenged him to a match that very night, which of course I lost.

It was a great pleasure working with The Rock. The two of us hadn't hit it off at first. It was entirely my fault—I gave him a bad impression of me the very first time we worked together.

I was supposed to be involved in the finish of a match Rock was having with Chris Benoit. I must have misunderstood my cue, because Chris had to hold on to Rock for a few seconds longer than was planned. Rock got a bad taste in his mouth for me after that. He used to rib me about missing my cues in the dressing room. I took it with a smile, because I really liked and admired him.

When I finally got the chance to wrestle The Rock myself, I was definitely out to prove myself. I must have earned his respect that night, because after that, he was incredibly gracious and friendly.

Some time later, Rock told me how glad he was to see how far I'd come.

"I'm proud of you, Eddie," he said. "Two years ago, I never would have thought you'd be here."

That made me feel so good, knowing that I had The Rock's respect. For him to tell me that he was proud of me meant a lot.

The Rock has given so much to this business. The things that he has accomplished—like crossing over into a mainstream movie star—have elevated wrestling in people's minds. The fact that he remains so nice and so humble makes him even more special.

If anybody has the right to a big head, it's The Rock. Ego is a monster, and anybody can fall victim to it. Everybody does, in one way or another, but life has a way of humbling us. *God* has a way of humbling us. What goes up must come down. It's what you do when you're humbled that counts—how you deal with it, how you use those lessons to better yourself as a person.

The best way to describe The Rock is to say that he is the consummate professional, by which I mean someone who does what's best for the business, while still doing what's right for him and the wrestler he's working with. In our match together, The Rock took care of everybody—the company, himself—and he took care of me. He made sure I looked as good as he did. That's a pro. There's a reason he was the star of the show. The Rock got everybody over.

There's only a handful of wrestlers that I believe consistently reach that high level of professionalism—The Rock, Ric Flair, Stone Cold, Triple H, Undertaker. There's a reason that those five guys reached the top of the business and were able to stay there for so long.

These guys, that's what I aspire to. That level of professionalism. I try to live up to those standards every day. I try to do everything I can to put over the show, my opponent, and myself.

I consider myself very lucky to have forged good personal relationships with all of those guys, especially Undertaker. He has been an enormous source of encouragement to me in recent times. Not only does he have my respect and admiration as a worker, he's become like a big brother to me. I'm able to open up to him as a person. We've developed a nice intimate friendship.

'Taker is always supportive, reminding me that I've earned my spot in this business. "Don't doubt yourself," he's said to me. "You're here because you deserve to be here."

For me, that's as good as it gets. When Undertaker compliments you in that way, you know you must be doing something right.

CHAPTER 38

Chris Benoit called me on my cell phone. "Guess what?"

"Okay," I said. "What?"

"We're going to *SmackDown!*"

To be honest, it didn't make a difference to me. WWE had split into two separate brands while I was working the indies. When I came back, I was placed on the *Raw* roster. It just made good sense to put me wherever Rob Van Dam was working. There was an instant rivalry between us, based on the fact that we both used a frog splash as our finishing move.

I had no problem moving over to the other brand. Chris and I were traveling together at that time, so as long as we were both going, being on one roster instead of the other wouldn't have all that much of an impact on my life.

The storyline was that *SmackDown!* General Manager Stephanie McMahon was competing against *Raw* GM Eric Bischoff. Considering our long history together, it made perfect sense for me and Chris to want to screw over Bischoff.

As it turned out, *SmackDown!* was in fact very different from *Raw*. Right away I could feel a subtle difference in the overall atmosphere. Because it's not broadcast live, there seemed to be a little less pressure. The whole vibe was a bit more kicked back. Not that the production or professionalism was decreased—there simply wasn't the stress of going out live.

SmackDown! is just as exciting as *Raw,* with its own distinct, different energy. That's exactly what WWE was trying to accomplish—two different shows. It's not just about having separate rosters. Each show has to have its own unique style.

Another thing that was great about my coming to *SmackDown!* was that Chavito and Rey Mysterio were working there. We hadn't worked together since WCW. Chavo had joined WWE when Vince purchased WCW during my year away from the company. Rey came aboard a year or so later and went directly to *SmackDown!*

Being on a roster with Chris, Rey, and Chavito, guys that are my true family, made life a lot easier for me. I was still struggling with my sobriety, and it was very helpful for me to be with people that I knew would always have my back.

There was a tremendous group of workers at *SmackDown!*—Chris, Rey, Edge, Chavito, and Kurt Angle, among others. It didn't matter what the combination was—Singles matches, Tag matches, Triple-Threats—each week saw at least one four-star match.

It was a very satisfying time for me. I was working hard and having a great time. I was producing without having to pull teeth and argue with people that didn't know what the hell they were talking about.

That makes a huge difference in my overall state of mind, the knowledge that when I walk back through the curtain, I've delivered. I thrive on that feeling. I need to know that I've had a great match, that I've done my job.

My first major feud on *SmackDown!* was with Edge. The two of us had never worked together before, and when our program was first booked, Edge's defenses went up. He didn't believe I was there to work for the match. He was worried that I was only looking out for myself. I don't blame him—he'd been around this business long enough to justify being cautious.

But once Edge realized that my only concern was putting the program over, his walls came down and we developed a nice friendship. As we got to know each other, I was happy to discover that Edge is a tremendous human being. I already knew he was an incredible worker—he's also a very warm, genuine guy.

Edge and I had some tremendous matches. The most memorable was on September 26 in San Diego, a wild No DQ match on *SmackDown!* It was among the most brutal matches of my career—and I've got the scars to prove it.

At the end, Edge hit me with the Edgecution off the ladder to score the pinfall. He left me lying in the ring, and when I picked myself up the fans gave me a standing O. It was a great feeling because they were cheering me despite the fact that I was the heel. I was flipping them off and they still applauded me!

When I got to the back, Shane McMahon shook my hand and hugged me. That meant a lot to me. It let me know that my putting my ass on the line out there was appreciated.

FEELING THE LOVE OF THE CROWD.

CHAPTER 39

Not long after I'd arrived at *SmackDown!* I teamed up with Chavito against Rey & Edge. The office liked the chemistry we had and began putting us together more and more. Before long, Los Guerreros were a full-fledged tag team.

I was thrilled to team with Chavito. It was something that we'd always wanted to do. We used to play tag team in my father's ring. All of a sudden we were living out our childhood dream.

The reason Los Guerreros worked so well is that Chavito and I have a natural chemistry. Our whole family has it. Any time two Guerreros team up, the results are phenomenal. Chavo & Hector, Hector & Mando, Chavo & Mando, me & Chavito, all the combinations have been great. It comes from having the same schooling, from sharing the same basic psychology. Put us together and it just flows.

Too often, tag teams are two guys thrown together because the creative team can't

291

find anything else for them to do. That rarely works, because there's no way to fake chemistry. You either have it or you don't. It's a gift.

In no time at all, Chavito and I hit that magical place where we each knew what the other was thinking. All we'd have to do is look at each other and we'd know what the other one wanted. Sometimes I'd turn around and Chavo would already be doing what I was about to ask him to do. Neither of us ever had to wonder if the other one had his back. I always knew Chavo would be there.

It was awesome. It made me feel so good inside, like I was out in my dad's backyard again, playing tag team with my nephew.

My Latino Heat character had been growing in popularity for some time, but it wasn't until Los Guerreros that people actually started *liking* me.

It wasn't supposed to be that way. We cheated every way we could, and it ended up charming the fans. We tricked and conned everybody, always coming up with new ways to fool the refs. Instead of hating us for it, the fans ate it up. They looked forward to seeing us lie, cheat, and steal our way to victory.

In the beginning, the cheers confused the shit out of me. We were supposed to be heels! I would get to the back and say to Chavito, "What the hell are we doing wrong out there? What do we have to do to get them to boo us?"

Then I remembered something my dad used to say. "Son," he'd tell me, "it doesn't matter if it's good news or bad news, as long as they spell your name right."

I never understood that until Chavito and I started getting over. I realized that he was telling me not to worry whether they were cheering or booing, as long as they were reacting. It's when the fans stop cheering or booing that you've got a problem.

One thing you can never do is force-feed the people. You can try to relay the story you want to tell, but in the end, it's the fans who decide. If they want you to be a babyface, then believe me, you'll end up a baby-face.

Even though Los Guerreros did all kinds of heel things in order to be the bad guys, we did it in such a fun and entertaining way that the people liked it. They enjoyed the fact that we weren't hiding it from them, that we were doing our lying, cheating, and stealing right there in the open. Obviously we were hiding it from our opponents, but by making the fans a part of it, they turned us into babyfaces.

If I'd done the things I do—like hitting my opponent with a title belt, then faking out the ref like I was the one that got clocked—back in the eighties, I'd have been booed as the biggest heel ever to hit the ring. But nowadays people go for a character that walks the line between babyface and heel, like Stone Cold Steve Austin. The crowd goes off their rocker every time they see me getting ready to lie or cheat or steal.

To Latino Heat, it's all just part of the game. Lying, cheating, and stealing is just the way things are. The only time it's wrong to do those things is when you get caught. If you don't get caught, you win.

That's been the psychology all along—cheat to win.

Los Guerreros went on to become one of the most popular WWE tag teams in years. People loved the hilarious vignettes we did, which were like little three-minute Cheech and Chong movies, only without all the weed. Each one was based on the idea of us lying, cheating, and stealing—we talked our way into a rich lady's house and threw a pool party, we hustled a couple of racist Anglos at golf, things like that.

I'm very proud of the work Chavito and I did in those vignettes. It demonstrated that we had talents that went far beyond what we did in the ring. But perhaps the most satisfying thing about the success of Los Guerreros and Latino Heat was that I was able to really celebrate my Chicano roots.

293

There's never been a Chicano wrestler that has gotten the exposure that I have. Certainly, a lot of Chicanos and Chicanas have had a tremendous impact on our culture over the last ten years—George Lopez, Edward James Olmos, Paul Rodriguez, Cheech Marin, Selena, to name just a few. These are people that I look up to, people that came from the Chicano community and became larger than life without turning their backs on who they really are.

They say that the key to any great wrestling character is finding something that's within you and then exaggerating it. Latino Heat is a huge part of who I am. It's my Chicano heritage, taken to the extreme.

Obviously Latino Heat is a bit of a cartoon, but that doesn't make it a negative stereotype. Far from it! I don't think I would have been blessed with the love and support of the Chicano community if they truly felt Latino Heat was a bad representation of my people.

A lot of the Latino Heat character comes from how I use the Chicano slang—words like *ese* or *orale!* Some refer to it as "Spanglish," but I prefer to call it *Chicanics.* It's exaggerated, to be sure, but it's actually pretty true to life.

A writer in one of the wrestling magazines made the most moronic comment I've ever heard. He wrote that I have "the fakest Mexican accent ever." That's just so idiotic! How can I have a fake Mexican accent? I'm Mexican! But it's a perfect example of how Anglo culture doesn't get Chicanos. Ask any Mexican-American and they'll tell you that they know people that speak exactly the same way as Latino Heat.

In fact, it's exactly the way I talk on the streets, when I'm among my own people. I might not speak that way around everybody, but when I'm around my buddies, that's exactly how I talk. When I'm with Tury and Hector, it's nothing but *"Ese* this" and *"Ese* that." We're very proper when we're doing business or around other non-Chicano people, but when we're among ourselves, that is our lingo.

I've also heard from people who complain that lying, cheating, and stealing reinforce negative stereotypes of Chicano people, but name one politician that hasn't done that. Forget that—try and name any *person* that's never lied or cheated or stolen. Shame on anyone who thinks those are Chicano characteristics. Those things aren't exclusive to Mexican-Americans, they're something we all do at one point or another. Latino Heat is just being honest about it.

Besides, it's not like I live my life that way. As true to life as it might be, Latino Heat is still, after all, a freakin' character on TV!

VICKIE IS MY TRUE TAG TEAM PARTNER!

CHAPTER 40

I had so many reasons to succeed in my sobriety. It had never occurred to me before, but I had a lot to live for.

My whole life changed after I got sober. Everything was different from the way it was before. My world became smaller and more focused. I found that I honestly didn't have any interest in being with anybody other than Vickie and the girls. My time is so limited. Any time that I'm not working is for my family. I wasted ten years' worth of time. Now the time I have is for my kids, for my wife.

The fact that I became quieter and more introspective freaked a lot of people out. Everyone knew me as a happy-go-lucky guy, always laughing and having fun. I'm a much more serious person now. People see me keeping to myself and they don't understand that I'm actually happier than I was before. I'm at peace with myself. I don't have to be yelling from a mountaintop to show the world that I'm joyful.

There are people who mistake my focus for arrogance, like I look down my nose at people who can drink. They assume that I think I'm better than them, which is totally untrue. I just know what works for me, what I personally can and can't do. I don't look down on anybody.

What people don't seem to get is that I've grown up so much in

SHERILYN WITH MY SISTER LINDA AND SHAUL.

the last few years. I behaved like a child for most of my life, but I'm not that person anymore. I'm a responsible adult.

Being an alcoholic gives you an excuse to act like a teenager long after you're supposed to have grown up. You stop growing emotionally. So it's kind of like I've gone from sixteen to thirty-seven, just in the last few years. That doesn't mean I can't still act like a big kid—now I just do it without a drink in my hand.

Some members of my family had the most difficulty accepting the changes I've made in my life. They all wanted me to get sober, but then when I did, they couldn't relate to me anymore. I guess it just takes time for

CHEATING DEATH, STEALING LIFE

HECTOR AND MARIA, CHRISTMAS 2003.

people to get adjusted to the idea that you're not the same person you used to be.

I know my family are happy for me, but at the same time, they don't know how to deal with the new me. They want to protect me and respect me, but at the same time, I don't think they know how to behave around me. All I ask is that they understand my boundaries and accept where they fit into my life.

My sister Linda had an especially hard time understanding the changes I've made. There was a point where we simply couldn't talk to each other. We had a big knock-down, drag-out fight over the phone. "You don't call me anymore," she said. "I feel like I don't know you anymore."

THE EDDIE GUERRERO STORY

ME AND CHAVITO AFTER *WRESTLEMANIA XX*.

It was like she took my sobriety very personally. We made peace once I helped her understand my new life, that I needed to close the walls around myself and devote my time to Vickie and the kids. Now our relationship is better than it's ever been. Her family—my brother-in-law, Gilbert, and all the kids, Melody, Nicole, Eric—they're so great to me.

Unfortunately, my relationships with my brothers have deteriorated over the past few years. I believe that God will reinforce those bonds again and they'll get back to what they were and maybe even better. It's just a matter of them understanding my new life. I think they haven't had time to get used to this new Eddie.

It's not just about my sobriety. I've had some success—by which I mean what the world calls success—and that's had its effects on my family. I think

CHEATING DEATH, STEALING LIFE

it's hard for my brothers to enjoy what's happened for me in WWE. They can't help but think, *Man, why didn't I get those breaks?*

It's not that my brothers didn't accomplish amazing things—each of them was extremely successful in this business. It's just that the opportunities were very different in their day. The business didn't allow for a Chicano wrestler to reach the levels that I've been blessed to achieve.

I hope my brothers know how much I miss having a good relationship with them, and how much not having one hurts me. There are days when I wonder if I'm the one to blame. Am I doing something wrong? Am I disrespecting them?

But I don't feel that's the case. Because I'm the younger brother, I've lived my whole life thinking that they're always right and I'm always wrong. I've learned that that isn't true. Now I hold my ground. I'm not going to let myself be stepped on. My boundaries are set, and I don't think they like that. I'll always be their baby brother, but I'm not a baby anymore.

I think the people that had the hardest time accepting that I'd changed were the ones who were there with me when I was at my worst.

About a year after I got sober, Chavito and I were at the airport together, checking in for our flight. He went ahead of me and when he was done, he stood to the side and waited for me. "Go ahead to the gate, bro," I said.

"No, that's cool," Chavo said. "I'll wait."

"Chavito, go. I got it."

"No, no, no, I'll wait and make sure you're okay."

I looked at him and realized what he was thinking. "I'm not fucked up anymore, bro."

Chavito smiled sadly. "I'm sorry," he said.

Seeing him standing there, waiting to clean up after me yet again, hurt me deep inside. I thought, *My God, what did I put this guy through?*

I realized that it wasn't just Vickie that had been taking care of me. I had a whole laundry list of friends and co-workers that had been looking out for me over the years, making sure that I didn't screw up or get into trouble.

THE EDDIE GUERRERO STORY

I never wanted to be a burden to anyone. It just became second nature to me when I was drinking—people would start babysitting me and I would let them do it.

I'd get so loaded, people would have to carry me to my room. Some of the boys joke about that to this day, which really hurts my feelings. It's embarrassing to think of myself like that. It wasn't until after I went through rehab that I began to grasp just how much people took care of me.

I understand that I had problems, and the people that love me were just looking out for me. When someone is sick, you take care of them. It's what you do for the people you love. You take care of them and you don't hold it against them. That doesn't mean I'm not ashamed of how reliant I was on everybody.

Through everything, one of the few people that never judged me was Chavito. God knows, he has the right to, but it's just not in his nature. I'm sure he's got his resentments, but he is so full of love. I've apologized so many times and he forgives me for everything.

"I took care of you because I love you," he said. "You'd do the same thing for me."

"That's true, bro," I said. "The difference is, I've never had to do it."

Chavito's gotten to spend more time with the new me than anybody else in my family. I think that's why he's able to appreciate the changes I've made, the fact that I'm not the same Eddie that I used to be.

In a way, Chavito still takes care of me. I can talk to him like no one else, releasing all my doubts and issues and bad feelings. "Just let it out, man," he says. "That's what I'm here for." I'll always love him for that. He's my buddy.

Chris Benoit is the other person that never complained about taking care of me. At least he never told me that he was sick and tired of it. That's something that I'll always love about him.

When we traveled together, Chris looked out for me every step of the way. It reached a point where he would bang on my hotel room door every morning, to wake me up and get me on the plane. "Come on, man," he'd say. "Get up! Vickie's going to kick your ass if you don't get home on time."

When I got sober, I sat down with Dean and Chris and apologized for what I put them through. "Don't worry about it," they both said. But I do worry about it. I know that it's a debt that I can never fully repay.

Unfortunately, I haven't had the chance to say I'm sorry to everybody that took care of me over the years, people like Perry Saturn. I hope they know how grateful I am for their kindness, for their love and support when I needed it most.

TURNING HEEL AT LAST!

CHAPTER 41

WrestleMania XIX was in Seattle, at Safeco Field—a great house. When you wrestle in a stadium, everything is different. Because of the size of the building, it takes a moment or two longer for the crowd noises to get to your ears. It really changes your game. I was taught to always listen to the crowd, to let the cheers and boos help guide the match.

In a stadium, you have to be patient. It takes time for the noise from the back rows in the upper decks to reach the ring. You have to trust your instincts. You've got to really believe in yourself and what you're doing out there.

Los Guerreros were in a Triple-Threat match for Team Angle's WWE Tag Team Championships, along with the team of Chris Benoit and Rhyno. I'm always happy for the chance to get in the ring with Chris. No matter what else happens, the two of us can go in there and be more than okay.

I was a little disappointed when I was told we would only have nine minutes or so. That's not a lot of time for a big three-team match. But I understand that there's only so much time available and a lot of people on the roster also want to be a part of WrestleMania.

About a month after WrestleMania, Chavo was in a dark match—a match that takes place before the televised event begins. I was in the back, watching on the monitor. I turned away to talk to somebody, and when I went back to watching, Chavo was down in the corner. I could tell right away that he was injured. He was holding his arm and shaking his head. I knew something was up.

They rang the bell right then and there. I ran to the gorilla position to meet Chavo when he came back. He got checked out by Larry Heck, the *SmackDown!* physical trainer, who knew right away what had happened—Chavo had torn his bicep.

Obviously, he was pretty upset. I did everything I could to make him feel better. "Hey, man," I said, "these things happen. You'll be back in no time."

No time was wasted in getting Chavo taken care of. The next day he flew to Birmingham, Alabama, to see Dr. James Andrews and had it fixed. But he still had to heal up from the surgery, which guaranteed he was going to be out for six months.

As his uncle, I was concerned for Chavo. As a wrestler, I was a little more philosophical—the show must go on. I've been in this business long enough to know that you've got to take it as it comes. I learned that in my very first WWE match. I popped out my elbow and thought my career was over.

But Vince told me not to worry, that one way or another, they'd make it work. And it was true. They adapted. Now whenever one of the boys gets injured, or something unexpected happens to change the course of a story-line, I tell them not to worry, because Vince will make it work.

So when Chavo got injured, Vince and the creative team adapted. Rather than make me a singles wrestler, they decided to pair me with someone else.

The first instinct was to team me up with Rey, but he was in the middle of a successful program of his own and no one wanted to ruin that for him. When Michael Hayes suggested Tajiri, we all agreed that it was a good idea. Tajiri has great charisma and he's easy to work with. I've always liked him and thought it could be a lot of fun being in a tag team with him.

There was some worry about the language barrier, but I knew Tajiri spoke more English than he let on, as well as a little Spanish. Plus, I've picked up some locker-room Japanese over the years, so we didn't have any trouble communicating.

Tajiri and I didn't go the old-school route. We never traveled together, we just worked as a team in the ring.

In the old days, we would've become a team and then had no choice but to travel together. That said, I think it's important for tag teams to travel together. It's how you get to know each other. And when you know each other on a personal, more intimate level, it just opens up the door for chemistry in the ring.

In this case, I think everybody understood that my tag team with Tajiri was only temporary.

Tajiri did a great job. He fit right in after Chavito got hurt. There wasn't a beat skipped, and that's a compliment to Tajiri's work. Not everybody could've done that.

It wasn't the same as what I had with Chavo. We were a completely different tag team. The thing that benefited us was we didn't try to be Chavo and Eddie, we were Tajiri and Eddie.

Los Guerreros was a special situation. We didn't have to struggle with different psychologies—we'd both been taught the same one. Sure, there were rough edges at first, but once those edges got smoothed out, we had a bond that made us unstoppable. That's a kind of chemistry that you don't get with many people. The only other person I've had that connection with was Art Barr.

My first big match with Tajiri was at *Judgment Day*, a Ladder match against Team Angle—Shelton Benjamin & Charlie Haas—for the WWE Tag Team Championships.

Tajiri had worked with ladders back in ECW, but Shelton and Charlie had never been in that kind of match. Needless to say, they were both a little scared.

I took the leadership role, explaining that the only way to go was balls-out. "If you don't go in with that mentality," I explained, "either the match is going to be the shits or you're going to get hurt. The only way is to just go out there and do it. Trust me—you're going to take a beating. It's going to hurt, but if you're willing to go for it, we can have ourselves a hell of a match."

We went out there, and I could tell that Shelton and Charlie and Tajiri were all a little nervous and a little hesitant. It was just an okay match, not up to the standards I'd set with Rob Van Dam or Edge. I would've preferred to have taken more bumps, but that's me. We came out all right. Nobody died, which is always good.

Ladder matches are very good for me now. I know what to do and what not to do. I'm not afraid of them—I can improvise and make them work to my advantage. But no matter what, it's going to hurt.

Tajiri and I won the titles at *Judgment Day*, then continued feuding with Team Angle for the next two months. There was good, simple chemistry among the four of us that enabled us to put on some decent matches. We retained the tag titles the entire time, usually through some classic Guerrero cheating to win.

The whole time with Tajiri, I kept pushing for a heel turn, only to have people try to convince me to become a total babyface. "You're already baby," they said. "People like you!"

CHEATING DEATH, STEALING LIFE

But I wouldn't listen. I wanted to be a full-blown heel. I knew that was the only way I could continue to get my character over.

I got my wish when we did *SmackDown!* in Rochester, New York. We had another Tag Team Championship match with Team Angle. I got distracted when Shelton dropkicked Tajiri onto the hood of my lowrider, allowing Charlie to roll me up for the pinfall.

I got hot—not about losing the titles. I was much more concerned about the state of my car. I flipped out on Tajiri, beating the daylights out of him, then putting him through the lowrider's windshield.

People always assume when we do that kind of thing that the glass is gimmicked in some way, but take my word for it—it's a real windshield. The trick is knowing just how to do it. You have to think of it in terms of physics— where are you going to put him so he gets the least cut up when the glass shatters?

Obviously we take certain measures to protect each other. We just don't go and kill each other's bodies. But you never really know what's going to happen.

Beating the hell out of my tag team partner did the trick—I was positioned as a vicious heel, just in time to compete in a tournament for the United States Championship.

Unfortunately, I had forgotten my dad's rule. It didn't matter how much I wanted to be a bad guy. Ultimately that was a decision made by the fans. And judging from the pop I got when I came out and did an interview explaining that I had "anger management issues," the fans were determined to keep me a babyface.

When WWE has a title tournament, there is usually some idea of how it's going to play out in the end. But Vince always tries to keep the people guessing. He's like an amazing magician—you know he's creating an illusion, you just can't figure out how he's doing it.

In the case of the U.S. Championship tournament, I think the creative team knew all along what the final match would be—me vs. Chris Benoit. They know that you can never go wrong putting us together in the ring.

I consider myself truly blessed to have been able to work with Chris for so

THE EDDIE GUERRERO STORY

many years. Every time I wrestle Chris, it's special. His natural intensity forces me to raise my game.

I didn't know it at the time, but our U.S. Title Tournament final at *Vengeance* is one of those moments in my career when I've made a distinct change to my work.

That was the night that Latino Heat came into complete focus. It was a huge revelation, realizing that I didn't have to be a badass like Stone Cold or a kick-ass heel like Triple H.

Latino Heat was a character that nobody else had ever done, which made it something special. I wasn't a babyface or a heel, I was something in between, and the people loved it.

It didn't matter how mean or evil my behavior became—the people were cheering every bad thing that I did. There were endless variations I could do with lying, cheating, stealing—hitting my opponent with a title belt, then tossing it out of the ring; taking the timekeeper's hammer and handing it to my opponent so the ref would see him holding it. As long as I was entertaining, the people would let me get away with it.

In the finish, Rhyno came out and gored Chris, setting me up for the victory—and the crowd cheered. That was the moment it fully dawned on me—the fans *wanted* to see me lie, cheat, and steal.

I shrugged my shoulders, like, "Oh well, shit happens," hit Chris with a frog splash, and won the U.S. Championship. I got a hell of a pop, too.

A few weeks after winning the U.S. Championship, I took on John Cena in El Paso. Any time you work in your hometown, you're going to get a babyface pop.

Even though I live in Florida, El Paso is my home. Everybody knows me there. They love seeing one of their boys on TV. Back in WCW, I was getting "Eddie sucks!" chants everywhere I went. But when we got to El Paso, the crowd cheered me like crazy. Even when I was beating up Chavito, they were on my side.

I kicked off the *SmackDown!* broadcast that night. The fans' reaction to my entrance and to my opening interview was so over-the-top, I finally became a full-blown babyface. There was no middle ground anymore.

The following week, Cena "stole" my lowrider, which of course ticked me off in a big way. General Manager Stephanie McMahon offered me the chance to take John on in any kind of match I wanted. I chose a Latino Street Fight, to be held in the arena parking lot on the next *SmackDown!*

I had a good talk with John before we went out there, giving him the same advice I'd have given him if we were going to be doing a Ladder match—we were going to feel pain. We might even get hurt. There was no way around it.

That didn't mean we couldn't be smart about it. John and I made sure we had everything down in our minds before we started the match. The only safe way to make it through those next eight minutes was to be as prepared as possible.

The Latino Street Fight was one of the most innovative matches of my career. We did it in the parking lot, surrounded by a circle of cars.

John and I beat the living hell out of each other, suplexing each other onto the hoods and roofs of the cars, smashing each other's head through windows and windshields.

In the finish, Chavito made his long-awaited return. He laid John out on the hood of a car with a hubcap, setting up my frog splash from off the roof of an SUV.

If it sounds dangerous, that's because it was! But it was also pretty creative. I look forward to working with John again in the future. I think the two of us could do great things together.

I was glad to have Chavo back, but at the same time, it was a little difficult. Not just for me, for the both of us. I had gotten used to working single, and I knew Chavo wanted to work single too. He was tired of playing Robin to my Batman, and I don't blame him. When he came back, we were both definitely looking to go in different directions.

Instead, we picked up right where we left off. Literally. The first thing we did after Chavito came back during the Latino Street Fight was take the

WWE Tag Team Championship belts from Charlie Haas and Shelton Benjamin. They weren't Team Angle anymore—they were now the World's Greatest Tag Team, which is way too much pressure to put on a couple of young guys.

It wasn't a problem going back to being Los Guerreros. The chemistry between Chavito and myself is always going to be there. But at the same time, we were both hungry for something new. It's like eating steak—it's delicious, but if you eat nothing but steak, you want to taste something else. That's where Chavito and I were at. We were ready for a piece of chicken.

For the next few weeks, I was carrying two titles—the U.S. Championship and the Tag Team Championship. It feels good coming out with two belts—it's a real compliment—but they also get pretty heavy!

Being a dual champion has its pros and cons. On one hand, you're definitely getting pushed, but you're also expected to deliver twice a night instead of once. Believe me, working two matches a show isn't easy. And even though you're pulling double duty, the pay stays the same.

Not long after Chavo's return, we went up to Canada for a weekend of house shows. We were in Winnipeg—Los Guerreros vs. the Basham Brothers.

In the middle of the match, I got bumped to the outside and hit the rail. I was out there selling, when all of a sudden, I felt some liquid hitting me. My first thought was that I'd knocked over somebody's drink when I hit the barricade, but whatever it was kept spilling down on me. I realized that it wasn't an accident—some asshole was pouring beer on me. I looked up and this guy is standing over me, holding his empty cup. He looked me right in the eyes and smiled. He gave me a look that said, "Yeah, I poured beer on you. What are you going to do about it?"

Before I could react, security grabbed him and started pulling him away. I was going to let it go, but as they took him away he looked right at me and started laughing. That was all it took. I saw red and lost it. I jumped over the rail and made straight for this jerk.

Luckily for him—and for me—security broke us up before I could lay my hands on him. I was hot, but I had a job to do. I went back to the ring and finished the match.

After the match ended, I stayed in the ring and called for a microphone. I needed to explain my actions. I had done an interview with the local newspaper, selling the show, but also talking about my sobriety. The fact that this guy poured beer on me struck me as a personal insult, like he read the article and decided to fuck with my sobriety. It hurt me a lot. I'd laid myself out there and this so-called wrestling fan thought it would be funny to throw beer in my face.

Where I come from, doing something like that is personal, and I reacted in kind. Still, I thought it was important to apologize to the fans for behaving the way I did, for not responding in the Christian way.

"I believe in turning the other cheek," I said, "and I'm sorry for being hypocritical from what I profess."

The people started chanting my name, letting me know that they were standing with me. It was very moving, knowing that with the exception of this one moron, I had the fans' love and support.

When I got to the back, I jumped into the shower as quickly as I could. I had to get that beer off me. I'm sure my pores were trying to swallow every bit of it! I actually had to throw away my knee pads, because they were soaked with beer. I worked the rest of that run in borrowed pads.

L os Guerreros got into it with Big Show for a few weeks. We did some real toilet humor in that angle, doing things like feeding Big Show some "special burritos" to give him the runs.

The following week, I drove a sewage truck to the ring and hosed Big Show with "shit." It was actually dog food and water, a tanker truck full of it.

I almost wrecked the set trying to drive the damn truck out there. I just couldn't get the clutch down. I usually have no trouble driving with a clutch, but this one required me to be pretty delicate. I tried driving it out before the

show and came this close to tearing down the top of the set. We decided that probably wasn't such a good idea, so when we taped *SmackDown!*, I had somebody else drive it in. Then we edited it so that I hopped out and sprayed Big Show with the sewage.

Blasting Big Show with gallon after gallon of stinky, disgusting brown liquid was a lot of fun. Unfortunately for me, the bit that it set up was no fun at all.

The next week, I lied, cheated, and stole a win over Rhyno, then I got into my lowrider truck to leave. It was a Godfather Customs lowrider truck—they're a great outfit. WWE uses their customized cars and trucks whenever we can.

All of a sudden, an extremely angry Big Show came storming out and smashed in the rear windshield with a pipe. He pulled me out through the window and continued beating the truck with the pipe, coming close to destroying the front windshield. Then he picked me up and threw me onto the

CHEATING DEATH, STEALING LIFE

hood, so that my back went right into the damaged windshield, shattering the glass.

I rolled off onto the floor, with blood running down my back from all the cuts and lacerations. Show lifted me back up and powerbombed me onto the hood.

Let me tell you, it was brutal. I have a big old scar on my arm and a few more on my back to prove it. As I've said, the only way to prepare for something like that is to take a deep breath, try to protect yourself as best you can, and accept the pain.

People see us doing things like that and think we've got the truck rigged up, like a stunt in a movie. Unfortunately, we don't have the luxury to create an illusion through special effects or other gimmicks. The easiest way to show someone getting powerbombed into the hood of a truck is to powerbomb them into the hood of a truck.

Three nights later, I dropped the U.S. title to Big Show at *No Mercy*. I always like working with Big Show. When you work with someone like him, you have to adapt your style to suit his size and technique. But I believe that to be true in every match. The key to being a good wrestler is being able to have a good match with anybody they put you with. Not everybody can do that. That's a gift that, by the grace of God, I'm blessed with.

For such a huge man, Show is very talented in the ring. When we worked together in WCW he used to jump up to the third rope and stand on it. He had to be slowed down for his own good, for both his character and his physical well-being.

Obviously Big Show can break you in two any time he grabs hold of you. But he's a professional. He's not going to kill you.

He's also a really good guy, with a huge heart. Literally.

Show doesn't have it easy. He looks big on TV, but trust me, he's even more enormous in real life. He's a massive human being, so he can't always do the things regular people do. For instance, he can't sit in the regular seat on a plane. It's just not comfortable for him. Every now and then, Show will charter a jet for himself. He lives in Florida, and whenever he can, he asks me if he can give me a ride home.

THE EDDIE GUERRERO STORY

I've still had a few run-ins with him, but I've had run-ins with everybody. That's pretty normal for life in a dressing room.

Chavo and I kept working with two of WWE's most gifted young wrestlers, Charlie Haas and Shelton Benjamin. Our feud with them went on for what felt like months, and before long, things began getting pretty tense. There was some definite frustration, as well as various issues that had built up between us.

A lot of it was my fault. Because I'm the veteran, the responsibility for any given match falls on me. It's my job to be a leader out there, and if something goes wrong, I'm the one that gets bitched at. If the match goes bad, I get the heat.

I was acting very old-school with Charlie and Shelton. The old-school way of dealing with rookies was to yell at them. More than just yell—the veterans would verbally beat the younger wrestlers down. And the rookies weren't allowed to respond. They were supposed to just stand there and take it.

Well, I've got a lot of old school in me. We would get back to the dressing room after every match and I'd ream them out. But instead of listening, they put up a wall.

It all came to a head in San Diego, a week or two before Christmas. In the middle of our *SmackDown!* match, Shelton hit me with a flying armbar and popped my left elbow, the same one I'd injured in my first-ever WWE match.

I tried buzzing him—"Hey, I'm hurt!"—but I guess he didn't hear me. Shelton and Charlie kept picking me up, throwing me around, and pulling on my injured arm. They were just making a rookie mistake, but I was hurting pretty bad and started getting hot.

When we got to the back, Chavo said, "C'mon, let's go talk to these guys." It turned into a screaming match, right from the start. The four of us got into each other's faces and before long, Charlie and I started pushing each other. Fortunately, the boys got in there and split us up before things could escalate any further.

Incidents like that happen all the time backstage. The only thing to do is apologize and let time run its course. Life in the dressing room is a lot like a marriage—not every fight is the end of the world.

In hindsight, I know that I could've handled the situation differently. I've learned that you've got to talk to people calmly. You can't just put somebody down, you need to talk to them like a human being. That's true in all aspects of life—you can't yell at people and expect them to listen. It's just not nice.

The longer you have in this business, the more responsibility falls onto you. As a veteran, I have an obligation to take on a leadership role in the dressing room, especially where the new wrestlers are concerned.

First I lost the U.S. title, then Chavito and I lost the Tag Team belts to the Basham Brothers on the following *SmackDown!* It didn't matter to me. What was important was that they finally started to split up Los Guerreros by having Chavito turn heel. No question, that was the best thing for us at that point.

The timing was perfect. We'd been trying to talk Vince into doing it for months, but he kept saying, "No, no. We'll do it when the time is right." God bless him, he knew what he was talking about. When we finally did it, the fans were ready.

Chavito began getting angrier and angrier, picking fights with me after our matches. The fans hated that—by God's grace, Latino Heat was hugely over at that point, one of WWE's most popular babyfaces. Everywhere Chavito went, the crowds were chanting my name. They seriously wanted me to kick his ass.

Though we'd developed serious tension between us when we'd feuded in WCW, this time Chavito's attitude was totally different. In his mind, that program had him being punked out by his mean uncle Eddie, and he couldn't see how it was going to work in his favor. Now Chavito was the heel, an actual bad person and all-around unpleasant guy. Plus he had a lot of input in how the character and story developed, which helped us both to be comfortable with the storyline.

When Bruce Pritchard suggested bringing Chavito's dad, my brother Chavo, into the angle, I thought it was an awesome idea. Chavo is one of

the greatest wrestlers alive, and I thought this would be an amazing opportunity for a new generation to see him at work.

It must have been great for Chavito to be able to work with his dad. At the same time, there are positives and negatives to everything. I'm sure having Chavo around put major pressure on Chavito.

Over the years, my brothers have put a lot of pressure on me. I've felt that I could never do the right thing. One of them was always telling me, "You've got to do this," or "You've got to do that." Always nitpicking. There comes a time when you get tired of hearing it. I wanted to scream, "Aren't you guys ever happy?"

I found myself doing the same thing to Chavito: "Do this," and "Do that." That was wrong. I learned that the proper way to treat somebody—anybody, not just family—is to respect their decisions, their business psychology. Once I understood that, my relationship with Chavito really improved.

When his dad came to work in WWE, I think Chavito might have had to

CHEATING DEATH, STEALING LIFE

live with that kind of thing all over again. Our family thrives on perfection, especially when it comes to wrestling.

The Guererro boys have always made good tag teams because we were trained to work together and think as one. But that only applies to what happens inside the ring. Outside the ring, we've all got very different opinions. It's not a bad thing—everyone in the family wants the other guy to be the best wrestler that he can possibly be—but it's not an easy thing to live with.

God help us, we Guerreros can't seem to stop ourselves from telling each other what we think is right or wrong. That can lead to a lot of wounded egos and hurt feelings.

For my part, I thought Chavo could be a great help to me. I've always believed in Chavo's psychology. I've learned a lot from him. I also thought it would be good for our relationship, which had undergone a lot of ups and downs over the years, especially since I got sober.

The original plan was to use Chavo for a couple weeks, but Vince really liked him. Vince has a lot of respect for the old school, for people like Chavo, who really have a great mind for the business.

Chavo Classic, as he was known, was part of *SmackDown!* for a few months. It just about broke my heart when I heard Chavo had been released. It hurt so much, watching my oldest brother fighting some of the same demons I fight.

CHAPTER 42

Vince called me aside and said, "We're considering making you the WWE World Champion."

I was shocked. All I had ever wanted was to come back and wrestle in WWE, for one more opportunity to give my best. I had not the slightest thought of actually becoming the champion. I'm not trying to sound humble— I honestly never imagined the possibility.

"I'm so honored you've even thought of me as champion," I said. "And of course I'd be grateful for the opportunity."

Even as I thanked Vince, I didn't really believe it was ever going to actually happen. Not that Vince didn't mean what he'd said. It's just that I've been in this business a long, long time. I've had promoters tell me all kinds of things, and if I've learned one lesson, it's that things change.

When I reflected on the idea of becoming WWE Champion, I realized that I'd achieved just about all that's required to wear that gold belt.

Perhaps the most important thing that's needed in order to be the WWE Champion is consistency. You have to have the complete package. Just being physically able to do it isn't enough—you've got to be mentally able as well.

At that time, I was as steady and solid as I've ever been in my career. I had no major injuries, I was in great condition, I was feeling positive about my life and my career. I was *on*.

On January 25, Chris Benoit won the 2004 *Royal Rumble,* then jumped to *Raw* in order to face Triple H for a shot at the World Heavyweight Championship at *WrestleMania. SmackDown!* GM Paul Heyman announced that we were going to have a Rumble match of our own, to determine the Number One Contender for Brock Lesnar's WWE Championship.

Just before the match started, I got beaten up by a mysterious assailant. The EMTs stretchered me out and took me to a nearby medical facility. Fortunately for me, I managed to make a remarkable recovery and get back to the arena in time to be the lucky #13 entrant in the Rumble.

It ended up with me and Kurt Angle as the last men in the ring. We went back and forth, each of us coming close to eliminating the other. Finally, I reversed Kurt's suplex and tossed him out over the top rope, officially earning a title shot in the main event at *No Way Out.*

Even after I won the *SmackDown!* Rumble, I didn't allow myself to believe that I had any real shot at becoming WWE Champion. I refused to count my chickens before they were hatched.

No Way Out was scheduled for February 15, at the Cow Palace in San Francisco. That gave us three short weeks to build toward the Pay-Per-View.

Those weeks were an opportunity for me to mainline my work and show off what I can do. I immediately started working with Brock Lesnar, which was a total change of pace from working with Chavito. Working with Chavito wasn't easy, but it was comfortable. Being in the ring with Brock pushed me to work on another level. I had to dig deep and find a strength I didn't know that I had.

I felt really blessed to be able to work with Brock. First of all, he's an incredibly gifted athlete. Anybody that can suplex Big Show—really suplex him at will—man, that's strong. He's an animal.

When it came to business, Brock had a great work ethic. He's a perfectionist and was willing to work as hard as he needed to in order to achieve perfection.

Brock was very focused. He knew what the office wanted from him and he was determined to deliver. Before he left, he was consistently giving great matches. He picked up the pace and stepped up another level. I know that people felt that Brock's early success was forced, but at the end he was carrying the title like a true champion.

I owe Brock a lot. He went out there and busted his ass for me. I'll always love him for that.

Brock and I spent those three weeks learning how to work with each other, going thirty minutes at every house show. We needed to get a feel for each other. Working night after night with a bull like Brock really helped me get into shape for our match.

The pressure was definitely on. I'd worked dozens of Pay-Per-Views, but this time the show was riding on me. It was my face on the poster.

I'd had title shots before, but never one where I actually had a chance of winning. Basically I'd been in matches where I did the job for the champ.

No Way Out was different. This was the real deal.

I worked my ass off to make No Way Out a success. I had gone to Vince and really pushed the idea of working the Hispanic market. He put his faith in me and really made an effort to focus on our Latino audience.

It really felt like a do-or-die situation. WWE had made a point of pushing me as a Latino wrestler, especially as far as the house shows were concerned. In return, I sacrificed almost all of my days off to go and do promotion. I went on Telemundo, on Univision. I did TV and newspaper interviews in all the Latin markets.

The thing is, all our efforts produced—we were drawing great houses in

all the Hispanic communities. Now the only question was what kind of house we'd do at the actual Pay-Per-View.

On the day of the show, only eighty percent of the tickets had been sold. By the time Brock and I hit the ring, they were turning people away. The walk-up was tremendous. The Cow Palace ended up selling three thousand more tickets than they had expected. We had to move the curtains back to make room for all the fans that had shown up.

CHEATING DEATH, STEALING LIFE

The best part was that the majority of the walk-up business came from Mexican-Americans. *La Raza* turned out in record numbers to see one of their own get a shot at the WWE Championship. Seeing all the Latino faces in the audience was such a great feeling. It felt so good to see all the hard work pay off.

Those fans got to witness the match of my life. I only wish my dad could've been there to see it. It was everything in my life coming to a point, everything that I busted my ass for my whole life. Not just the last few years—my whole life.

The response I got in return was so moving, so powerful to me. They didn't care whether I lied, cheated, or stole. They didn't care whether I was a heel or a babyface. They just were happy that a Latino was representing them, that I was out there busting ass.

The match began building to its conclusion when Brock ducked away from a frog splash and gave me the F5. Unfortunately for him, my legs swung out and I kicked the ref, knocking him out. Brock covered me, but the ref was bumped, so there was no one to count me out. He went out and got the WWE Championship belt, but before he could do anything with it, Goldberg—who Brock was slated to fight at the upcoming *WrestleMania*— came into the ring and speared him.

In the back of my mind, I was concerned that the fans weren't going to pop for me, that everything was going to go to Brock and Goldberg. I needn't have worried. The crowd was chanting "Eddie! Eddie!" as I came to.

I made sure I respected his finish, but at the same time, I wasn't going to get the win through Goldberg's actions. I was going to get it through my own. It was important to me that I truly win the belt, as opposed to winning it by accident.

With Brock down from the spear, I took the opportunity to roll on top of him for the cover. The ref was still groggy and Brock kicked out at two. I couldn't believe it!

Then I saw the title belt, lying there in the middle of the ring. It was the perfect opportunity for Latino Heat, the pot of gold at the end of the rainbow.

I picked up the belt and waited for Brock to get up so that I could nail him with it. When I went to hit him, Brock ducked out of the way. I dropped the belt as he picked me up for his finish. As he started to spin me through into the F5, I reversed him into a swinging DDT, planting his head onto the belt.

Boom!

I shoved the belt out of the ring and quickly went up top for a frog splash. I landed it perfectly and went for the pin—One! Two! Three!

All these feelings were running through me as the ref put the WWE Championship belt in my hand. I'm a very emotional guy, and that was easily one of the most emotional moments of my life. It was almost like I was numb from all the many emotions.

But I didn't have time to dwell on my feelings. I had some more business to do. Before the match, Vince only had one instruction for me—to celebrate like crazy.

Well, he didn't have to tell me twice!

I was so happy and excited, I wanted to share it with everybody. I ran down to the rail and hugged my mom and Mando. There was nothing worked about my excitement—it was as real as real can be!

Then I jumped over the barricade into the arms of the crowd. I hadn't told anybody I was going to do that, but it was something I'd been planning all night. I wanted to get the fans as involved in my celebration as I possibly could. It was my way of saying, "Thanks. You guys did this with me."

I was especially grateful for the support that the Mexican-American community had given me. Everywhere I went that week, Latino people were coming up to me, saying, "Hey, man, thank you for representing."

Eventually I climbed out of the audience and headed up the ramp. I reached the stage and got down on my knees. First I thanked God, then I looked up toward heaven and said, "This one's for you, Dad."

It was something I had always wanted to do. I'd only ever dedicated a match to my father once before, at a tribute event held right after he passed away. In my heart, I knew how proud he would have been to see me reach this place in the business—I was the first Guerrero to compete for the World title since my dad's 1954 match again Lou Thesz.

Finally, I went through the curtain, still overflowing with emotion. I certainly didn't expect the reception that I received from the boys. Everybody was clapping, people were shaking my hand and congratulating me. Goldberg was one of the first people to meet me through the curtain. He threw his big arms around me and said, "You didn't need me out there."

That was such a nice thing for him to say. A lot of the boys came over and hugged me. "Man, this is great," Bill DeMott—Hugh Morrus—said. "I didn't think it was gonna happen, Eddie, I really didn't."

I think guys like Hugh see me as one of them, a lifer. There are wrestlers whose careers are designed to take them to the role of champion, but that's not me. Getting the chance to represent the hardworking boys really meant a lot to me.

Chavito and my brothers Chavo and Mando were also there, waiting to congratulate me. I could tell Mando was proud of me from the way he kept patting me on the back. He didn't tell me verbally, he told me with his eyes. He was crying, which said more than any words ever could.

Chavo looked truly happy for me. He gave me a hug and said, "I'm so proud of you, man." It wasn't the same as having my dad there, but it was close. I've been wanting Chavo's acceptance for so long. It was a small validation, something I'd been fighting for for years.

I really wish Vickie could've been there, but she was doing her job as a wrestler's wife. She was home, being a mom, taking care of the family.

She was almost as emotional as I was when I called her from the dressing room. She was crying, telling me how happy she was for me. She sounded pretty overwhelmed, which made me even more emotional. Even though she wasn't there with me, it meant so much that Vickie was a part of my life.

Once the cameras were off, my mom and I got down on our knees and thanked God for blessing me with such an opportunity. I know I could've never done it without Him, without the power and the grace of God.

I asked God to give me the strength to carry the WWE Championship with dignity and respect and honor, to be a good representative of what the belt means. To not only do Him justice, but also myself and the rest of the boys.

I didn't sleep a wink that night. I was on too much of a high. That might be the one time I can remember that my not sleeping came from feeling good.

THE EDDIE GUERRERO STORY

CELEBRATING MY TITLE VICTORY AT *WRESTLEMANIA XX*.

CHAPTER 43

Everything was different after I became the WWE Champion. The belt changes a person, the way you look at the business, the way you approach your job. You become a different worker once you get the belt. That also goes for after you stop carrying the title. You're looked at differently. You're a member of a very elite club. Starting with Buddy Rogers back in 1963, only thirty other men have been WWE Champion. And being part of that elite club, you're expected to perform at a higher level.

The responsibility is enormous. Everything you do is for the greater good—of the match, of the show, of the company. It's a huge honor, to be the focal point of a promotion, to have everything ride on you.

That's a hell of a lot of pressure to live up to. In the old days, I'd have gotten drunk and numbed myself up. Without that option, I had to work through the stress and anxiety by focusing on my Bible and savoring every moment that I wore the belt.

Along with the added pressure, the WWE Championship also presents all kinds of wonderful new opportunities. As champion, your celebrity quotient increases to where you get to do all kinds of exciting extracurricular activities. For example, *TV Guide* did two collector's editions before *WrestleMania,* one of which had me and Kurt Angle on the cover. That's big, being on the cover of *TV Guide.*

Right after I won the title, I was invited to appear on *MadTV.* It was part of the big promotional push that always comes before *WrestleMania.* I was on with a few other Superstars—Big Show, Chris Jericho, and Trish Stratus—doing a skit where we were coming out of the gym and got interviewed by Jay Leno. I only had one line, and Frank Caliendo, the comedian who played Leno, made it real easy for me.

It wasn't all that different from doing a *SmackDown!* vignette with Theodore Long, though there was a little bit of pressure simply from being in another element.

It was a neat experience. It was very rewarding for me personally, because it made me consider all the different possibilities of things I can do in my career.

I'd love to try doing a movie at some point. I think it would be so much fun to act in a comedy. Doing so many vignettes on *SmackDown!* has really helped me grow as an actor. I feel I've gotten pretty good at doing comedy.

I also filmed a commercial for Stacker 2 YJ Stinger energy drink out in Los Angeles. It was hard work, but a huge amount of fun to do. There was a big fiesta, with sexy girls and cool lowriders. Plus, I was the star. It was a real kick being catered to like I was a real movie star.

My brother Mando joined me on the set. He's worked out there for years, as an actor and a stuntman, so he was able to help coach me on my lines and how to be comfortable working on that kind of a shoot. I was grateful that he was there. Any time I get to work with my brothers is special to me. We have our issues, but we also have good times together.

It was a long day. We shot the commercial twice—once in English, and then again in Spanish. Doing it in Spanish meant a lot to me, because it meant WWE and Stacker 2 were paying attention to the Latin market. That's something I'd been suggesting for a long time. It's the fastest-growing demographic in the country. Every time we acknowledge the Latin market, the Latin market responds. It's foolish to ignore them.

CHEATING DEATH, STEALING LIFE

I'd love to do more things geared to that audience, whether it's guest-starring on something mainstream like *The George Lopez Show* or appearing on one of the Spanish language networks. It would be so much fun to be a guest on *Sabado Gigante*.

One thing I pushed for after becoming WWE Champion was getting myself into *Lowrider* magazine, which is hugely popular in the Chicano community. John Cena actually hooked it up—he was talking to the editor and told him about how I'd been using lowriders on the show. He told John to pass along his number, so I called him and set it up.

I was the first male ever to grace the cover of *Lowrider*—a very big deal. It's always been a beautiful girl and a badass ride. I'm so proud of that. It showed how much I represent to the Latino audience.

No one gets the belt overnight. In my case, it took close to two years working nonstop since coming back to WWE. By the time I actually became WWE Champion, I was already tired. You have to work so hard to get there that when you finally make it to the title match, you're exhausted. But you've got to keep going.

In my case, it was especially hard because *No Way Out* was the last Pay-Per-View before *WrestleMania,* meaning that everything that happened from that moment on was geared toward the biggest event of the wrestling calendar.

And this particular *WrestleMania* was one of the biggest ever—the twentieth anniversary event, being held at the world's most famous arena, Madison Square Garden.

If *No Way Out* was my big night, then *WrestleMania XX* was to be Chris Benoit's moment. I wouldn't have had it any other way.

There is probably no one in this business that I'm as close to as Chris. We lived out on the road together for a long, long time. As tight as we had been since becoming friends in Japan, these last few years have brought us even closer. When I first returned to WWE after being fired, Chris was home, healing up from surgery to repair a broken neck. We started traveling together again after he came back. I'd been on the road, all by myself, so it felt so good to be with a friend again.

In the past, we had never really gotten deep as far as releasing our most intimate emotions. Obviously we had talked about our personal lives and

A HARD-FOUGHT BATTLE WITH THE GREAT KURT ANGLE AT *WRESTLEMANIA XX*.

various issues, but never in a way that truly went below the surface. But after my experience in rehab, I became much better at expressing my emotions. And the more I opened up, the more unguarded Chris became with me.

It wasn't just our pain we shared—it was our lives. Not everything is doom and gloom. Chris and I share the beautiful moments too.

I was booked to make my first title defense against the always amazing Kurt Angle. The main event, however, was a *Raw* brand Triple-Threat with Shawn Michaels and Chris Benoit challenging Triple H for the World Heavyweight Championship.

Kurt and I had a pretty satisfying match. It's hard not to have a good match when you're in the ring with a tremendous talent like Kurt. Very few wrestlers have his natural gifts, especially considering the relatively short time he's been a professional.

We used old-school psychology, with Kurt spending the majority of the match working over my leg to get his ankle lock over. He locked his trademark hold in three times—the crowd popping louder and louder with each twist of my ankle—before I resorted to some classic Latino Heat maneuvering. I managed to send Kurt to the outside, giving me the chance to sneakily loosen the laces of my boot. When he came back and locked a fourth ankle lock on me, I used my free foot to push him—and my boot—into the ropes, allowing me the chance to roll him up for the three count.

I was very happy with the match, though I don't think it was as great as people have told me it was. Still, it was pretty thrilling, defending the WWE title at *WrestleMania*, in Madison Square Garden.

Right before my match, one of the road agents had come to me. "Hey, Eddie, I forgot to tell you, you're running out after Chris's match."

But the main event match was so exciting—a true classic—I completely forgot that I had a role to play at the end. I had to be reminded to go out and celebrate with Chris.

I went out there and we held the belts together as a huge cloud of confetti blew around the entire arena. It was such a buzz. After so many years, there we were, side by side at the very top of the business. It's moments like those when you've got to pinch yourself to make sure it's really happening.

It sure felt like a dream. I was standing there at *WrestleMania* in Madison Square Garden with my best friend in the business, a man who is as close to me as a brother, both of us carrying the gold.

But as soon as the right moment came, I got out of there. It was his night in the spotlight, something that he so rightfully deserved and earned for himself. Chris deserved that title for so long. He had it in WCW for a moment—literally. I know back then I wasn't close to ready to be champ, but Chris most definitely was.

Chris and I prayed together after the show ended. We got on our knees and thanked God and when we got up, I put my arms around him and gave him a kiss on the cheek. "I love you, man," I said. "I'm so happy for you. Nobody deserves it more."

TELLING CHRIS HOW PROUD I AM OF HIM FOR WINNING THE WWE WORLD HEAVYWEIGHT CHAMPIONSHIP AT *WRESTLEMANIA XX.*

UNDER THE CHRISTMAS TREE WITH MY BEAUTIFUL WIFE, 2004.

EPILOGUE

No question about it, things have been coming up roses for me. But the thing about roses is that they've got thorns. Nothing has come easily. Everything that's happened to me in the last four years has been through God's grace and lots of hard work.

I've hit so many walls, and each time I've come back stronger. I believe that's the true definition of strength—the ability to fall down, then pick yourself up and walk taller than you did before. To learn from your mistakes and strive to be better.

I try to keep a positive outlook, which is never easy for me. My faith in Christ keeps me strong. And when I don't believe in myself, I thank God that there are a lot of people who do—Vickie and the girls, Chris and Dean, Vince and Stephanie and Hunter.

Sobriety is an uphill battle. And the moment that I feel like I'm winning is when I'm in trouble. The moment I feel I'm in control, I'm screwed. That's when I'll get sucker punched.

It makes me feel good when people tell me how proud they are of me for kicking my addiction's ass. It brings a smile to my face, but at the same time, it puts my guard up. I'm proud of what I've accomplished, but I also have to remind myself, *Don't get cocky.*

That's the attitude that leads to a relapse, thinking that you've gotten it beat. I have to fight my addiction every day. I know I should take some pride in what I've accomplished so far, but I'm not quite there yet.

I'm still new at this. I've only been clean for a few years. The person that

SHAUL AND SHERILYN, CHRISTMAS 2004.

I am now is only three years old. Those three years have been spent learning how to live a new life. I'm confronted with something new every day. These feelings come over me and I think, *What the hell is this? What's going on with me?*

It's gotten a lot easier, but that doesn't mean I can ever let my guard down. That might be the hardest thing of all, the knowledge that every day is going to be a new struggle.

What keeps me going are the positive things in my life—my relationship with Vickie and the kids, my work, my spirituality. It took a long time for me to start seeing them. I had to be sober for a good while before I realized that, without a shadow of a doubt, the positives outweigh the negatives.

It's hard sometimes. I'll come off the road and know that I haven't turned off my wrestling mentality. So I take some quiet time, I pray and I meditate, whatever it takes to separate myself.

One positive step I've taken is that I don't call myself an addict anymore—

I'm a *recovering* addict. You live what you profess. If you have a negative attitude, you're going to live a negative life. I prefer to be optimistic.

I admit, I've been down a lot of the time, always beating myself up for the past. There was so much chaos and so much turmoil for so many years that I was scared to accept anything good in my life. But you can only kick yourself in the ass for so long. I realized that God doesn't want me to be in bondage to the mistakes I've made. In a way, living like that is as bad as being drunk. You're still in bondage. The disease is alive in you, telling you that you're guilty, that you're not worthy.

So I'm recovering. It's an everyday thing. It's important to acknowledge that I've changed. I'm trying to get on the other side of my addiction.

By the grace of God, I'm never going back. I promised Vickie, I promised the kids, I promised myself. I'm never putting another drink in my mouth. I'm never going to get high again. I will stand by that commitment, no matter how tough it gets.

KAYLIE, CHRISTMAS 2003.

Cleaning up the mess that was my old life also extended to practical matters such as my disastrous financial situation.

When I came back to WWE, it was for a third of what I was originally making. I was basically starting from scratch. And then I couldn't even begin

THE EDDIE GUERRERO STORY

MY CRAZY DOG, FRIJOLITO!

paying back the IRS for two years. They want to be sure you're current before they'll allow you to set up a payment plan.

I never would've been able to dig myself out of my financial hole without the help of my new CPA, Fred Hoffman. Not only is Fred a fantastic accountant, he's a remarkable person. He has done so much for me, getting my finances in line, helping me get organized. Not only that, he's been advising me on how to do the right thing for my family's future, for the girls' college, for my retirement. He has stuck with me through thick and thin.

The smartest thing I did was not run from the IRS. It was very hard at times, because I felt like I was working for nothing. But I'm very glad I dealt with it, because now, by the grace of God, it's over. I can move on with my life and begin thinking about my financial future.

I've paid back all my debts. I don't have a lot of material things to show for it, but I'm free again. I lived with that burden for close to four years, but that monkey is finally off my back. It's all taken care of now.

Perhaps the one aspect of my disease that is truly cured is my addiction to spending. Believe me, not having any money is the fastest cure for that particular disease!

I still try to lead a generous life. I continue to tithe, of course, and I still believe in giving lots of gifts—to my wife, to my kids, to my brothers and sisters. What good is money if you hoard it?

The difference with me now is that I understand that the cost of the gift is not what's important. It's the thought that makes a gift special, not how much you spent on it. It took me a long time—and a lot of money—to learn that lesson.

Buying things for myself, that's another story.

CHEATING DEATH, STEALING LIFE

I have a hard time accepting that I've earned anything, that I deserve to buy myself a new TV or a new car. It took me more than two years after getting sober just to buy something for myself.

My wife has to really get on me about it. "Go ahead, buy something for yourself. You've earned it."

One of the most important lessons I've learned is that nothing lasts forever. That's why it's so vital to savor life's special moments—like renewing my wedding vows with Vickie or the feeling of being carried around the crowd after winning the title.

A few months after *WrestleMania XX,* I dropped the WWE Championship to John "Bradshaw" Layfield following a pair of hard-fought and extremely bloody Pay-Per-View battles.

I confess, in a great many ways I wasn't prepared to carry the company on my shoulders. For right now, all my inner strength is better suited to maintaining my sobriety and keeping my life flowing smoothly. There will come a time when I'll be fully prepared to wear the belt again. And when that time comes, I promise I'll be ready to carry that title with all the dignity and strength it deserves.

At the moment, I'm learning that being an ex-WWE Champion also has its responsibilities. From this point on, I'm obligated to lead in the locker room. At first that made me a little nervous, but as I consider my life's experiences, I believe I can bring a lot of knowledge and wisdom to the table.

There's more of a need for veterans like me than ever before. The business is so different. When I was coming up, it used to be ninety percent of the locker room were veterans and the other ten percent were the rookies. Now it's the other way around.

As a veteran, as someone who's survived a lifetime in this brutal, beautiful business, I believe I have a lot to give back. I want to be a light. It's not up to me to change people—that's God's job. My role is to live my life the best way I can and give of myself. I believe I'm here to give of myself through wrestling, whether it's in a match or talking to the boys in the back.

Now I've got a new fire lit under my ass. I want to give back to this business by serving others. My heart belongs to Christ, it always will. But I believe I have a lot left to give to the business. There are many different ways to give my heart. I want to give my heart to the dressing room, I want to be there for the boys so that no one has to go through some of the things I went through.

I'm not just talking about my knowledge of wrestling—I'm talking about *life*. God had a plan when He blessed me to be in this business. I believe that He wants me to do anything I can to help the boys who might be having the same issues as I do. I just want to be there for them when they're in need. I want to be their friend.

When Christ came into this world, He didn't stay in a monastery or in church. He went out into the world and ministered. He taught us to go to the world and spread His gospel, which is love. That's the true message of Christ, spreading love. I know that in my heart because that's what He has been to me.

Working with boys that are just coming into this business, that's a way for me to follow Christ's example and spread love.

I think about my dad a lot these days, about how he loved teaching young wrestlers. It was so important to him to pass along the foundations of this business to the next generation. He was a stickler for the basics. My dad was nothing if not old school.

In a lot of ways, those are the same lessons I'm trying to get across to the new boys. The only way to survive in wrestling is with a solid foundation. Not just as far as the business—you also need to have a strong spirit and a clear sense of purpose if you don't want the pressures of this life to take you down.

God forbid something were to happen to me where I couldn't work anymore, I can honestly say I am satisfied with the effort that I've given these past few years. I have given my all, my full heart. I can walk away and know that I've given the best I had to give.

My dad taught me early on that wrestling is bigger than any one person, bigger than any of us. If I retire, the show is going to go on. Another person will step into my place. That's just the way it is.

Stone Cold Steve Austin described it beautifully. "We're just little pistons in a big machine," he said. That's one of the hard truths about this business—if one piston wears out, it's going to be replaced so that the machine can keep going.

When my current role ends, there will be a different one to play. The role that I'm playing now might not be the role that I play when I'm forty-five, and that role is not going to be the same one I play when I'm fifty-five.

Still, it's hard to accept that reality, especially when I've lived all my life in this business. I was nursed on wrestling. It's all I've ever wanted to do. What do you do when you work for something with all your might and all your soul, and when you get it, you realize it's not what you thought it was going to be?

I'm at a crossroads. I'm not going to be able to live this life forever. I have to realize what's real in my life—God, my family, my friends. I had a dream about Dad recently. We were in the ring, surrounded by hundreds of wrestlers. "None of this is real," he said. "Look at everything you've got around you—your family—and be thankful for it. It's time to stop struggling and start living."

Wrestling is still my passion. It continues to give me the greatest natural high, second only to my relationship with Christ. There are bigger reasons than wrestling for me to be here. I have three beautiful daughters that are always going to need me, even when they're all grown up. I have a lovely wife that I'm going to live with till the day I'm gone.

There is so much in my life that I need to be thankful for. Not just my family and my career. One of the best things about being a WWE Superstar is that we get the opportunity to visit with people less fortunate than ourselves. Whether it's sick children or disabled veterans, it reminds me how much I have to be grateful for. Human nature is to simply look at our own lives, but to really get a sense of the world around you, you have to broaden your view.

Even in my own world, the world of wrestling, I have to remind myself that I'm doing okay. Not everybody is blessed with a happy, healthy family, not everyone has a life to come home to. The lifestyle we lead isn't easy on a marriage, and a lot of the boys haven't been blessed with what I have.

In a lot of ways, I'm the luckiest man in the world. I got a second chance at life. I got my career back, my family, my spirit. I got a chance to earn back all the things that I had lost.

I hope my story, my message, can help people out. I'm not God—I'm just an extension of His grace and His glory. I'm just an extension of His power. I'd be so proud if my life could inspire somebody to do something to better themselves. If all this pain that I've gone through helps one person avoid pain, then I'm happy. If it helps one million people, I'd be extremely happy.

But the main person it's got to help is me. I can never forget that. If I try to fix the world and forget myself, I'm going to fall again. I've got to always remember that. If there's one message I need to get out there, it's that you never beat addiction. You get up every morning and hope that you can conquer it all over again. It's never over. It's an everyday thing.

Life turns on a dime. I don't have any idea what tomorrow will bring. I'm just very blessed to have been able to live what I've lived today. Sure, life would be a lot easier if we knew what was going to happen. But that's not the way it works.

You've got to live by faith, one day at a time.

ACKNOWLEDGMENTS

First of all, I want to thank the Lord Jesus Christ. Only through His strength have I been able to live through these years.

Thanks must go to my family, for their lifelong support and inspiration— my mom, Herlinda; my sisters, Maria and Linda; and my brothers, Chavo, Mando, and Hector. Of course, I'd also like to thank the rest of the Guerrero and Llanes families, for always being gracious and loving.

A special thanks to Art "Tury" Flores, who was there for me when no one else was.

I'd like to thank all of the amazing people at WWE, starting with the entire McMahon family. All of you have been nothing but supportive to me through all my issues, and you continue to be there. Vince, thank you for being that part of my dad that I've missed so much. I am blessed to have you in my life. Jim "J.R." Ross and Johnny Laurinaitis, both of whom believed in me and never lost faith.

My love goes out to all the boys who were supportive of me throughout my issues, especially Chris Benoit, Fit Finlay, Dean Malenko, and Darren Matthews. Xavier and Joel, thank you for your prayers and love. Lastly, a special thank-you to Oscar Gutierrez and family.

For their encouragement and friendship, I'd like to thank the following people: My sponsor, Bob, who, after Christ, is a big part of my sobriety. My grand sponsor, Bill, as well as all the people in the rooms that didn't judge me, but gave me nothing but love. Dirty Dan—thank you for making me laugh. Dave Cohen—you are like a brother to me. Fred Hoffman, who was with me from the very beginning and who never lost faith in me. Diane Mohr—thank you for all your love. You are like a sister to me. Jim Weigel—thank you! Thank you! I love you! Dr. Moreno—thank you for your prayers and taking care of my mom. Waldo—thanks for always being there. Hector Rincon and family—thank you for your hearts. Hector, you are beyond a friend. You are my angel sent from heaven.

My gratitude to Michael Krugman for helping me to tell my story, and to Margaret Clark at Pocket Books for putting it together.

A very special thank-you to my beautiful girls—Shaul, Sherilyn, and Kaylie. You all have loved me unconditionally, and that is why I never gave up. Shaul, you have a heart of gold. Sherilyn, thanks for always making me smile.

Finally, to my incredible wife, Vickie, thank you for your effort to make peace with me. Thank you for learning about and understanding my disease, which has led to the best relationship I could have ever imagined. I will love you forever . . . unconditionally.

CO-AUTHOR'S ACKNOWLEDGMENTS

Eddie, I am truly honored by your trust and friendship. My love and gratitude go out to your wonderful family—Vickie, Shaul, and Sherilyn—for welcoming me into your home and making it a singular joy for me to assist in the telling of your extraordinary journey.

Many thanks to the good folks at WWE, notably Mark Carrano, Steve Pantaleo, Jimmy Noonan, Tim White, Chavo Guerrero Jr., and Rey Mysterio, all of whom supplied important access and information without which Eddie and I could not have told this story.

None of this would've been possible without the hard work of Abby Royle. Her remarkable efforts made it all come together with ease.

My eternal gratitude and respect go out to two publishing giants—superagent Dave Dunton at Harvey Klinger Inc., and the incredibly patient and understanding Margaret Clark at Pocket Books.

Major thanks to Dr. Vladimir Santos for giving me my voice back. Also, cheers to Dr. Carl Berg for his invaluable support.

ACKNOWLEDGMENTS

Much love must go to my family—David, Cynthia, and Michele Krugman—as well as those dear friends who saw me though the long process—Jonathan and Caitlin FitzGordon, Ken Weinstein, Jason Cohen, Mike Flaherty, Nick Stern, Nevin Martell, Bob Kaus, and Tracy Zamot.

Finally, I must declare my unceasing love and appreciation for the fabulous and beautiful Carrie Hamilton. You're the light in my life, the film in my projector, the cream in my cannoli. Hi, honey!

ACKNOWLEDGMENTS